The Boy in the Yellow Dress

VICTOR MARSH

Clouds of Magellan | Melbourne

© 2014 Victor Marsh
First published 2014

ISBN: 9781742984087

Clouds of Magellan, Melbourne, Australia
cloudsofmagellanpress.net

Dr Victor Marsh is an honorary Research Fellow at the University of
Queensland and does sessional teaching at Southern Cross University. His
doctoral dissertation *The Journey of the Queer 'I'* focused on identity positioning
in gay men's spiritual autobiographies. In 2010 he wrote *Mr Isherwood Changes
Trains: Christopher Isherwood and the Search for the 'home self'*, a critical discussion of
the often-misunderstood religious life of the British writer whose relationship
with his guru, a Swami in the Ramakrishna Order of Monks, lasted nearly 40
years. In 2011 Victor compiled and edited *Speak Now*, a collection of essays on
issues surrounding same-sex marriage in Australia.

Contents

prelude – 1

exile – 5

return – 134

hometown blues – 272

coda – 334

Acknowledgements

*

For Prem

prelude

funeral suite—my old man

That's me, up on the platform, wearing sombre clothes. The crematorium chapel is packed and expectant faces look toward me standing at the lectern. Beside me a no-frills coffin is poised before a curtained portal on the narrow runway that leads to the fires. The funeral director has shown me the switch for the microphone, and the large red button I'll push to send the coffin on its way. I may look comfortable, even in charge, but I'm bluffing. I was never good at improv.

The chapel is a stark, comfortless place, its décor bland enough to accommodate all shades of belief, from theism through to atheism and anything in between. They provide the space, we must provide the meaning.

In the cemetery adjacent there are headstones for my brother (who died in his twenties), my mother, and my grandmother. Now it's my father's turn to be interred. He died just a couple of days before his birthday—his 82nd—and today just happens to be my own. My sister Valerie and I are all that remain of our nuclear family, one that has been coming apart, in slow motion, for decades.

Although I am the one directing proceedings I have had little time to prepare. I live in Los Angeles, where I work in television production, and I didn't get in to Western Australia until late yesterday.

We are not a religious family but perhaps they imagine the years I spent in an ashram as 'religious', and it has fallen to me to officiate. My father seldom went to church but among the mourners here today is a sizeable contingent of his Lodge cronies and I know they're fond of a bit of ritual. I've canvassed for potential eulogists among his terse mates but only one of them has stepped forward. I improvise a running order with the help of a *Book of Common Prayer*. I'm not Christian but as I *ad lib* through my makeshift service I weave in snatches of a Psalm: 'The Lord is my shepherd, I shall not want'.

Earlier today, in the funeral parlor in Fremantle, I saw his body laid out, open casket, his fine hair washed and fluffed out across the pillow, in a style he would never have affected. For most of my 47 years we have had a difficult relationship but if I feel uncomfortable doing the honours here, it's not the first time I've been presented with a difficult situation and little know-how. How can I do justice to my father's memory, feeling as I do? A son trying to give his father's life its due—it shouldn't feel perfunctory. Recently I've come to recognise and respect the effort he made, in what must have been a difficult life. But there are issues dragging at me like an undertow that I wouldn't know how to articulate. I hope I provide enough grist for the grieving assembly and that they're satisfied with my sketchy efforts.

I push the red button. As the coffin trundles over the tracks and noses bluntly through the curtains, I intone the Lord's Prayer, invoking a rough consensus among the crowd. They follow my cue, grateful for a little familiarity.

As the next group of mourners moves in to take up the space Val and I receive condolences outside before we re-locate en masse to the old family home in Attadale, where the aunties have arranged sandwiches and sponge cakes. The uncles will bring beer.

In spite of the inquiring looks, with their implicit expectation of grief, I feel detached. One of my father's cronies looms into view. He grips me by the elbow as he shakes my hand.

'Your father was proud of you.'

Do I recognise the face? Do I recognise the sentiment? Another fellow, equally unfamiliar, mutters that we should have had a proper minister up there to do the ritual, and leaves. I am inclined to agree. The whole scene is blighted with doubt for me. This is my 'home' state, yet I live far away. Here am I playing the dutiful son, yet we have been estranged for decades, living out deeply different versions of what makes a man a man.

The next few days I'm too busy to mope. With little time before I return to work in the United States, we have to prepare the house for sale. Val's partner Kaite swings into action to disassemble the household. She packs up what can be donated to charity, advertises a garage sale and flogs the car to a Triumph aficionado for spare parts. Cousin Billy repairs a crack in the roof tiles and patches water-stained plasterwork in the dining room ceiling beneath. I paint the worst of the inner rooms.

I get some satisfaction from ripping the place apart, selling ancient knick-knacks, tearing up the piss-stained carpet in my father's bedroom, but when I see strangers load the kitchen table onto the back of a truck, it's like watching gruff stagehands striking a set, and I know it's finally over.

The only thing I retrieve from the bric-à-brac is a small china figurine. It's Nipper, the little dog from the old HMV ads, listening to his master's voice. I remember him fondly from my time in Tokyo, of all places. A canny secondhand dealer who swoops in early for the 'estate sale' spots the little figurine, but Kaite whisks him away … and he's mine. I will place him alongside the picture I carry of my guru wherever I go. My niece collars the big *Webster's* that has sat on its own stand for two generations, since my American grandmother first installed it in its place of honour.

Val and I haggle over photos from the family albums. After years of traveling I have none, I never thought them important enough to collect and carry; but one grabs my attention. It's a photo of a boy, seated on a sofa, dressed in Sunday best. From the chubby hands he can only be three, or at most four.

Shining face, slicked back hair, alabaster skin; those little fists. I remember the day the man came and put his head under a black cloth bag, and … whoosh! exploded a flash of light. 'Kingsley Watson': the photographer's name still visible in brown pencil to match the photo's sepia tones.

Something about the trust caught in these bright eyes makes me squirm.

The photo was taken in Victoria Park, in the first house I lived in. I try to describe the place to Val, who would have been too young to remember. I recall the velvety upholstery on the couch, the heavy drapes, and the big square of carpet on the floorboards. I don't recall the fabric of the little beige jacket in this shot as well as something else I loved to wear in that room.

child's play

1948. In the formal sitting room, the curtains are drawn. Thick carpet and upholstered furniture muffle all sound. The boy seeks out this place to be alone. But first he goes to the room across the hall, to the cupboard where his mother's dresses hang.

He climbs into the wardrobe to reach for one of these that is special to him; it glows, dappled yellow, flecked with green. Clambering down from the cupboard, he slips the gown over his head to hang loose around him, its folds cascading onto the floor. Silky texture is cool where it skims his skin.

Women's voices murmur in the kitchen.

Suitably attired, the boy returns to the sitting room, where he twirls slowly in the half light, head cocked, gazing down at the skirt as it rises around him in the air. Entranced by its golden glow, he settles down to sit on his heels, spreading the ample folds of fabric in a perfect circle around him on the floor.

Eyes closed, he rests in peace, ears singing in the silence. A cone of light coming into space above where his head was, its base coinciding with the dress's circled shape upon the floor. Dust motes float, lazy, in the light.

But one day, when he reaches into the cupboard, the cool fabric isn't there to meet his touch. He wants to catch the magic feeling, wrap it around him, disappear. He tries the cupboard again, but no matter how carefully he repeats his actions he fails to make the dress appear. A heavy feeling, like dread, drags in his chest.

Another day: he's in the washhouse, in the back yard. A copper tub squats above the fireplace where they boil the water to wash the clothes, on Mondays. Sifting through the ashes, he finds the charred remains of the dress ... this lovely thing banished to dirty dust in his hands.

In the fowl run a hen murmurs cluck cluck, *slow. The heaviness returns to roost in him as, inside the house, a door clicks shut.*

Back at work in Los Angeles, as the tape editor shuttles back and forward through video footage, different scenes from my own history keep pushing forward to be reviewed. I am surprised how much I can remember, how easy it to summon up parts of the 'past' into the present.

exile

victor/victoria

They never say anything to me about the dress. Apparently I have done something so shameful it can never be mentioned, and I am left to deal with the loss alone. I have become an exile, shut out from the place of peace, and I have to learn to live in this new reality.

I live at 6 Howick Street, Victoria Park. That's a girl's name, Victoria. They've named me Victor, shorten it to Vic; that's a boy's name. My brother David, who is definitely a boy, goes to school at Victoria Park State School but I don't go to school yet, I go to kindie. My brother walks me there in the morning and after school I have to wait for him. We walk back home together. When I am six, I will go to big school like him.

There's a boy named Teddy living across the road. He is the same age as me and has a sister. I go over to their place sometimes. One time me and Teddy's sister are playing in a tent in their back yard. She takes down her panties and lets me look at her bum. She has two holes under there. Her mother comes out the screen door and yells: 'What are you kids up to!' and we stop playing, quick.

Another time, we're all together in the back lane behind our place. Teddy is going to pull down his pants and show me his thingie but my mum comes through the gate and she is shouting, so I don't see it. My mum says 'That's very bad, what you kids were doing.' She sends me in the house to wait 'til she comes back and strides across the road to their mum's house. Something awful is going to happen.

I go inside like I've been told and hide under the Singer sewing machine, on the black iron treadle. It's hard, and cold. I wait for a really long time but my mum never says any more about what we did.

Next door, at number four, live the Trumpeters. Their mummy is
Enid and there's a dad, he's Basil, and one of their girls is a grownup. One
day she tells me to come inside, in her bedroom, in the front of their
house. It's dark in there. She sits on the bed, high up, and she doesn't
have any panties on. She tries to put my peanuts in her front hole, but it
doesn't work, she says. She has hair there. It's dark, like the room.

I know it's called a peanuts because my mum told me when I was in
the bath.

One afternoon, after kindie, I am waiting for my brother to bring me
back home, and this other boy is there with me, at the see-saw. He points
out a girl at the swings and he says I have to give her a kiss.

'Go on. I *dare* you! Go on.'

I don't know what to do. I never thought of doing that, kiss a girl or
anything, but the other boy keeps saying go on do it. They play games I
don't know.

'Go on. What are you, a *chick*-en?'

I want him to shut up so I go over to the girl and give her a peck so he
will stop. I don't know who she is. She smells different.

Later on, the headmistress tells me to come into her office and asks
me did I do this terrible thing. I don't understand and I feel bad when she
tells me I have to talk to one of the men teachers. The men are from the
big school. I have to stay late. My brother won't know where I am.

The man teacher is very serious. He says I have to explain myself.

'You don't want to be called Georgie, do you?' I don't say anything.

'You know Georgie Porgie?' I don't know.

'*Georgie Porgie, pudd'n 'n pie, kissed the girls and made them cry!* You don't
want to be like him now, do you? You want to be called Georgie Porgie
for the rest of your life?'

I shake my head. I don't understand. But the man teacher lets me go.
These grownups are serious.

It doesn't get any better when I get to primary.

During recess and lunch breaks I like the tricky games with skipping
ropes. But that's girls' stuff. Playtime is separated. If you cross over you'll
be called a 'sissy' by the other boys. And by the teachers, too. They shoo
me away to the boys' yard, where I flinch at the bruising bounce of a hard

cricket ball. Prissy as well sissy, when some boys grab at each other's balls, shrieking dirty words, I am shocked.

I am friends with Ronny Hetherington, who is 'sissy' but he doesn't seem to know it. Ronny lives with his parents and a young brother. Their house is on my way home from school and sometimes I stay and play in their yard. They came from England and still talk posh. In a photo of us together, Ronny's posing with his head on an angle and his finger pointed under his chin. He thinks he's a starlet in a movie magazine. I want to be left right out of frame. What Ronny the starlet is ready to flaunt, I am already trying to hide.

Three grades ahead, my tough brother David is certainly not a sissy. He is always getting into fights in the schoolyard, and proudly wears the scars of boyhood that I shrink from. He breaks his arm doing the 'rooster chute', a tricky manoeuvre that requires you to stand atop the horizontal bars, a good six feet above the ground. With your feet still planted you swoop backwards, somehow grabbing the bar with both hands on the way down. You swing under the bar, kick out your feet and throw your body forward as far as possible and land, feet first, in the dirt.

David's broken arm is a sign of manliness, not failure. I admire his bravery but I cannot match it. David is so strong he can travel the full length of the monkey bars, swinging arm to arm. My arms won't even support my weight just to hang there with both arms, let alone swing from one rung to the next.

The next time David breaks an arm, by falling out of a tree, I seethe with envy, distraught that my brother has captured everyone's attention again. When David returns from hospital, his arm set conspicuously in plaster, I wail: 'Nothing ever happens to me!' And the whole family laughs at me.

Here's a photo of the two of us together at Victoria Park Primary. David's probably nine or ten and I am around six. See the tough guy, with dark hair and calm, secure eyes. He's the image of our mother, Tish, but with the ferocious hormones of a boy. And the gap-toothed, sandy-haired one next to him, he'd blow away if you said *boo*! That's me.

The house in Howick Street swims in female energy, fat and nurturing. I feel safe there. I don't see much of my father, Frank; he's a salesman and often comes home after we kids have gone to bed. One night sitting in the kitchen, with the lights off and the hiss of the gas rings burning, mum says, 'Let's give Dad a big surprise, eh? When he comes in, we'll all shout WELCOME HOME!' There are tears on her cheek.

For the first three years at primary, the teachers are women. But they're not all soft, like my mum. Miss Watts in second grade has thick hair chopped short. Her stockinged legs smell of nylon and they swish when she walks. She has false teeth that sit too loose on her gums. When she's at her desk, marking papers absent-mindedly she sucks on her teeth until the top set drops down to clack together with the bottoms.

Me and my classmate Timmy stay out of trouble for the most part, except for one of those times when you truly hope the floor could open right up and swallow you completely. Timmy is called up to face the class and recite some poetry, or recall the events of his holiday, or something, but Miss Watts calls him at the exact moment when, for some reason known only to himself, Timmy has his tiny white dickie sticking out his fly.

Given no time to gather up his dignity and re-button, Timmy goes through the entire recital exposed for all to see. I share his anguish, but nothing is spoken (am I really the only one to notice?) and the trauma recedes. No one, not even the teacher, says anything.

But really it is the men I have to watch out for.

Mr Clifford is on roster during recess and he bristles with a harshness that my instincts say: Avoid! He teaches Grade Five and I work out, in dread: if I move on up through the grades, I will inevitably arrive before that steely gaze. So, when Grade Five does come around I enter Mr Clifford's classroom in a state of high alert, studying the man hard to learn the means to please. His thick glasses make his eyes look crazy.

One day some foolish boy makes a face behind the teacher's back, his need to be popular overriding his sense of safety. Mr Clifford catches him at it, and erupts. His face turns red and he becomes a puppet in a Punch and Judy show. With a screech, he fires off a fusillade of blackboard dusters. His eyes are rolling and his pepper-and-salt hair quivers, not just on his head but from his ears, his nose, his throat, and his animated eyebrows too, ready to shoot out like quills from a porcupine.

The cheeky boy ducks, and most of the missiles miss their mark, but Mr Clifford's anger needs to be satisfied. He drags the boy from his desk and starts to whack him, hard, with the wooden ruler that he uses to mark lines on the blackboard, for writing lessons. The more the boy wriggles to get away, the harder Clifford hits him.

I am frozen, immobile, like the rest of the class, holding my breath. The violence registers as if it is my own body being dragged around and beaten up in front of us.

Soon after, I am rescued from the cauldron of Mr Clifford and his rages. My father relocates the family across town to a new suburb, south of the river. David continues into high school, in Victoria Park, while Valerie and I move to Attadale Primary, where there is a new fifth-grade teacher, the entirely pleasant Mr O'Hara. I have swapped the pit-bull for a lamb and school life assumes a different mood.

During craft lessons, Mr O'Hara has me sing to the class. I croon true love tunes that I hear on the radio, copying Bing Crosby and Rosemary Clooney. When you sing, if you close your eyes, you can disappear into your voice until it comes out clean, right on the note.

Inside and outside, everything turns smooth. At least at school. At home David has taken to bullying me, trying out his superior muscle strength, and something seems to be rankling my father.

quarter-acre block

1955. It's a new house.

My mother trills her joy to all her friends: 'It has curved architraves. And they're French-polished! It's truly my dream home.' I don't know what 'architraves' are, but I repeat her puffery to my new classmates. Father speaks in more muffled tones of the financing. The house was built for a bookie who went broke and the builder decided to put it on the market to recoup his costs. Uncle Bill's a bookie too, but he seems to be doing OK.

Initially, I am disappointed with the house. A week or so before, I went with my mother and her sisters on an outing to see it from the outside but none of them knew the street number and I took a fancy to a grander structure further up the road. Wrong house.

This one is part of a new development, in bushland, and it feels like I have moved to the countryside. In reality we have come south of the river to Attadale, halfway to Fremantle on the new Canning Highway. Howick Street, in Victoria Park, was part of an established neighborhood, houses shouldered side by side, with English-styled gardens, footpaths, well-worn roads, and an orderly procession of trees spaced neatly up and down the streets. The trees and verges were clipped like clients in my Yankee grandma's beauty salon. Here, all is a confusion of native trees, in smoky olive greens and greasy black. Off the highway the back roads are little more than graded dirt tracks and the bushland has been sacrificed to make way for more and more houses, all the way down to the river.

At first I don't know how to take this in. It seems primitive. I try out some jungle calls atop a mound of tree stumps and other debris that has been cleared to make way for the highway but my voice rings hollow even to my own ears, so I come down from the mountain to wait for some more authentic feeling to come to me another time.

Soon I am into a familiar routine, padding off bare-footed to Mr O'Hara's school. I feel more at ease in the bush, mimicking bird songs, enticing them to follow me, wondering what I am really saying in birdspeak. I pay close attention when a teacher tells of poisonous snakes and spiders, describes correct procedures for snake-bite, and the places where they are likely to snooze, such as under fallen logs. There are dark holes to be wary of, too, where deadly redbacks lurk. The letterbox is a likely nook for these nasty little spiders and I resent being sent out to collect the mail. As for the snakes—tiger snakes and dugites, mostly—I take comfort in the news that they feel the vibration of your steps through the ground. They are just as likely to want to avoid an encounter as I am. The best strategy is to avoid surprise. So I tend to stamp out my way, until I realise that I never actually encounter any.

I plunder the bush for wildflowers, spider orchids and blood orchids, miniature miracles waiting to be discovered among the drab, olive bushland. I stuff thick bunches into jars as proud trophies of my explorations until Aunty Gwen, a family friend familiar to these parts, advises me that, really, I ought to pick only a few and leave the rest to reproduce. Better to see them in the wild than dying indoors in glass jars.

Other members of the new household are not making such an easy adjustment. One evening my father summons the family to the kitchen. Everyone is in pajamas, ready for bed: my brother David, sister Valerie and I collect with our mother, Tishie. Dad has come home late from work, as usual, but this will be different, I can feel it already. A strange charge fills the air.

'Get up, go on. Climb up there.' Dad tells my brother to climb up onto the kitchen table. The mood is heavy, dragging with dread.

'Now I want you to jump, and I'll catch you.'

David hesitates.

'Go on, *jump*, I tell you. I'll catch you. *Jump*! Go on …'

Is he drunk?

The more my father urges, the more tightly he commands our whole attention. Finally when David is provoked to leap from the table top, instead of catching him our Dad steps back, making no effort to break his fall, and allows him to crumple to the kitchen floor.

'That's to make sure you never trust *anyone!*'

It wasn't far to fall, and David isn't hurt, but I am puzzled. Is that it? Or is there something else that I am supposed to read between the lines?

'Oh, Frank. Why did you have to go and do that?' my mother the peacemaker might have said. But she is overawed. This is not the kind of family spirit she grew up with. She knows about the struggle with his business partners that has precipitated the family's move across town, so perhaps she can make allowances, but if she does raise the matter in muttered private conversations in their bedroom, we kids don't hear about it. Without any other interpretation available, Father has demonstrated only one thing: *he* is the one who cannot be trusted.

As the years pass, other dramas are acted out around the laminex but few words break through the net of resentments. Most weeknights Dad comes home late, half-sozzled.

'There's your dinner, then. Ruined as usual.'

Mum plonks down the dinner plate. She keeps his meal warm by placing it on top of a saucepan, with the lid of the pan over the plate and hot water simmering beneath. By the time he gets to eat, the food is usually gray.

'Ah, get off my back, woman.'

This is muttered only half strength. If he feels guilty, it's expressed only obliquely, in a kind of mute belligerence. He eats his food in silence, eyes down, obsessively clearing every part of the plate, seething with unspoken ripostes. We kids watch this tight-jawed procedure from the sidelines as hints of thunder and lightning flash around.

Mother's authority in the domestic sphere is seldom challenged but Dad keeps her under control with parsimonious disbursements of cash. She keeps him in his place, in turn, with sheer moral superiority. This tension simmers away under the surface, like the water on the stove, as he shakes copious amounts of salt onto the food and grimly divides the dinner into gulp-sized portions.

'Can't you taste it first?' she complains. 'All that salt ...'

Frank is the good boy who works to finish all his food. At the same time he's the angry man who has bloody-well paid for it, after all. The bone-handled knife bends, threatens to break, as he scrapes the plate clean of the last traces of gravy.

Frank makes sure that the benefits of domesticity don't unduly compromise his freedoms. Mum is a homebody, but he keeps up memberships in two or three men's clubs where he can gather for after-work drinking sessions with his business buddies. Saturdays he spends at the East Fremantle Bowling Club.

Mum stretches the household budget with purchases on 'time payment' plans. A new lounge suite takes a year to pay off, and Marshall's drapery keeps a card on file for her clothes account. She and her sisters, Lucy and Verna, swap visits on weekdays to do each other's hair. They all trained in Grandma Evans's salon, The Vanity Box, in the Perth suburb of Leederville. All the aunties play canasta and when we're lucky, Grandma teaches us kids the rules so we can join in the fun. A raucous afternoon with our Yankee 'Grammaw' around is sure to be a giggle. We kids crowd around as out come the ciggies and the swear words.

The tension rises as the discard pile grows larger.

'Shit. How many of those black threes did you have, Verna?' Lucy complains.

'For goodness goshness Agnes' sake, somebody freeze the pack,' Grandma protests. 'There's at least a canasta of sevens in there by now.'

Lucy swoops and takes the pack.

'You little bugger!' Mum tries to swipe it from her.

'I thought she had kings in *her* hand.'

Everyone is cackling and hooting protests.

'But you just threw *out* a king!'

'And you fell for it …'

On school mornings we kids have to wait until dad's leisurely visits to the 'library'—the toilet off the back verandah, where he works his way through the morning paper—to sneak loose change from the pockets of the trousers left hanging on the bedroom door the night before. He won't give us any pocket money but when we ask Mum for money for school she says 'Check your father's pockets'.

Dad's woollen trousers smell of stale sweat and cigarettes. He would wear the same clothes every day if Mum let him. She whisks away the worst for cleaning to keep him looking, and smelling, respectable. She has more trouble with the shoes though. They always stink, and even if, after much wheedling and nagging, he gets a new pair, they become the ones he wears, day in day out, until they too get that ineradicable, musty odor. We are glad when Saturday comes so he has to wear his bowling shoes, with special smooth, flat rubber soles that don't ruin the hard flat greens at the club, and gives his daily pair an airing.

Out in the yard, Frank heaves and strains to bend this piece of virgin property to his will. A foster child, he left home at an early age to earn his keep felling trees in the great timber country of the South West. Now here he is, thirty years later, in his own brick house, the seasoned battler on his quarter-acre block, face to face with the unkempt tangle of the land. If not quite 'his' yet, then the bank's; or the Repatriation Department, which arranges housing loans for war servicemen.

'Frank, will you please get out of those office clothes,' Mum complains.

He throws off his office shirt and resumes his part-time chopping and digging in his singlet, keeping a tally in a ledger of every palm, shrub and tree he uproots, as if he is doing the office accounts. I wince at his gruesome bookkeeping: so many zamia palms, so many banksia trees; the list tracks down the page. For months, little bonfires smoulder here and there, small funeral pyres for dead natives and the yard becomes a bleak and barren place.

Father's hard-won property pushes back the bush with a stiff, upright fence on three sides, joining the ranks of other fences from street to ordered street. Naked wooden pickets cut from timber from some other place, chopped and stripped and planed, sawn into regulation lengths, lined up man-height in even rows, and nailed impersonally to cross beams, in yard after yard, unwilling recruits in the great war of obliteration.

In the back yard, one last gum tree stands, a silent reminder of what has been. Morning magpies come to chortle their songs there, waking me in a state of wonder. But this remnant tree drops messy twigs and leaves into a yard that is now bare, save for the stiff form of the Hills Hoist. This marvelous new invention, a 'rotary clothesline', is a pyramid shape of metal tubes and the wires on which you peg the wet laundry, supported by a central metal pole, with a handle you turn to raise it up and down. Every home should have one. Most of them do. The Hills Hoist is like a huge radio antenna through which the force field of conformity is beamed directly to every home.

Frank wants to create a surface in the backyard on which to practise lawn bowls. He splits the yard in two and levels a broad section of ground along the back fence line. The 'bowling green' will be grown from a certain variety of fine 'couch', a grass that lends itself to compacting into a dense, hard surface smoothly suitable for play. The rest of the yard is seeded with the more rugged buffalo variety, and a strip of narrow timber, sunk into the ground, runs right across the yard to separate the two sections of lawn. The would-be bowling green requires a hard surface and the straggly buffalo is inimical to the plan. For years he will struggle to keep them apart.

A two-stroke mower is bought and juiced up to blare out growls and petrol fumes and we boys are dragooned to drag about a heavy roller, crushing the dedicated strip of lawn into the required flatness, just like the felt-covered billiard tables at the Commercial Club. The harder and more even the surface, the truer the trajectory of the biased bowls will be, and Frank intends to spend his leisure hours perfecting his delivery.

The one last tree stands, quite literally, in the way of Frank's genteel vision and on the day of its demise he enlists the help of my brother and me to bring it to its knees. I am reluctant to be recruited into his relentless war on the environment, but Dad has manly lessons to teach his sons and wields the axe with great authority. He explains that if you cut a wedge into the trunk just so, the tree will be inclined to fall in a particular direction, and he wrestles guy-ropes into place to ensure its fall across the yard, away from the hard-won fence line. He grunts each time the axe thuds into the trunk and his sweat smell, mingling with the metallic tang of the axe blade, bites into my nostrils. The heavy blade chops hard, and hard again, against the tree, a dull ringing sound softened each time its sharp edge gouges out rough chunks of tree flesh, exposing the inner red and ochre tones at the timber's heart. A difficult death, the greatest left until last.

As it falls, the tree heaves and shudders. I am writhing inwardly, in sympathy, so I feel a surreptitious thrill when, contrary to all of father's theories, with a great ear-cracking heave of defiance the timber skews the wrong way across the yard, falling heavily across the triangles of the stiff Hills Hoist, which quivers now in shock, insulted, steel limbs twisting awkwardly, tree branches poking through among the wires.

My old man bellows with rage, blaming everyone and everything—us boys, the ropes, the laws of mechanics themselves—cursing the tree for its perversity. He chops to disentangle the branches, struggling to bring the twisted clothesline upright, grumbling about the cost. Thrilled as I am at the outcome, I must hide my glee but for years after, the broken teeth of the clothesline's rotary mechanism will remind me how the tree took its revenge.

Over many days the trunk's well-rooted stump stubbornly holds its ground as fire, the final solution, burns into its foothold in the earth. At night, from my bedroom window overlooking the back yard, I watch subdued embers glowing red against the dark.

A sure but sterile order reigns, bounded by the pickets, with every sign of native life banished for good. Sandy soil that once supported well-adapted life forms resists attempts with topsoil, seed and fertilizer to support its alien garden. Wild untidy life recedes throughout the suburb and I must roam further afield to catch the swirl of natural forms. Magpies, displaced refugees, skirt the great desolation to sing to me from a tree in a neighbour's yard.

Father's dream of a perfect practice surface is never fully realised. My brother and I shirk our heavy-roller duty and, as tough weeds and interloper strands of buffalo invade the bumpy green, Frank is forced to confine his practice sessions to rehearsing his stance on the mat, refining the proper grip and perfecting the smooth initial delivery of the bowl onto the lawn. (He plays pennants as well as club games.)

On the carpet in the living room we play the indoor version, *en famille*. This is something we can all do safely, kids and grownups. I learn to use the bias to effect a backhand draw, nudging out a closer bowl and nestling my own closer to the white 'kitty', to take the shot.

Dad recites a little ditty doing the rounds:

> *Girls are made to love and kiss*
> *And some are very pretty*
> *But best of all, I'll tell you this*
> *Is kissing little kitty.*

The verse is immortalised on a kitsch ashtray illustrated with a sketch of a bowler levitating with atypical glee. The 'kitty' in question is the white ball around which you need to cluster your bowls to score. A bowl that touches, or 'kisses', the kitty is marked with white chalk and is kept in play, even if later it gets knocked into the ditch. Technically speaking, 'kissing kitty' is good insurance for the endgame. I miss the smutty double entendre.

Wives might yet take comfort from the ditty; better to have a husband getting close to this little kitty than having him off chasing another Kitty, or Colleen. The smart ones, like my mother, follow their men into the clubs. She joins the ladies' bowls club at East Fremantle, where Dad plays, at last finding something she can share with him and she soon has her own stories to tell over the kitchen table, of nervous near misses and triumphant draw-shots that saved the game. We kids make fun of the way they use the salt- and pepper-shakers, and whatever else comes to hand, to reconstruct the more dramatic games the oldies played in pennants and club games.

Frank has asserted his claim on the land and we nestle nervously around him. He still comes home late, his meals ruined, but now Mum has won her own access to a wider world, away from the strictly domestic confines of the house.

dream sequence—dark circle

'Would you mind sleeping with your father tonight, honey? I'll swap with your bed. Ok?'

I don't ask why. I am not at an age to be consulted over the logistics of the household and as a passive boy I don't demur. It's a private adult drama being acted out to a script that I have not read but they know well, so the usual sleeping arrangements will be different tonight. Perhaps they've done this before and, after all, it will be rather special to sleep in the big bed with my father alongside.

The bedrooms are at the other side of the house from the kitchen, along a hallway, past the bathroom. Mother retreats to my bed in the sleep-out, where part of the verandah has been enclosed, and I go to hers. The generous expanse of my parents' mattress is quite a contrast to my own narrow single. Their room is laid out differently and there are new smells here. There's a dressing table with a mirror, up against one wall, where her few feminine toiletries are arrayed. A bottle of 4711 Eau de Cologne is there in its box, for use on special occasions. Against the opposite wall are matching his-and-hers wardrobes in shiny wood-grain and between them is the big bed, with the same wood-grain, head and foot.

I am asleep before my father joins me.

In the depths of the night, a dark dream disturbs my rest. A group of tall male figures gathers in a circle. Each figure overshadows a smaller one in front of it, and they are all turned towards the centre. Their shadows loom upward, elongated, forming a gloomy vault-like canopy, as a mysterious rite unfolds. I am one of the smaller shapes, and the larger presence behind makes me uneasy. The mood is oppressive and my body churns with dread.

Next morning I wake to find my pajama bottoms down around my ankles. I am puzzled to find the lower part of my body naked. As I draw my pants up and clamber out of bed, a heavy feeling lingers with me like a musty smell.

In the kitchen, they're laying a brand new floor, with rubber tiles to replace the linoleum. A friend of my father, expert in these matters, has been brought in to help and the two men huddle over the plans. Men's business. I had better pay attention. They've drawn the design on grid paper with the colour marked out against the squares. Most of the tiles are grey but at one end, around a section of cupboards, a different cherry-red has been coloured in to highlight the cabinet's shape against the grey. At that edge, instead of a neat right angle, the cupboard curves and the arc of colour against the square shapes has thrown them a problem. It's geometry. Square tiles needing a curve. They'll have to be cut to shape.

The issue has been discussed in detail in preceding weeks, so I have had a chance to observe the process and enjoy the choice of colour, especially that cherry red as a highlight, and I reckon the curvilinear flourish in the floor plan is a pleasing variation on the grid. In the weeks to come my mother will master a new electric floor-polisher, with contrary spinning wheels, experimenting with different products to buff the surface to an impressive gloss, her friends applauding her prowess.

But this phase, the cutting, gluing and laying, this is work for men. I watch from a distance as they discuss the plans.

Father's friend has strong legs and calloused hands and he knows this flooring business. He wears a leather tool belt around the waist of his shorts. Pots of smelly glue and a couple of Stanley knives lie scattered here and there among the stacks of tiles.

I gather up some nerve and sidle up alongside, to join in.

'Aah, that curve, it's a real problem,' the men concur.

'Mmm …Yeah, it's a real problem,' I echo, auditioning my style enthusiastically. My voice doesn't match.

'YOU,' flares my father, his mouth an ugly shape. 'You stay OUTTA this!' And with a sweeping backhander he dismisses me. 'Just get out,' he growls, turning back to the task at hand.

My rehearsal at manliness rebuffed, I stumble down the hallway to my room at the back end of the house and sink down onto my bed, too shaken to be able to think or cry. He hasn't struck me, not physically, but he might as well have. I sit there, with an overwhelming sensation of the world spinning out of control. Last night we were so close.

My mind revs weakly, like a car with a flat battery, unable to turn over a spark. What to make of it? From the intimacy in bed, to the harsh rebuff in the tile-strewn kitchen, and now this spinning void. My heart feels like it is choking. I am drowning in a feeling I can't contain, struggling to get back to the surface somehow, but I can't reach the banks of this deep, dark pool.

I remember diving off a jetty into the river, in Como, and hit my head on the shallow bottom. I must have come close to breaking my neck that day. Slipping away, underwater, like I was tired, and sleep was pulling at me. But some force summoned up a shred of will before I could welcome in the water, and snapped me out of the warm pull of unconsciousness, stood me upright, head reeling, coming back to breathe in air.

Slumped on my bed, I grope to get some traction. Slowly, something brings me back from the brink of disintegration. But I don't know this new shape I am in, as if there's space between the pieces. My makeshift strategy for survival will rely on shutting this unpredictable man out of my life, at least from the inside. This is a difficult decision to make, because the inconvenient realities of life as an eleven-year-old make me dependent for food and shelter on the arrangement as it stands. I will depend on my father as little as possible, beyond the minimum required to stay lodged here in his house, until …? Until I can find some other place and safely leave? But where else can I go? Wherever I belong, long term, I know it can't be here.

This decision, unnoticed by my father, will cost me in many ways. I accept (perhaps too readily) that I don't belong to the world of men. If I can't con the ways of masculinity and gain entry to that fierce tribe, I will find another way, eventually, but at this time there's no way out. As much as I hate the taste of beer, the crude jokes, the rough manner, the loud voices and the mocking smiles of the brutal brotherhood, I don't know how I can totally avoid trying to be like them, so I must study their ways.

My mother is my comfort and her unstinting caring is so much a part of the fabric of my life, it's easy to take it for granted. Without her I would be crushed. But I do know that I am not a girl. Shamed out of that identification since the early years at primary school, with the stinging accusation 'sissy' ringing hotly in bright red ears to warn me away, I have tried to fit in. Now I am on my own. Neither/nor. In some ways absences can be even more powerful than presences; the men are the puzzle.

While the option to stay is a passive one, it has activated a new level of self-protecting alertness. My dark secret tightens into a denser knot as I withdraw a part of my being to hang on and wait for my release, however that might come. The decision troubles me enough for me to raise a flag in this lonely place, somewhere in my psyche, so that one day I can find my way back and re-consider, a day when I will have better resources to handle my choices. Meanwhile, I have to pretend that I belong.

In the brick and tile house on Canning Highway, the family watches telly in the living room. I am usually reading a book; the programs hardly demand my complete attention. Frank chides me: 'Stop biting your nails!' But he fails to attend to the possible sources of my anxiety.

caterpillar dreaming
for Van Tan Vuong

My mother asks me to bury some rubbish in the back garden. As I dig a hole under a hibiscus bush I come across the decomposing body of a cat, a family pet that died some months ago. I push away the ghastly testimony of decay, quickly shovelling sand back into the hole, wishing I had paid more attention when it was buried. This encounter revives a fear in me that I too will be laid in the ground one day.

My chores require me to clean up leaves in the yard from time to time. One day while raking I find a glistening capsule that I must have squished in passing, its inhabitant ejected prematurely from a private hibernation. I pick it up and hold it in my palm. It has blue-green swirls, like that *pāua* shell from New Zealand, but reds and some yellow, too, and a burnished copper swirls across its surface. Lustrous, like the inside of an oyster shell, but not hard. A little more than an inch long, it lies still across my palm.

I find the dry brown husk that was its cover, before I came along.

There's no one to ask what this creature might be but I guess that, even though it's dormant, it's probably alive. Perhaps there's an insect body rolled up inside. Yes, that's it: no longer a grub, nor yet a butterfly, suspended between two states of being. The caterpillar has gone but no butterfly has yet emerged to spread its wings to dry, then fly away. Look how beautifully protected it is as it goes through the changes.

I worry I might have killed it and check for signs of damage. Luckily it seems whole, and after a moment to enjoy its opalescent beauty, I slip it back into the brown sheath and hide it among the leaves. How long will it take to make its transition?

I wait two weeks, anxious to know if it will survive, but when I return there is nothing there. Did I mistake the spot? I check across a wider area, but there's no sign to mark its passing. No brown husk, no glistening capsule, no grub … and no butterfly.

The golden dress may have been lost to me, but this chrysalis proves to be a kind of talisman from the natural world. It tells of a larger mystery taking place, a very personal reminder that whatever this process is that I am living, I am going through the changes, too.

I will recall the chrysalis when a friend commits suicide, decades later. Disaster after disaster piles up on his head and he can't take it any more. Will it ever get that bad for me? The chrysalis is a warning and a promise. It's not for me to abort the outcome before its time.

wake-up call

1956. It's morning. 8.11 am. I can tell the time to the minute from the sound of the traffic on the highway, out front. Everyone else is up. Mum is in the kitchen getting breakfast together. My fourteen-year-old brother and roommate, David, is already dressed and heading to school. Father is installed in his stinking library, slowly working his way through the morning paper, and Val is whining that she can't use the loo.

'Come on Frank,' says my mum. 'Sitting there so long. You'll get piles.'

I'm in the sixth grade now and my school is close by. I lie in bed listening to the traffic, calculating how long I may linger in the warmth before rousing myself at the last possible minute to take my turn in the shower, where I luxuriate in the steaming water, washing scudding foam from hot pink skin.

As I shower, something catches my eye. I look down and see a dark intruder. Is that a spider?

A black hair gleaming through the suds, close to the skin. Just one—is it two?—down near the little appendage that scarcely attracts attention on an average day. Black? The hair on my head is blond, slowly turning brown. Why that? There. Now. I want to push the discovery away, as if I have a choice. My body, inhabited without reflection up until now, is insisting on its own agenda, betraying me from below. I almost panic, sensing something will soon be lost. Panic soon shifts to resentment: does this mean I will have to become like all the others, this weird tribe I have learned to live among? Reluctant to surrender, I lapse briefly into depression.

By the time I have my first wet dream—a mix of fear (have I wet the bed?) and stronger, inchoate, feelings—it is clear that this alien state of being is not going to evaporate; its sheer inevitability threatens a sense of freedom that I have been unaware of before. I don't yet associate the phenomenon with any sensual pleasure that might compensate for the sense of dread.

A friend of my brother chortles lewdly as he squirts water from the garden hose in spurts: 'Hah! What does that remind you of?' David hushes him with a glare, not knowing that jerky rhythm is a message I can decode already. Snigger words like 'stiff' and 'fat' leap out of conversations. At school, I blush, awkward at girls' attentions. One wants to polish my desk.

David has never hesitated to accept his own invitation to adulthood. Unlike me, his pansy brother, he just can't wait to get into everything. He wants to leave school already, a horrific prospect to me, and is desperate to own his own car. He slicks his black hair back with Brylcreem, and flicks a kiss curl forward over his forehead, like Elvis Presley. He really likes girls, and it's clear they like him back. With a car, the opportunities will multiply. He sneaks a visit to the legendary 'Snake Pit' in Scarborough, where bodgies and widgies hang out and dance to the new rock and roll music, and he likes to disparage the 'Neddy boys', soft types from the other side of the river, from upmarket suburbs like Crawley, Nedlands, Peppermint Grove, home to private schools and the university.

I discuss the possibilities of penetration with another boy. Bill lives a few houses further up the road and wants to know a lot more about it than I am comfortable with. I am becoming curious about animal sexual behaviour—I keep pet rabbits, a cat, and a cage with budgies—but I am still prissy when it comes to people. Girls have two holes, one at the back and one underneath, I remember that.

It must go in the front hole, we decide, and I put off thinking about it as long as I can.

It will be a couple more years before my own longing finds a form to fixate upon, and Terence Johnson's well-turned limbs briefly inhabit the contours of my desire. I haven't quite put the two together yet: that 'sissy', or 'homo', equals what I will feel for Terence. Humiliation has not yet become my caustic counsellor.

fluffy due

My mother marks the calendar behind the kitchen door: 'Ethel due'. A friend is going to have a baby. So when my white rabbit is due to give birth I mark the calendar too: 'Fluffy due'. I get the facts on lapine gestation from a library book, and count the days from the time a friend brings around his young buck and together we watch them mate (with very close attention). While it is a little off-putting to see how they fight, and how the buck bites out tufts of fur from her back in his fierce and rapid copulation, I suppose it is as good an introduction as one can get, in a family that would never talk about sex.

Fluffy will happily sit in my lap, like a pet rooster I had years ago. (Before my father chopped off its head and it became our Sunday lunch, that is.) While sympathetic to my doe's violent initiation into the act of love, at the same time I am just as interested in the male's lusty thrusting.

My calendar notation draws shrieks of outrage and delight from my mother and her friends, but in the context of her own diffident essays at adult-to-child instruction I see that she is grateful that I can put one and one together to make three. She handed over a booklet, *What Every Boy Should Know,* a few months ago, without comment, but I found its cross-sectional diagrams of male and female reproductive organs less than revealing. Father must have resisted her entreaties to offer me a 'Q & A' on the issue, and the opportunities for mutual embarrassment, mercifully, lapsed.

I don't recall if Ethel is as prompt at delivering her offspring as Fluffy, but on the appointed day, when I go to check the hutch, I find her nest box meticulously prepared. As a foundation for her nest she has used some of the straw I provided but she has torn out clumps of her own fur, too, to make a soft, warm cocoon on top.

As I enter, she sniffs around, agitated by my attention, and I know something is up. When I lift one of the tufts of fur, a writhing mass of pink forms is revealed there, snug within their mother's fur bedding. Tiny blind bodies, hairless as yet, looking more like mice than rabbits. Maybe five or six of them. Some have mottled markings in their skin.

The kittens (that's what they are called) take on different colours as their fur grows through; the mottled skin markings must have been some kind of indicator. Both Fluffy and the buck are white but there are a silver and some chocolate browns mixed in among the whites flip-flopping on the lawn. I know nothing of genetics, but I do see how a mother and father can produce offspring quite unlike them in many ways.

crushed, a love song

For an athlete is enamour'd of me, and I of him,
But toward him there is something fierce and terrible in me
eligible to burst forth,
I dare not tell it in words, not even in these songs.
—Walt Whitman 'Earth, My Likeness' from *Calamus*

I wonder if you notice, Terry Johnson, that for a brief few days I have a
crush on you. I am that sandy-haired, softer boy, quite popular in school,
but shadowed by a secret.

One day after school we ride our bikes down to the river for a swim
and for the first time I have to struggle with the pain of the pleasure of
another boy's company. Do you see my eyes snatching thirsty glances at
the swelling shapes of your thigh and calves? You're wearing royal blue
swimming trunks. Your skin glows and your perfect limbs make my blood
beat harder. Fine hairs dust the hollows where your spine meets your
buttocks' rise.

My gaze lingers along your arm, across your firm shoulder muscle,
along the biceps, to where your forearm, accented with rising veins,
curves into the magical square that holds your wrist and man/boy hand so
right. You're a sketch by Leonardo, sprung to life, 3-D.

As we frolic in the warmth of this early summer afternoon, my longing
almost bursts its banks. You are in chest-deep water, near the jetty. As we
splash about I long to cross the gap and grasp you in a dizzy embrace:
bodies wriggling, struggling; hands gripping arms. This urge lifts free of all
constraint and I lunge against the water to grab at you but, as I push off
the river bottom, I kick my big toe hard against a sharp-edged rock and
slice off a part, unseen. Instantly snapped back from the brink of desire,
my attention is drawn one-pointed to an acute, searing pain where my toe
should be.

Poor Terry, suddenly pressed into service as paramedic; you bundle
me onto your bike and urgently pedal us both back home, me
uncomfortable, riding side-saddle on the cross bar, you afraid, as I am,
that I will bleed to death before you make it there. If our bodies brush

together as you carry me to safety, no frisson of pleasure rises through the stark pain for me to savour the occasion. Love abandons me before I can speak a single syllable of its dirty, secret name.

sticks and stones

What is secret doesn't stay that way for long.

A friend and I (his name is Daniel) have started sneaking out at night to prowl the local lovers' lane, on the sandy tracks down near the river. On a Friday or Saturday we can be sure to come across a few cars snuggled under the low, scrubby paper-bark trees. We hope to find out exactly what goes on between men and women there but are afraid to trigger pursuit by young men, angry at having their *coitus* interrupted. Reluctant to peer boldly through the steamy windows, Daniel and I are left to imagine what kinds of acts might be under way. One Saturday night we find a discarded condom. I know that it's called a 'prophylactic', commonly a 'franger', or 'French letter', and that it's used to guard against disease as well as impregnation. We take the rubber back to my place, wash it out in the bathroom sink, then roll it in some paper towels to dry, before my pubescent friend decides to try it on for size.

Daniel is a short boy with an inordinately large penis that I soon discover features a fleshy, dark red head. When it gets hard its hole drips with sticky fluid. At thirteen, these are mysteries for which we have only rudimentary instruction. We haven't yet worked out that we could masturbate, so our fumbling repertoire consists of looking and touching and whispered debates about what we could do.

One afternoon my sister catches us comparing notes in the room off the back verandah; nothing hard-core, but we do have our dicks out. Val turns on her heel and storms through the house, bellowing 'HOMOSEXUAL' at the top of her lungs; rolled out, syllable by outraged syllable: HO - MO - SECKS - SHOO - ALL, the emphasis bunched on the third syllable, like she wants the forbidden fact to splatter onto the walls and hang there dripping for days, so no one can fail to recognise what I am reluctant to have anyone, even Daniel, see. I sit shivering, like that time in Victoria Park, huddled on the cold black treadle under the Singer sewing machine, after my mother interrupted us in the laneway behind the house. I cringe, dreading the imminent discovery in which denial will be unmasked and I will be caught in shame's glaring headlights.

Daniel slinks out the side door.

Val knows she has something on me. There's no one else home but she might tell them later, so the threat hangs ready to unload whenever it finds its mark, like the 'sissy boy', 'fairy', 'pansy', 'poofter', 'queer' darts I have ducked until now, hoping they won't home in on me.

The next few days are fraught with caution. My phone calls to Daniel's house meet with a frosty reception, his mother won't even call him to the phone. What has Daniel said to her? Does he suspect that I am more into these games than he is? Now that he has caught a whiff of what this might imply about his own manliness, he withdraws completely from our pre-love games. I am popular in school, and active in sports, so to a degree I am shielded from suspicion, but I fear my cover has thinned.

It isn't as if the word is foreign, exactly. If Val already knows what it means at ten, I must too, at thirteen. I have been avoiding even the short form 'homo' but somewhere I have learned not only that its nastiness applies to me, but now, especially as the physical aspect is manifesting, what it might mean. It has never landed so squarely on its target like this before, let alone in (semi-)public.

My Yankee grandmother has a Webster's on a stand. The entry after 'Ho.mo sa.pi.ens' ('the scientific name for the only living species of the genus *Homo*') is:

ho.mo.sex.u.al *adj.* of or characterized by sexual desire for those of the same sex. *n.* a homosexual individual. Opposed to *heterosexual.*

This identity seems ready-made, and I suspect it's loathsome. Will I become one of those invidious caricatures who mince across the screen occasionally at the pictures? No handsome leading man takes another man into his arms for a kiss, or more.

I do some furtive research in a public library, uncovering the term in a volume by Von Krafft-Ebing, a book so grim it ought to be enough to drag me from my wayward path back onto the straight and narrow. This is what I have to go on:

von Krafft-Ebing, R 1924. Psychopathia Sexualis with especial reference to the Antipathic Sexual Instinct. A Medico-Forensic Study. Only authorised English adaptation of the Twelfth German Edition. New York: Physicians and Surgeons Book Company.

I flip to the index at the back: p. 616. There I am, right after 'Hermaphroditism, psychical':

Homosexuality (vide Antipathic sexuality), p. 286
Homosexual feeling as an abnormal congenital manifestation

followed closely by *hysteria,* then:

ideal sadism, 118
Impotence, 13
Immorality, 502
Incest, 612
Injury to women, 105

And

Insanity among the Scythians, 302.

So that's the company I keep … A little further on, right after a lengthy entry on 'masochism', is the dreaded:

Masturbation, consequences of, 286.

Then follows a lengthy entry on 'pederasty', and various references regarding:

pathology, special, 462
psychopathological cases, 554
sexual instinct, homosexual, 282
—perversions of, 79, 462.

I must be seriously sick. Flicking back to the listings for 'sodomy', I go to page 561, where the German expert has listed kindly for my perusal:

7. Unnatural Abuse (Sodomy).
Sub-section 7 (a) records information on *Violation of Animals (Bestiality).*

So this is my condition: a 'mental condition', in fact, an 'abnormal perversion'. I am not so much a legal problem, I see, as I am a specimen for the scientific study of 'Inverts'. My sister has spoken with more authority than she knew. If she and her scientific allies already know me better than I know myself, are they telling my future, too? On page 573, I find that for 'many neuropathic individuals' (and *Urnings* are almost always 'neuropathic' apparently):

Before them lies mental despair—even insanity and suicide—at the very least, nervous disease; behind them, shame, loss of position, etc.

Nothing to look forward to but despair, insanity and suicide … I search out 'neurasthenic' in the index, and flip through some case studies. For example, the one on 144:

hysteria gravis … there was no amnesia. Thoroughly virile. Decent appearance. Genitals normal. Short imprisonment.

Imprisonment! But you said I was not a criminal, I was an 'irresponsible insane person'. Even before being identified as a psycho-medical disorder I have already achieved the status of criminal offender, now a sexual, medical and social outlaw. Moreover, Victor Marsh, aged thirteen, living in a suburb of Perth, Western Australia, in 1958, has already found his way onto the path to perdition, for on page 447, I read:

puberty teaches the youthful sinner to know his true sex soon enough … the homosexual act committed after puberty has set in, is the decisive step in the wrong direction.

A *moral* outcast, too. Even the scientist names me as sinner.

There were many messages folded into Valerie's accusation: this is shameful; you had better hide; there is danger in this becoming public knowledge; there are other people who don't *need* to hide; you're sick, you're 'one of nature's mistakes'. The admonitions speak clearly to me. This naming project is part of a coercive conspiracy to call me into line. I'm a boy, not a girl. I have been warned not to gush. I shouldn't use my hands when I talk. In fact, it is advisable not to be too … 'expressive'; too 'theatrical'. I should be careful not to flap my wrists, nor to stand with my hands on hips (a dead giveaway), especially on the football field. My brother recommends that if you clench your teeth, the muscles make your jaw look stronger. The size of your biceps matters. There's a way to walk like a man does, but I am not getting that right, I'm a little 'loose in my loafers'. Real men don't use words like 'gorgeous'. And the way your voice goes up at the end of the sentence? You need to bring it down, level it out. Train it into a lower register, talk like a man. Gruff is good. Better still, don't talk so much.

In fact, wouldn't it be better if you dumped that enthusiasm entirely.

dream sequence—drowning

Here it is again: I come to, to find myself plunged deep underwater, so deep that I know I can't make it back to the surface. That I will certainly drown. That with all the life force within me, I will struggle to reach the surface, yet I know that I am down far too deep to make it, and this lungful of air I hold will certainly be my last.

The dream plays so regularly that on later reflection I wonder if it is a memory. Did I drown in some past life, go down with a ship in a storm, or crash an airplane that plunged so deep I never made it to the surface? Was I tangled in debris and spent too much time freeing myself? Or is this a memory from birth itself?

Nonetheless, it's the same sequence playing out every time the dream occurs: I struggle to hold the last lungful of air and the only thought my body speaks, with increasing intensity, is that when I finally have to let it go, the next breath will be water, and I will die. But I have to try. Desperate, I push upward, and the pressure to release my last breath is overpowering.

The outcome of the dream is always the same. After holding on for as long as I can, finally forced to surrender I do give up, breathing in my watery death. Yet letting go does not kill me. Instead, the next breath bursts through into new life. What I have been so afraid will be my ending releases me into a fresh beginning, in an utterly unexpected continuity of being.

The feeling of relief is immense, yet whenever the dream recurs I never see past the struggle, nor can I jump forward to know the outcome. I must go through the entire process; the tension and the mounting fear are always the same, and the breakthrough just as exhilarating.

The dream continues for years; into my late twenties. It never occurs to me that rather than being a recall of a previous death, I am drowning in my ordinary life.

the ways of men

David isn't large, but his physical courage is the source of much praise and admiration among my father's cronies when he emerges as a star in Aussie Rules football. Typically, he plunges headlong into a tangle of growling fellows, barrels the opposition aside and emerges at full speed with the ball in his firm possession. And he has the complete set of ball skills required to make the damned thing go wherever he wills it. He can hand-pass adroitly and, in the kicking department, he can punt accurately, even the torpedo variety—the one where you have to drop the ball across the line of your boot—and he times a dropkick perfectly, on the run.

It isn't long before I feel expectant eyes turn in my direction. But the skill doesn't run in the family. Certainly, I have the speed to get to the ball sooner than my foes but that inflated object, so essential to the game, is *pointed*, and it has an unnerving tendency to bounce unpredictably. What to do? If ever I manage to lay my hands on it, before I have time to gather my wits and try to dispose of it, constructively, by kicking it to a team mate further down the field, the great galumphing pack of screaming schoolboys quickly catches up and descends, whooping and hollering, upon my nervous person. My panicky attempts either to punch the ball away, or kick it in a forwardly direction, are to no avail. According to some mysterious law of physics, the ball will invariably spin off on a tangent that one could never reasonably expect and some more useful boy will leap at his good fortune to show that unlike me he has what it takes.

In the stands, age-worn faces grimly shake their heads and wonder, *sotto voce,* what might be missing from my make-up.

'Aargh … Plays like a bloody girl …'

Instead of football, I prefer to run, especially the out-of-your-body abandon of the shorter sprint distances when you enter a zone of silence as though you're in a tunnel. One glorious day I do my dash for this sort of (physiological) freedom on the sandy oval at my high school's athletics day, competing in the 100 yards sprint, in my age group and again, over the same distance, in the open division, and win both. I do the same for the 200 yards and, in the final race of the day, run the last leg of a 4 X 100 relay for my team. When I receive the baton at the final change, in the curve that leads into the top of the home straight, my team is coming third. I grasp the baton with my trailing hand and, determined to peg those others back, run down the two boys in front of me, passing them both before they reach the finish line.

I leap about, gasping, elated. Our team has carried the day, on accumulated points. Personally flushed to have a challenge tossed back at me like that I am pleased by the strength I found to come from behind and win. To see the finishing tape at the end of the straight and just pull myself towards it with sheer willpower, my body responding to my will. That was thrilling.

The silver-haired headmaster comes up to me and says: 'Well done. You won that race by sheer determination.'

He seems to be congratulating me. Having never won praise from a significant older male figure, for this brief moment before the day rushes on I puzzle at an unfamiliar feeling, soon forgotten. Besides, it wouldn't do to boast or be proud.

For athletics training I go to a nearby club at the recreational field ('the rec') in Melville, where some luminaries of track and field train. One guy, de Gruchy, whose speed has brought him into prominence at state level, works hard at these training sessions. One evening after practice in the clubroom, when he is having his tired muscles rubbed, de Gruchy shocks me:

'Don't stop now,' he grins, encouraging the masseur. 'You're rubbing me in all the right places!'

Although I have never done it to myself, I recognise the invitation to the attendant to masturbate him. Just horsing around, of course; he's a man, he has no time for sissy boy stuff. De Gruchy overheard me earlier, out on the track, asking someone how to set up my starting blocks. I have never used them before, and no one gives tuition. 'Work it out yourself,' he sneered, and the implication is clear: it is a sign of weakness for a boy to ask for help. After that, in my own mind I re-name the sprint champ 'de Grouchy', although I would never say it to his face.

In school cadets, we are instructed by teachers playing officers (with occasional visitors from the regular army). Sometimes we spend school holidays at a military camp in Northam, my father's old stamping ground during the War, about sixty miles north-east of Perth. A sergeant-major from the regular army gives drill demonstrations and rehearses us in the art of giving orders.

'Haaa!' (the first syllable barked to capture attention, and slightly eee-longated, but not so much as the second); 'Teee-en' (a protracted diphthong, to build suspense before the ultimate crack of command); 'SHUN!' (The last syllable to be snapped out with the kind of crisp delivery you'd like to see responded to in kind by the raggle-taggle squad you will, supposedly, be whipping into shape.) 'Ha-Tee-en-SHUN!' Initially I shrink from filling out the contours of command, but with the sah-major's encouragement, I get into the performance of it and soon learn to enjoy a certain sense of power that accrues with giving orders convincingly.

In the all-male setting of army camp, the yearning stirs interesting feelings. We adolescent boys warm to the sah-major as a kind of surrogate father, one you'd like to have giving you some of his time and care. He is gruff but kind and his patient attention almost makes you want to make a mistake deliberately, so he will come over and rehearse you until you get it right. If the feeling is new, I seem not to be alone in craving the attention and approval of an older man. 'Father hunger', that's what therapists will call it.

Under the sah-major's avuncular attention we learn to march crisply. He teaches us to chant a song to march by and shares an important piece of information about military rations. An official-issue rations kit provides only three sheets of toilet paper per evacuation, says the sah-major. In the interests of efficiency, this only allows for 'One up, one down … and one to polish!' We enjoy the flush of camaraderie his humour brings on, even if it is released by such patently foolish means.

Another kind of attention from the adult males rouses my curiosity when, during the second year at cadet camp, all the young men in the unit have to attend a compulsory, so-called 'medical parade'. For the two-week duration, we are housed in spartan huts with wooden floors and roofs of corrugated iron. We sleep on straw-filled hessian 'palliasses', a new term instead of the 'mattresses' at home, just as 'straw' is the substitute for 'comfort'. On the day of the medical exam, each platoon has to line up in its respective hut. We are to stand to attention alongside our bedding, facing the wall, clad only in the regulation army-issue, khaki woollen 'great' coats (our other clothes have been removed beforehand, folded, and set off to the side on the bedding, which must be rolled up and presented, just so) until the 'medical examiner' comes to us one by one, at which time each boy will turn around, opening his greatcoat for inspection. The oldest among us are fifteen, and the youngest probably thirteen or so.

I don't recognise this inspector as one of the weekend warriors who plays at being in the military via the cadet corps; the 'officers' in our school unit are drawn from the teaching staff. Perhaps he is the genuine article, an army medico.

When the medical officer comes to me and I turn to face him, I am surprised by the size of his entourage, for two or three other inquisitors accompany him on his rounds. The teachers who get to play at being officers have insinuated themselves into the retinue.

'Your coat, sergeant Marsh.' I open it as I have been told.

'Cough.' I do so nervously, avoiding eye contact with all these men as they inspect my genitals. We are not preparing for war; we are schoolboys. Why are they all here, sneaking a look at my privates? Even if such a medical examination were a requisite for true military service, it puzzles me that these other hangers-on—grown men with wives and families— should need to be involved in the intimate inspection of the genitals of an entire unit of adolescent boys, one at a time.

I am in charge of a platoon and we get quite good at drill. Otherwise it would be boring. Rather than bossing the boys around, I try out another technique, with a sub-text that reads: 'We're-all-in-this-together, let's-show-these-drongos-what-we-can-do' kind of attitude, and the boys really perform for me. It helps that the school-teacher-cum-CO, or 'Commanding Officer', with the rank of captain, is an authoritarian blusterer and never earns our respect, so I tap into an 'us against the idiots' kind of camaraderie to bring them all together into a snappy, well-knit squad.

In fact, my platoon is selected to do a drill demonstration before the entire 5th Cadet Brigade (that includes all the schools in the region) during a day of official parades and demonstrations. My parents drive from Perth to attend. In addition to the brisk marching, smart turns and so on, our well-rehearsed routine includes a lot of business with rifles, and climaxes with firing a round of blanks, scaring the daylights out of everyone.

Frank reminisces warmly about his days as a staff sergeant in the same camp, during the war. He notes my three stripes and we discuss the chevron and crown insignia Frank wore as a staff sergeant. I wonder how he enjoyed the all-male military monastery. I don't tell him about the brief grope I shared in another boy's palliasse, or the weird hazing ritual some kids acted out in the lavatories—'nuggeting', with boot polish applied to the genitals—that has got them sent home early. (Not in my platoon, of course.)

Back in regular school, the CO of the cadet corps is my instructor in geometry. At this time teachers are required to be generalists and neither they, nor their students, have any clue why one of their number might suddenly become the English teacher, the maths teacher, or the historian. In some cases their knowledge of the subject is only a day ahead of that of their students.

This one loves to creep noiselessly up to the door of the classroom, fling open the substantial sliding door with a sharp crack, and storm around the room, opening all the windows—even on the coldest days— to shock our dozing brains awake. Watching for reflections in the glass covers over the ceiling lights we try to spot him coming so that he won't catch us by surprise.

Angry if any other teacher has left information from previous lessons on the board, he appoints someone to clean it off (even if it is clearly marked 'Please Save' by his predecessor), making it perfectly clear that he is the master of this domain; other teachers be damned.

The teacher chalks up a new theorem on the board, with the injunction: 'Required To Prove, blah, blah, blah,' whatever it is, written under the lead diagram. From RTP, we are supposed to work our way through to the proof, QED: *quod erat demonstrandum*. The Latin phrase is the solitary thing I will recall from arduous hours of geometry with its exceedingly obtuse squares on the various hypotenuses.

Having presented the problem he stands and glowers at us, all six-feet-plus of him, with his eyes bulging. 'Weeeell?' His voice rises accusingly, defying us *not* to come up with the solution. No other instruction is proffered. Mostly we squirm in ignorant silence, until we are rescued— usually by Chris Rathbone, or one of the others who seem to know geometry already even before we have begun instruction. Certainly we receive no clues from this teacher. Rathbone *et al* discern the pathway from RTP through to QED and talk their way to the solution. While it breaks the prolonged and barren silence of the lesson, this triumph is a mere sop to this teacher and, for all his personal brilliance, Rathbone does not rescue the rest of us from the Captain's scorn.

The teacher's bug-eyed bombast hardly seems out of place in the military. So I am surprised, on one occasion, to find that I can stand my ground in the face of his apoplexy. A shooting practice has been organised at a rifle range and it falls on the same Saturday as a theatre outing for the Drama Club. When the CO demands my attendance at the former, I inform Captain Bombast that, frankly, I would rather attend the theatre, as my interest in drama and literature is likely to continue beyond the range of a .22 rifle.

My resolve leaves him smouldering. In spite of being only a weekend warrior, perhaps he has swallowed the requisite unquestioning obedience admired in military culture, whereas for me, a crossroads has presented itself and I instinctively veer left. One of my angels among the staff (Styles, a significant ally of the Drama Club) must prevail, in another conversation, somewhere off-stage, because the issue is never forced.

At army camp itself, in Northam, he has a go at me again. After lunch on the second day I take the platoon into one of the huts and proceed with the prescribed lesson, on the correct procedures for dis-assembling, cleaning and re-assembling our weapon (the heavy .303 gauge rifle), when a breathless messenger arrives with the news that we are to assemble on the parade ground. I get the lads together, marching them smartly up the roadway and into place on the small parade ground (with the rest of the Unit waiting).

'Pla-tooon … HALT! Le-eft TURN! Three paces for-ward, MARCH! Stand at … EASE!'

'Nice of you to join us, A platoon,' says the CO.

After the assembly, as the Unit breaks up and each group heads off, Stewart calls me over for a dressing down.

'Where were you, Sergeant Marsh?'

'Hut 'C', SAH!'

'You should have been here.' Pause. 'Wee-ell?'

'Schedule says: *Rifle Cleaning, hut C*, SAH!'

'After lunch we assemble here first!' Pause. 'Weee-ell, Sergeant Marsh?'

'Actually, sir, with all due respect, we arrived yesterday. This is only the first day of the schedule, so no routine has yet been established. SAH!'

'Well, I don't care about that!' he snaps, as if I am trying to pull a swifty on him. 'Be here at 1 pm, before the afternoon session.'

'Yes! Sir! We certainly shall. Tomorrow. SAH!'

I am not really auditioning for a career as a rebel any more than I want to be trained to kill. The tacit assumption here is that we'll just shut up and give respect, even to buffoons. While I would never dream of open defiance I am surprised to find in myself an innate resistance to bombast and a kind of courage that enables me to hold my space against male authority figures. I am reluctant to be dragooned into a state of mindless surrender to a chain of authority, none of whom—when it boils down to a one-on-one with the people in charge—automatically inspires respect. While others do seem drawn to the life (two outstanding cadets from my year will go on to officer training for the real-world army, at Duntroon Military College) it doesn't feel like a route to survival for me; more like extinction. I feel that familiar urge to *crush* me, taking the imperative to 'curb my enthusiasm' to a potentially lethal extreme.

I am getting a first inkling that there might be more than one model of authenticity in the masculinity stakes. If I don't formulate it in quite these terms at the time, I am surprised to find that there are responses available other than just wimping out.

My under-explored assertiveness does bring an end to my tenure as School Captain, however. One day in class the senior year French teacher gives a girl a nasty verbal bullying for her late arrival. The headmistress has commandeered two or three of the girl prefects to assist in some administrative tasks and hasn't released them promptly when the bell sounded for the next lesson. Moody *Monsieur le maître français* thunders at the meekest of these, a hapless young woman who utters scarcely a squeak in class.

Some gallant, if foolish, impulse to come her defence springs up in me.

'It's not really her fault,' I offer, and the atmosphere takes a sudden turn south, towards the Antarctic. After the class, the black-browed *maître* excoriates me in turn, darkly suggesting that being the Captain of the School has somehow inflated my sense of self-importance. Having spent fourth year as the Captain of the School, in my final year I am demoted to an ordinary prefect.

father god

1959. Some teachers do win my respect though, either by dint of their personal qualities, or because they take a real interest in individual students. Ted Styles, an expatriate Englishman, runs the drama club. Styles, who was a policeman in Malaya before he put himself through the Western Australian teacher-training program, is a geography specialist.

Towards the end of the school year he comes up with some original and challenging theatre productions, most with a Biblical theme. When other institutes might be trying out your run-of-the-mill 'nativity play' fashioned around the legendary birth of the baby Jesus, Styles turns one of the quadrangles into an open-air theatre and sets me up to stagger around half-naked and mud-caked as John the Baptist, haranguing the audience of parents:

'Re-*pent!* You don't even know the meaning of the word!' I roar.

My brother's girlfriend (and my future sister-in-law) Jan is sitting with my mother in the second row and tells me afterwards that I had them all ducking for cover with my hellfire-and-brimstone rant. As I am deeply confused about my own identity, playing someone who had no doubts about who he was might have shown me a way, conceivably, but for all my borrowed certitude, the bizarre sagas of Biblical times remain opaque to my understanding. The tribulations of a tribe of homeless ancient Israelites don't engage me any more than the Jesus narrative does.

I am invited by a fellow student, Joan, to attend a lunchtime meeting of the Inter-School Christian Fellowship. Joan is the same age as the rest of us, yet she has an impressive certainty about the realities of God, and the lifetime guarantee that Jesus can 'save' us all from 'sin'. I have more than enough self-doubt for the notion of sin to stir unease in me, and I am guilted into going along to meetings until, on just my second visit, Joan alarms me by asking me to lead a prayer. Apparently I am supposed to say something of my own devising, without a script, and I cringe. I have no religious experience, and serious doubt (some would say, my conscience) undermines me. Maybe it is only stage fright, or maybe I have scruples about pretending to know what I clearly do not. I can't just make up something to say.

Talk to God? That's a leap, and more than a little presumptuous. I know, from personal experience, to jump off tables (trusting in the implicit promise that you will be caught) is not a reliable way to test one's father, neither in Heaven nor on earth, so any latent faith fails to respond to Joan's challenge. In church, a kid can stay hidden, no one would put you on the spot like that. Whoever this 'God' might be is inextricably bound up in a mishmash of stories from Sunday School, set in a culture that remains impenetrably alien to me and with little obvious bearing on my day-to-day existence.

One of the boys asks me accusingly one day: 'Are you a Christian?' implying that probably I am not. I have absorbed enough of the expectations of the society around me to know I ought to say 'Yes', an affirmation which could be followed by some order of confession, or a profession of faith; a weepy *mea culpa*; an inspirational story of revelation; perhaps even a Billy Graham-induced conversion experience, of being 'born again'. But no such personal epiphany manifests for me. To try and invoke it through prayer seems a dubious form of manipulation, with uncertain outcomes, especially as that Supernatural *über*-Male, Father God, is supposed to be all-powerful and all-knowing.

Clearly, I don't belong to the club. But what is the alternative? To be a 'heathen', perhaps? I haven't met any of that breed, but it is obviously not an identification any sane person would claim, at least, not in these parts. Intimations of hellfire flicker in the wings, probably in the same area offstage where my other awful identity lurks, waiting to be outed. To be flushed from hiding as a 'non-Christian' is probably of the same order of disgrace as 'non-heterosexual', even if I have not yet fully articulated the terminology, or the identification. Yet I resent the assumption that the affiliation is compulsory.

My mother is baptised, with my brother David—complete immersion, no half measures when you're dealing with sin—one after the other on the same night, at the Church of Christ in East Victoria Park. This church is a plain building, in the modern deadpan style. As part of the Protestant push, the kind of religion carried out here is clearly demarcated from that indulged in those Gothic piles with stained glass windows, rattling with ritual, stinking of incense, with organ music droning and a tragic Jesus figure impaled on a Cross. Here the hymns are earnest and plain, always in 4/4 time, and the large Cross is bare.

At the front of the church the stage has been stripped away to reveal a small swimming-pool sized space beneath the boards, and my mother and brother appear, suddenly re-clad in white, to take turns at being dunked by the minister. As a piece of theatre the baptismal ceremony lacks pace and drama, unless you're reading for the salvific sub-text. Mum tells me later that the pool was heated and the water warm, which seems sensible, if lacking a little rigour. Watching the dunking with some interest I fail to perceive any doves, or shafts of light and for a few days I observe my newly 'saved' family members carefully for signs of illumination.

We continue this church-going phase for barely a year before our attendance peters out. Initially, even my father goes to services, but before long my mother says she is disappointed in the 'hypocrisy' of some members of the congregation, without elaborating.

Unfortunately, I do well enough as John the Baptist to be cast a year later as the prophet Isaiah, and I have to endure the whole crisis again. At least Isaiah wears more clothing than John, and I don't have to bare my skinny physique, splattered in mud, for all the world to mock.

The more I hear about the bizarre behaviour of Jehovah, the less inclined I am to join His tribe. He's the model for all the angry men I know instinctively to avoid, from Mr Clifford through to (weekend) captains of cadets. If the Christian re-versioning promises to save me, from who knows what hell, its love is stained darkly with sin and guilt and The Awful Suffering of His Only Begotten Son. Heaven comes at quite a cost, it seems, and I am still trying to work out the basics of how to live on earth.

reverie on a bus

I am not entirely without sources of illumination. One day, on a long bus ride home from Perth, my mind drifts into reverie. I don't recall the train of thought that leads me there, but from within my day-dreaming a powerful feeling wells up, unbidden. As it expands it is as if I am somehow being opened up, from within. A passenger on a bus has little to do except go along for the ride. This passivity must have induced in me a kind of receptivity. It's hard to find the words to reflect the shift in inner topography: irruption? infusion? Some ineffably gentle feeling, spreading through me.

At rest from busy-ness, detached from doing, letting the body/mind just be, I am moved into a deep, calm state of non-specific gratitude. The mood feels so natural, I have no problem allowing it to expand and fold me into itself. 'I' disappears into the warmth. All feelings of 'difference' fade, minor variations in the field of warmth that, while it supports my very being, dissolves my little self entirely

I could call the feeling 'tolerance'—something that could be a starting point from which to relate to 'others'; a state beyond judgment, without discrimination of any kind—but that falls short. It continues as a deeply embodied feeling of kindness—kindness given and received; kindness like a lake with no shore. There is no sense of 'I' to claim this realisation, it simply is what is. I can't contain it, you could say it contains me; and 'other'; and everything else. It is the field of being and awareness itself, even if I don't 'know' that as an idea.

Looking back, I see that I have no 'cup' to hold the feeling at the time, and no training to retrieve the awareness, or cultivate it at will. Certainly I don't know what it 'means'. I would never have dreamt of calling it 'God'. Years later, I will read about the Buddhist notion of 'bodhicitta' and recognise something of the 'emptiness which is full of compassion' (to paraphrase Nagarjuna), and wonder how many other seed states a young soul traverses spontaneously like this. For these experiences slip out of awareness, especially when there is no cultural frame to highlight their meaning; certainly, it didn't happen in church. In present time it feels perfectly natural—a right 'fit'—and intuitively I recognise it as 'true', even without instruction.

Years later I read Lama Yeshe's lovely, simple description as 'the healthy mind'. *Citta* means mind in Sanskrit; mind in the sense of heart. 'No irritation; plenty of room … Heart feeling is what we need … not just an intellectual explanation.'[1]

[1] Lama Thubten Yeshe, *The Essence of Tibetan Buddhism*. 2001. p. 64.

enter, death

One weekend, on an outing to the port of Fremantle, Frank tries to interest me in the mechanical manoeuvres between cranes and ships on the docks but I find all that heavy metal oppressive. My interests are elsewhere. A passenger liner is disgorging its human cargo. I stand to the side, wide-eyed, as people come out of Customs, and find myself moved with a vague sense of longing. The world I live in suddenly seems very small. While I don't see myself as some backwater bumpkin, when a young man wearing a pair of svelte linen pants and Italian leather sandals strolls through the entry hall, I get a whiff of a cosmopolitan world just beyond the horizon that is enticing and, at the same time, painful in its allure. If not here, how will I find where I belong?

Our close neighbours include a migrant family, the Balzans, who live just two doors up the street, and they are my first contact with another culture, one focused on something other than footy, beer and barbeques. Mr Balzan is a Maltese Greek, brought up in Alexandria, and the family speaks French together. I am just being introduced to that mellifluous tongue at school, and my mother urges me to visit the new neighbours for practice. Such visits are hell, of course. Mangled accent aside, I can barely form a sentence. At school we are drilled into using the greeting: 'Comment allez-vous?'; a version sufficiently close in construction to what I might say in English; 'How are you going?' So when Mr Balzan asks me, simply, 'Ça va?' I am struck dumb.

No matter. If my non-existent vocabulary and tiny repertoire of phrases are inadequate to the task, the family nonetheless welcomes me warmly, encouraging me to try a simple phrase or two along with the Greek shortbread, the sesame cakes, the sugared almonds and thick, Turkish coffee sipped from tiny cups (so unlike the hefty mugs used at my place for our Nescafé instant). In Chez Balzan, except for the grandmother, everyone can speak English anyway, so they don't leave me hanging out to dry. They praise my tiny successes, beaming approval through my discomfort, and lay on their unstinting hospitality whenever I pluck up the courage to cross their foreign threshold.

Their son, Eric, is my age or a year older, but goes to a private school. One day I am surprised to read a postcard he has sent home from a trip away. Eric writes phonetically, as if he were sounding out words and phrases in French that he can speak fluently, but he is obviously untrained in grammar and the written form of the language. While I could correct the spelling, I envy Eric's ability to converse.

Mrs Balzan is very warm and flesh-padded, just like my own mother, and Mr Balzan is so kind and patient with my endless bamboozlement, that if I didn't feel so confronted by the inevitable language lesson I would visit them more often.

I squirm with discomfort by the old man's bed. This time it isn't the linguistic lack that has me tongue-tied. Mr Balzan is dying. I don't know what the illness is, or even how old he might be, but when Tishie finds out that he isn't going to come out of it she urges me to visit my indulgent tutor one last time.

I have never been into the parents' bedroom before and feel like an intruder in a private sanctuary. I wonder, annoyed: what is it I am supposed to do? I feel so unprepared, not knowing what to say to him— neither in English nor in French—and struggle with the feeling that I ought to be able to offer some balm to comfort the old man's anxiety as he lies there dying.

Fear is more evident than pain in the old man's eyes. It disturbs me to see that someone could be so close to the end of his life and apparently know so little comfort. The Balzans are religious; Catholic in fact; if not the Roman variety, then perhaps Greek Orthodox (there are icons on the walls). I would have hoped that by then you would know something that would make it be all right. No doubt there will be a priest who'll come and perform some ritual. Aren't they the experts at this?

For all his earlier kindness, poor Mr Balzan isn't getting any comfort from the adolescent me. I feel resentful in my inadequacy and I don't want that to be the last impression in the old man's pain. It isn't so much the imposition of being asked to come here, but more that life has served me up this too-real event without providing me with the means to respond to it appropriately, so I simmer in silence.

The old man moans quietly and turns his face to the wall.

I am no better prepared when my darling Yankee grandma passes away a year later. Her son William, a Captain in the Army, has died on the operating table while being treated for some problem with his kidneys and she takes the loss of her eldest very hard. She has been in and out of hospital herself with heart trouble and although I have finally got my wish that she could come and live with us, I don't want it to be for the last time. I shudder to hear her groans emanating from the bedroom at the end of the house, as she struggles with the pain of 'angina'.

From her room, whenever she hears visitors' voices hushed, she pipes up, demanding to know what they are talking about. When in good spirits, she tries to get up and 'make herself useful', mopping the kitchen floor, say, before my mother and the aunts bundle her back to bed, clucking in outrage. She is a brave and cheerful presence, even in her pain, but I can feel the dread behind the hushed conversations on the phone, as relatives share scraps of information gleaned from the doctors.

Grandma dies in hospital, but something wakes me in the middle of the night and I go into the living room where my mother, her eldest daughter, sits alone in the dark. We cry quietly together: no words, just hugs. We have had to share her with so many others and it hurts to let her go.

Before my voice broke I sang like a girl. Grandma heard my efforts and praised me, urging me to get some training. She read my future in a teacup and told me I would come second in something. That soon came true at an athletics meet. She taught me that my hands were good and said that I could use them to heal. She'd seen me with the animals, the baby budgies and rabbits. When any became sick, I would pick them up and, although I didn't really know what to do, I found that I could just let love flow through my hands and, often as not, they got better. So when she dies, this warm woman who really knows how to love, I feel I have lost something important and don't know what to do with that feeling. They say I am too young to go to the funeral.

The nurses at the hospital are from a Catholic nursing order, not that that was my grandmother's affiliation. I don't remember her going to any church, but years before, perhaps in America, she had been some variety of Baptist. I hear that Baptists are wowsers, but that doesn't fit Grandma Evans; she knew how to have a good time.

At school, the day after her death, I am lined up to go to Scripture class, so it must be a Friday. 'Scripture' period is strictly a Christian affair, a compulsory if minor part of the curriculum, whatever your affiliation. The visiting minister notices me joking around in the line and tells me that he will be officiating at my grandmother's funeral. The Reverend's intervention is a sobering reminder of her departure. With my smile fading, and before I have time to gather my wits, he asks:

'Did she … know Christ?'

These adults. They really have a way of putting you on the spot. For that is a mystery that remains impenetrable to me. 'Christ' is something I have more likely heard uttered as an oath, or with a chuckle, not at all in the same tone as the rumour going around that it is a sin to 'take the Lord's Name in vain'. I have cousins who are Catholic. They joke about how they can party on Saturday night and go to midnight Mass, or confession in the morning, to get cleaned up again. I had been sent off to Sunday school for a while, first with the Church of Christ, then the local Baptists, but religion has not informed my dreaming.

All I can remember is how loving and how loved my grandmother was, and even though I don't really connect that memory with the sanitised feeling of Sunday school, or the remote legends of the tribes of Israel, or the strange stories about Jesus turning water into wine that this minister has spoken of in class, something prompts me to affirm that, indeed, she did 'know Christ'. She was a fountain of love and support for a large clan. If God is love, I reason impulsively, she was connected.

I respond, 'Yes'.

After the funeral Tishie tells me that the minister has said wonderful things about Grandma, even though they had never met, and I am glad for that but the real confirmation comes later when I read a part of her diary. There aren't many entries around this time but the death of her grown son had obviously wounded her. An entry reads: 'I nearly lost all my faith'.

Even though I can't recall her going to Church, this line seems to be in the same vicinity as the rest of the mystery, so I breathe a sigh of relief that I probably said the right thing at the right time. I wonder what kind of thing this 'faith' is, that it usually carried her, but which sometimes drained away to so dangerously low a level.

And I wonder what that Minister would have said about her if I had said no.

achieve!

As a new school, built to cater to the first rank of baby boomers in the late 1950s, we have no history, no traditions. We are as raw as the concrete walls and as shallow-rooted as the flimsy grass on the sandy sports-field at Applecross High.

Somebody on the staff is given the task of creating a school crest. The school colours are red, green and white. One of the art teachers sorts out a design and he comes up with one incorporating a black swan, the bird native to Perth's broad-plained river, holding a book in its beak and a terse motto emblazoned beneath.

The exhortation reads: 'Achieve'.

Private schools have mottos in Latin, which take some learning to expound upon. But this motto is so stripped down, a single, blunt word devoid of charm or mystery. 'Achieve'. Is it meant to be inspirational? Or motivational? Or simply as pragmatic as it sounds? No one speaks of the larger picture, no philosopher-schoolteacher steps forward to address the metaphysical possibilities. Just this crude motto to urge us on, in non-specific striving, to … achieve. It proposes success, but how would this be measured? Even as it exhorts, it feels like such a letdown. Am I being encouraged to gear myself up for climbing high mountains, or just make sure that I acquire as much stuff as I possibly can?

Little do they realise what ponderous doubt they have loosed in my mind. This brazen command becomes a kind of Zen *koan*, a riddle thrown out unwittingly by a school teacher's urge to meet a deadline—'That should cover just about everything'—implanting itself in this earnest seeker's openness. It insinuates its directive into the very folds of my brain, revving up my adolescent anxiety as I endeavour to crack the codes of Life, and Meaning.

Haven't they have dodged the most important question? Achieve *what?* I ache to know. What do you do with a life?

To someone struggling with a crisis in identity, this is not idle philosophical speculation. They might as well have said: 'MU!' or, like Hisamatsu: 'Nothing will do. What do you do?' Or: 'Have a cup of tea'; and it would have made as much sense. I was transfixed by the awful certainty this implied of a people so confident of purpose that they could actually get on, not only with doing some major achieving, apparently unaware of their extraordinary feat, but blithely encouraging others to follow their intrepid example. I, on the other hand, wander lost in my private challenges, my mind transfixed by this dart. How do you parse the relative value of things? What is the real worth of *any* action? Is anyone offering advice on that front?

That is how I might have spelled it out. I am plunged into doubt by this riddle; is there something deeply wrong with me? And I pull back at that precise point where I am enjoined to go forward. *Achieve*. It is a toad of an answer, squatting fatly in the mind, even before the question has been properly formed.

A detached observer might have told me that achievement wasn't so far from my grasp. For a prematurely gay boy, being eaten up with self-doubt, the disguise seemed to be holding. Elected Captain of the school, as well as of the tennis team, the athletics team, the baseball team and the lifesaving team, I am popular and hardly know it. I am President of the drama club and the social committee. I receive a pennant for something called 'Outstanding Service to the School'. Pedalling furiously to escape my guilty shadow, I don't notice that, if anything, I could be in danger of becoming an *over*-achiever.

I win a citywide competition in ballroom dancing, first in the quickstep then, just a few weeks later, the *rumba*. As part of the entertainment at an end-of-year school dance I am booked to give an exhibition with a partner, Georgina. She is taller than me, and heftier, but with enough rehearsal and some well-worn sequences, we can usually bring it off. However, we have no time to rehearse with the hired band and when they plunge into the *cha cha* at a highly accelerated tempo, the routine becomes a panicked blur. I roll my eyes at the bandleader, but he misreads my desperate signal as enthusiasm and they rock on at full speed as Georgina and I try to jam in all those finicky steps.

Feet flashing, hips working to a rapid-fire cha cha beat, I feel like a character in one of those animated cartoons who has run off the edge of a cliff. He looks down in mid-air, his feet still whirling, and realises there's no ground under his feet.

The ensuing embarrassment is nothing compared to the awful realisation that I have flagrantly put myself right 'out there'; too far for safety, if I want my cover to hold. I might as well have been tap dancing.

The threat of discovery nips my ballroom career in the bud, and the Fremantle branch of Wrightson's Dance Studio loses its star sixteen-year-old male performer.

snookered

At home, things remain tense with my father. I feel safest when we can just ignore each other. Yet I find that there is another side to Frank that I had never discovered at home.

Under the state education system you aren't allowed to go to work, as David wants to, until after your fourteenth birthday. I want to stay at school as long as possible, for I recognise, dimly, that this could be a way out of what is becoming a City of Lies. Nonetheless, in the first long summer vacation from school, after I turn fourteen, Frank arranges for me to work in his office-supply business in Fremantle. This holiday job will continue through every ensuing year at high school and on into the first year at University. Each December, on the day that exams finish I head to work, recalled only briefly to perform in Mr Styles' Christmas specials.

Working in my Dad's business is less a chance to get closer to each other than it is for me to earn some money. Frank reminds me that by the time he was the same age he had already left school and started to earn a living. This way, I can buy some Christmas presents, pay for the materials for the birdcage and the rabbit hutch and a new pair of shoes for school.

It also gives me my first chance to observe my father in his work habitat and, sometimes, after hours with his cronies. After the bitter break with his former partners in Perth, Frank has built up a new business, from modest beginnings, in Fremantle. He's good at training new office workers in the rudiments of accounting, trial balances, the debit and credit registers, writing up invoices, and how to manage the other side of the business, re-ordering from wholesalers, and the annual stock-taking. In these one-to-one instructions with his employees he is more patient than at any time at home.

I watch my father at his desk, cigarette stuck to his bottom lip, squinting from the smoke drifting up into his eyes. The ash grows longer and longer, until he coughs. Then it topples, crashing noiselessly among his papers to be brushed aside, or not, as he checks the read-out from the adding machine against the columns of figures in the ledger.

Frank likes to hang out with some of his business associates after work; this is the favoured fraternity he leaves only reluctantly for the wife and kids at home. At the bar, he advises me that a man should always take his turn to pay for a round of drinks and that other men will look down on a bloke who doesn't pay his share. The trouble, as I see it, is if the group is larger than two or three, you would end up drinking quite a few middies or schooners by the time each fellow has taken his turn. I recognise early the roots of a tolerated, compulsory alcoholism that is part of being 'one of the boys' and, even while I am not insensitive to the bonhomie it generates, I am reluctant to accept it as part of my own *modus operandi*. But here, as I watch my father on his own turf, I see the respect in which he is held among his peers. Through their eyes I learn a different side of him.

In business he is an honest, reliable manager. All the clubs in which he holds membership trust him with managing the finances and he's famous for bringing the bar figures into the black.

It's at the Commercial Club in Fremantle that my father attempts to administer one of the essential initiations into the rites of passage to become a man. One Saturday morning, he takes me with him when he goes in to do a stocktake of the bar supplies, and we have the place to ourselves. Frank lights up a ciggie and switches on the low-hanging lights in the games room, where members play snooker and the even more difficult gentlemen's game of billiards, on splendid full-sized tables with impeccable, flat baize surfaces. Frank jokingly puts down his skill at these games as the 'sign of a misspent youth', but I recognise it as another exercise altogether. Expertise at games with balls is a sign of a youth *well* spent, assiduously cultivating a flawless masculinity.

It's unusual for my father to reach out like this but that still doesn't put me at ease. This is the world of men. Maybe I can learn something here in order to pass. It feels more like a test, like I am back in manual training class, and I am relieved that there is no one but my father around to witness me struggling. That's uncomfortable enough.

Frank gets me a shandy (lemonade with beer, a lady's drink), and himself a middie, and makes sure he puts money in the till. I wonder: am I supposed to buy the next round, to show that I know the rule? I'd have to ask him for the money; perhaps that voids the convention.

Snooker is played out across splendid reaches of felt, stretched impossibly firm over hard slate surfaces, and played with long, true cues. Frank shows me how to rack a set of reds and where to deploy the single colours down the length of the table (green, brown, yellow, blue, pink, black; not necessarily in that order). Pick out a cue; try it for size (how do you tell?) Feel the weight of it. Roll it on the flat green surface, make sure it's straight and true. Before shooting, apply chalk to the tip, just so (so it doesn't slip when it makes contact with the ball). No, not that much! Don't overdo it. (How much is too much?) Left hand placed flat on the table surface, drag the fingers back to form an arch, slide the pointy end of the cue into the webbed vee between the thumb and forefinger, with the cue stick gripped lightly in the right hand. Don't stand side on to the table like that. Face it. Spread your feet apart, plant them firmly on the floor, left foot forward of the right. Now get your head down so your eye can line up the cue ball and the pocket and *stroke* the cue stick through the white. If the tip slips, you haven't chalked it properly. Under *no* circumstances should you skid the cue stick off the ball and into the felt.

The upper part of the right arm is virtually motionless. All the action happens in the lower arm, from the elbow down. That is, of course, unless you have occasion to hit the ball really hard. Under *no* circumstances should any of the balls actually leave the table and hit the floor.

The possibilities for embarrassment multiply.

Then follows a lesson in applied geometry: dissect the angles. Visualise the line from the target ball to the pocket (with its small string bag). See the point on the target ball where the cue ball should intersect to pot it in the pocket.

For a sissy boy trying to negotiate entry into manhood, these are the exact coordinates of masculinity.

'Any dummy can sink the ball', Frank explains. 'A real player is always aware of where he needs the cue ball to finish to be positioned for the *next* shot.'

Needless to say, in the one lesson my father has the patience for, I don't manage to catch all of this. But if I can ignore the stale smell of beer and cigarette smoke from the carpets, it is an interesting foray into my father's reality. Instead of trying to relate face-to-face, we are doing it through the medium of a game of skill, and my father's detached manner holds a space open, briefly, for a scrupulously safe interaction. In spite of my awkwardness this is comfortable, compared with the forced interactions in the garage at home, where Frank is always tinkering on the car; usually something to do with the 'timing', or cleaning the 'carbie'. I would rather be curled up in my bedroom with a good book, but if David is not around Frank will drag me out of my cocoon to hold a spanner while he turns some nut on the other side of the carburettor, or adjusts the spark plugs.

Cars are an ongoing love affair for him. Every couple of years he springs a surprise and turns up, after dinnertime, in a new model, tooting the horn from the driveway. Initially reluctant to join the enthusiasm (he never consults her on big purchases), Tishie gets swept up in the general hubbub too as we all swarm over the vehicle, remark on the upholstery and the colour (usually bland) and go for test rides.

No matter how new the car, Frank will spend hours in the garage fine-tuning the timing, or trying to locate the source of some worrisome rattle. 'Hear that?' he'll ask, when driving some place. 'There's a knock.' Sometimes it's a 'ping'. Frank's ears are tuned to a different wavelength. None of us ever can detect the problem.

While I pick up some of the jargon, I have little interest in mechanics. My reluctance stems from more than just a hankering to get back to my books. I know that these sessions with the hood up will always devolve into wrestling matches, man against machine. There'll be the inevitable incident with barked knuckles, foul words and seething anger bleeding out among the engine oil. For something he spends so much time on, you would think he would have a better time doing it. And I can't help feeling that Frank's frustration has something to do with my own disinterested incompetence.

David gets his licence on his seventeenth birthday. For him it is more than just a licence to drive. He can't wait a single day longer to claim his freedom. While not quite so highly motivated, three years later I do get my learner's permit soon after the appropriate birthday and, for a few sessions, wriggle nervously under Frank's snorting attention during some sporadic driving tuition. I have read in the book of road rules that you should drive as close as possible to the left hand side of the road and when I take that quite literally, Frank curses me for trying to ruin the tyres.

'What are you doing? You'll break the bloody seal,' he protests as I guide the car carefully through the gutters. In spite of my wayward inclinations, or perhaps because of them, I am the most law-abiding person I can possibly be. (As for 'seals', that's something about air pressure in the tyres, or the inner tube, or something about where they connect, apparently.)

When the day for the driving test comes, we go into Fremantle together. I have already passed the written questionnaire to get my learner's permit and this is to be the practical exam. If I pass, I can walk out licensed to drive a Class 'A' motor vehicle.

My father pals around with the examiner and gets into the back seat of the car to ride along. All the guys together. The examiner jokes that most accidents are caused by a bloke being distracted when he spots a 'piece of skirt' on the footpath. I chuckle nervously to join in, picking up the cues as I have been trained, while keeping my version of that scenario to myself (a young man with his shirt off, say).

If my peculiar girlie distractions remain unspoken, my nervous, tightly-wound behaviour must be a tip-off. I manage to shift the gears without crunching as I proceed at a snail's pace away from the testing station but when the examiner tells me to 'go left at the next', I promptly turn into a driveway.

'No, not here! At the corner ...' he hisses, indicating the crossroad further along. In the back seat, father rolls his eyes, embarrassed that a boy could be so ... tight. This is my usual *modus operandi* among men. I think that if I am very obedient, and try really hard, I will qualify as a *real* male and they won't be so aware of my sissy tendencies. Thus, even my very best efforts conspire only to out me, a truly nervous Nellie. Possibly due to the instant camaraderie struck up between Frank and the examiner, rather than my diffident if earnest driving skills, I pass.

Frank brings home a reel-to-reel tape-recorder from the office supplies shop and I have my first encounter with objective feedback. I try out a bit of Shakespeare:

'To be, or not to be, that is the question. Whether 'tis nobler in the mind to suffer the slings and arrows of outrageous Fortune, or ...'

I cringe to hear my own voice coming at me through the audio speaker. What a dead giveaway. This is how it sounds to be a 'queer'.

Every time I have opened my mouth, my own voice has betrayed me.
And remember this: some men like to bash queers.

I am cursed with a natural sense of aesthetics, although I don't appreciate
it at the time, for that potential finds little nourishment in the harsh
environment where I am planted. My ear seeks out the ideal forms that
hover in and around sound. Drawn to the rounded vowels of an educated
accent, I know it would be risky to speak with a plum in your mouth, so I
vacillate between the hard flat tones of 'strine' and a surreptitious flirtation
with a well-formed, posher enunciation. How long will I have to deny
awareness of the subtle harmonics that shape the overtones of a voice; or
the inner shape that carves a movement through space, for that matter?
This must remain a hidden longing.

Television has demolished the already fragile dynamics of the family.
Almost immediately, we decamp from the kitchen to the living room for
the evening meal and Mum is relegated to an even more subservient role,
bustling in the kitchen to bring food to her demanding family. She
complains that we never talk anymore. The family circle, heretofore
uneasily enforced around the kitchen table, has been broken forever and
from that point on, television effortlessly deflects us from unwilling
interactions with each other.

'Isn't anyone going to help me with these damned dishes?' She wails,
and we all wriggle with excuses, until the demand subsides and the
opportunity to help her passes us by.

Already something of a social critic and aesthetic snob, I loathe most
televisual programming, usually retreating to my room, ostensibly to
study, but mostly to waste time drifting in clouds of non-specific thought.
None of my school subjects is sufficiently engaging to bring my mind into
prolonged attention to the textbooks. I prefer to curl up with a novel.

Nonetheless, I make a great show of complaining about the noise, and
pointedly slam my bedroom door to indicate to anyone who cares to
notice that they are interfering with more important things. 'I'm studying!'
I announce, outraged. On occasion, I storm into the living room and twist
the volume control down before beating a retreat, loudly closing, one after
the other, the three doors that separate my room from the inane laugh

tracks, the hectoring outbursts of advertising, and the overwrought scores from Hollywood dramas bleating nightly from the idiot box.

Needless to say, with only one receiver, negotiations over which programs to watch test the tenuous consensus which holds us all together under one roof. When I, the highly-strung adolescent aesthete, do deign to sit with them, my personal tastes are hardly likely to determine our collective viewing habits. Sometimes my mother will accede to my peculiar preferences, in the interests of further education, but mostly we are surrendered to the lowest common denominator.

On one occasion, however, I do prevail. Rudolf Nureyev, the passionate Cossack ballet dancer, has defected from St. Petersburg's Kirov ballet and he is partnering a rejuvenated Margot Fonteyn for the Royal Ballet in Britain. A performance taped in London is re-broadcast through the ABC, even here in Perth, the furthest outpost of Empire. The recording has been made from a stage performance, rather than in a studio, using the minimum number of cameras, so it is seen mostly in a locked-off shot from somewhere up in the balcony. The camera stays wide, with no zooming in and few cutaways to close-ups, positioning the viewer as a spectator in a reasonably good seat in a theatre, *sans* opera glasses. For this family, in Western Australia, it is Culture painted with a lavish brush. Thanks be to the Muse Terpsichore, something stops them from derisively switching channels and I can gorge on this rare feast.

I take up a position on the floor with my back to the doorframe, half in and half out of the kitchen, only as far into the room as will be necessary to see the screen. I am ready to make a rapid exit if my pleasure becomes too obvious, or if I am challenged to justify the aesthetic canons of balletic art, or of Rudi's rude, form-revealing attire.

Nureyev has revivified the stuffy world of British ballet and fluffed up the career of the *prima ballerina assoluta* Dame Margot, many years his senior, in an Indian summer of delirious *pas de deux*. The Russian's passion, combined with a powerful stage presence, great elevation and a bravura technique magnetise my attention, and even in black and white, on that small screen, and mostly only in a wide shot, Nureyev reveals some essential flame of ardent devotion to Art to which my spirit breathlessly responds. Tense, sitting only three feet from the screen, I have to suppress any overt spasms of recognition. Quietly casting discretion to the winds I will myself to become oblivious to my family's reactions, real or imagined, behind me. But soon I am past the point of caring if my naked admiration for this pansy performance art could expose me in their eyes. With one-pointed devotion I dare them to change the channel while I drink up inspiration like thirsty desert sand.

Nureyev dances a role nobly, in the best traditions of the form, knowing how to strike attitudes that in other men would look epicene but to which he brings a thrilling, earthy passion. He is the moving embodiment of a different possibility of manhood: unapologetic about its aesthetic sensibility, yet strong and virile to boot. While the frou-frou elegance of the ballerina's tutu and her chaste, opaque white tights draw the eye away from her crotch (occasionally exposed when she is lifted into the air) the *danseur noble*'s own high-cut tunic ends well above his waist, leaving his lower body—sculpted thighs, chiselled calves, strongly articulated buttocks and an awesome, bulging jockstrap—conspicuously displayed. Apart from the dangerous attraction of muscle, backside and basket through those skin-fine tights, watching Nureyev dance fans what has been a mere whisper of beauty into a full-fledged aspiration in this young viewer. It's as if my five senses have conspired with my inchoate yearning to produce a sixth, higher sense. As far as I am concerned, it could now be possible to use the body to reveal the soul.

I have dared to sense a grace that lies latent in every movement but I have also been aware that the potential eloquence in the body itself— whether still and poised, or moving through space—is dangerous. However it is that I have glimpsed the inner contours of beauty, I have had to suppress that awareness and, until this point, there has been little in my environment to support my nascent aestheticism. Now this refugee from Soviet oppression awakens in me some inner response that affirms for all time that beauty is truth and truth, beauty. His disciplined movement transmutes muscle, gristle and sinew into the shape of meaning itself; each stretch is the embodied form of yearning, capable of pulling love itself into physical space from its hidden recesses in the soul.

Thank God there is no ballet school in the neighbourhood.

service station

My mother has a little old car that she lets me drive. 'Betsy' is a beaten up, two-door Austin Seven. Green with a black soft top, she is like a car from a cartoon, a short, squared-off runt of a shape and window frames you can take out and store in the back seat until you need them. A 1937 model, still in service in the late 1950s, she has seen better days, but in the interests of mobility and a degree of independence, we keep her on the road somehow.

Toxic fumes seep up through a rusted-out floor, so when the weather permits it's better to drive with the windows out. The ancient gearbox requires a special technique: a 'double de-clutch', my brother calls it, and he teaches me to pump the pedal. If I mis-time this, there's an awful crunching of metal and the car will chug and jerk to mock my maladroitness.

What Betsy lacks in automotive muscle is compensated for by a certain comic flair. A car with character, I hope, perhaps too little-old-lady style for a young male with any macho pretensions but I play it like I am in on the joke, bluffing my way around with panache (just like I have learned to use a word like that) blowing as much smoke as Betsy's rear end to conceal my insecurities. If I keep my head up and avoid any kangaroo hops, perhaps no-one will notice what I am, and I can avoid the mocking glances. David wouldn't be caught dead in it, of course, and I am aware that I am trading far too many points from my masculinity quotient to drive this girlie car, but it's not often I get to risk scratching the Duco of Dad's cream Wolseley, so I make the most of any opportunity to escape the daily grind on the hard-arsed push bike I have to ride to school.

Today my mum doesn't need the car and I am planning to visit a schoolteacher who has befriended me; that's Mr Styles, who has become a mentor of sorts. It's quite a new experience to have a man take any interest in me and Styles and his wife Ruth are generous with their time and hospitality. I stop off at the service station at the foot of the hill to pick up a dollar's worth of petrol for the short trip. Tishie brings the car in here to have some work done on occasions and often stops in for petrol.

The proprietor, a short fellow, middle-aged, with sneaky eyes, comes out to dispense the fuel. There's very little traffic going by on this mild, mid-week afternoon, and even less coming in and out of the station. When I go to pay he asks me to wait a minute while he finishes with another customer.

When I give him the money he takes my hand, and oozes:

'Nice fingers. Very sensitive.' (That's odd. He's a mechanic—or at least he *runs* a garage. He has mechanics who work for him.) 'Come in here, I've got something to show you.'

No one else is working today and the place is deserted. We go back into a small, windowless room off the mechanics' bay, near the grease pit where hydraulic hoists sit idle, their gleaming shafts retracted, down not up, ready and waiting to raise cars for inspection and the periodic lube job. Rows of wrenches, tyre levers, hoses, drums and oily rags surround the pit. This room is small, with filing cabinets and a desk. Out front is a cashier's area, and a section for displaying auto accessories for sale, but it's a small suburban garage and there's not much call for parts.

He wipes his hands, pulls out a sheet of folded paper from a drawer and nudges it at me:

'Read this.'

'Uh, what is it?' I ask, nervously.

'I got it from one of the truckies,' he says with a leer. 'Go on, read it … I'll be back in a minute,' and goes out front.

Twirled out of my intentions for the day I stand inside the anteroom. I look through the story. It has obviously been passed through many hands. I skirt the distasteful descriptions of wet 'pussy', more explicit here than the pictures in the surreptitious stash of girlie magazines my father has secreted under the shelf liners in his wardrobe. No teasing here, it's explicit, even gross.

A part of me recoils from the crude storyline and, even while the male/female parameters of the narrative don't really work for me, the overtly sexual content stirs something in my loins, as Garage Man discovers when he walks back into the room and eyeballs the swelling in my crotch.

I wish I had more clothes on. I am wearing my usual, after-school knock-about gear: a pair of black football shorts and a T-shirt. While my upper body is still slim and undeveloped under my nondescript top, my sprinter's legs are lightly muscled, and brown hairs dust their length. As usual, I am barefoot.

The garage man checks me out and murmurs faux surprise, his hope confirmed, noting my arousal. Something shifts in the room's energy field and a note of urgency slips into the man's demeanour.

'What's this then?' He mutters thickly as he comes in close. He's experienced enough not to move too quickly or he'll scare me, but when he places his hand over my crotch, my penis uncurls and he eases it free from the leg of my shorts.

'Mmm, we should take care of that,' he murmurs, quickly checking out my face for any signs of panic. 'Try this on for ...' he says, the last word disappearing as he slurps the length of my penis into his mouth. Electrified, I nearly jump right out of my skin but he has me pinned back up against the desk and I'm too surprised to run. Yet more than that, I am dazed by my own gasping pleasure as he slurps away on me. Almost as soon as he begins, he stops, and folds my stiffness back uncomfortably inside my shorts.

'I'll be back in a second,' he says, massaging my crotch through the shorts.

He is on full alert now. In the service station alone for the afternoon, with no assistants on the roster, he's taking a chance that no one will drive in for petrol during this lull in the day. He has a system rigged up with a black rubber band across each driveway that dings a signal inside the shop so he'll know when a customer drives across it. It's a common arrangement in small garages, but he's putting it to another use. His urgent moves ring other alarms in me. He has moved into a quicker gear, and unfamiliar as it is, it mesmerises with the offer of unfamiliar pleasures. His intent arouses a kind of dread along with my erection.

This man is middle-aged, gone to fat, and his smirking desire almost turns my stomach, but curiosity wrestles with revulsion for control. The grubby pages of the stupid story in one hand, my mind is trying to keep pace with these unfamiliar goings on. I have fooled around with a couple of my classmates but we haven't worked out this sucking thing at all.

Having checked the coast is clear, Garage Man ducks back in to the cool anteroom where I am standing immobilised, wondering what the hell I am doing still here, yet unable to leave. His furtive manner throws off waves of guilt but another, more urgent need overrides all other considerations. I don't find him in the least attractive, and I am still stunned by his crude seduction, yet my senses have tasted something, and it seems inevitable that he should continue.

A nudge from the back of his hand rouses my erection and even a grossed-out wink as he goes down there is not enough to break the spell. He pulls down my shorts and lips the head of my penis into his mouth.

'You're going to enjoy this,' he grins as he pauses to take out his teeth. I blink to blot out the ludicrous sight: a complete set of falsies, hot pink in his hand.

'Mmmm,' he purrs through the saliva, gumming away.

'But aren't you …' I stammer incredulously, trying to change the subject, wishing I had some better way to resist than ask him if he's married. One part of me wants to pull away, but his slobbering chops are sucking down the full length of my erection. He pulls his head back and kneads my balls as he comes up again, his desire now raging full.

'Don't you worry about that,' he pants, face flushed the same color as his toothless gums. He's reached some reckless point of no return, his business, marriage, reputation all swallowed up in this stolen moment of desire.

My shorts now around my ankles, I close my eyes to block out the lurid scene and, as my head tips back, he reaches up with one hand to cup it over my nose and mouth to stifle my groans.

He flicks his tongue around, his head bobbing up and down, working my penis with fervent expertise. I gasp as long, drawn-out retractions stretch slowly along its length. He pauses to work the head with his lips and tongue before returning back to swallow me whole.

My breathing becomes heavier. Some dam wants to burst its restraining walls and heave its contents on the city and the plains beneath but, physiologically, I am too inexperienced to interpret the signals I am getting from my body. I already know the possibilities of ejaculation but here I am in a state of intense confusion, boiling with a thousand new sensations at the same time as I'm revolted by this guy. I can't sort out these impulses. As I approach a climax it feels like I want to piss; a *flood* of piss. I have never pissed into someone's mouth but I have to release, and soon. I try to pull his head away, and he grabs my hands.

'I … Uh. Aaaah. But … what if …?' He reads my grunts correctly and mutters, 'Yeh, that's ok (slurp). You just let it go,' as he nuzzles deeper, greedy for every stolen moment. Still reluctant to let loose into his mouth I hold back, boiling, uneasy, but his determination works loose all last shreds of resistance and I explode in ecstatic confusion, gasping ragged sounds, and it's not piss that comes, but jets of semen, straight into his throat.

I am jerking inside out and as my body spasms he drinks me in more deeply. I want him to stop but he continues to work his mouth around my still rigid dick, now almost unbearably sensitive as it twitches last drops free. I want to pull his head away, but he holds me still, and his mouth cradles me softly as I come down.

I can't look at him. I am disgusted with him *and* with myself. Panting, confused, I want to vomit in his face, yet part of me is still basking in a contradictory afterglow of pleasure. He grins sheepishly and palms his teeth back in. 'Just wait here a minute,' he whispers roughly and slips out to check the front of the shop. I yank up my shorts up and wonder how I am going to get outside without the whole world knowing what has just happened.

Garage Man slides back into the room. 'Just give it a minute will you, before you come out.' His own reality comes back into focus and the guilt he was holding at bay is rushing back at him. He's stolen himself an outrageous amount of pleasure, risking everything he has. But on this bland suburban afternoon he has awoken me and he knows it. Tearing my sensuality open this way has shredded the fabric of my sleepy schoolboy days.

I scramble to come back to myself before emerging into the bright light. I flash on an image of this man in bed with his wife, heads on pillows, a polished wooden headboard pushed up against the bedroom wall. It's a cartoon, and his hot pink dentures are magnified in a glass of water, clacking on the bedside table.

He is really nervous now but I won't look at him or let him off the hook with any kind of acknowledgement; no smile, no thanks, I just want to get out of there. I slam the Austin's half-door shut, crunch into gear and chug off, senses in a tumult.

No one is around to witness my confusion, but when I reach my teacher's house, my evident disturbance breaks through the usual bonhomie.

'Is something wrong?' Styles asks.

'Ah no, not really … No.' I flush.

What am I going to say? *This disgusting guy just sucked my penis until I peed in his mouth. You know, the guy who runs that garage?* How do I say that and leave reality right side up? I really want to say how much I love to sneak a look at the muscled legs of the blond phys. ed. teacher, and how I envy the shape of his chest and the gold shock of hair over his tanned face, and how impossibly speckled with gold are the irises of his eyes; how some boys make me feel this blind desire that I know I must hide, at all costs, and how incredible it feels to ejaculate! How I want to hold some guy and feel his skin touch against my own.

If I tell him that the married guy who runs the garage just sucked my penis there'll be an uproar but, as awful as he is to want to do that to me, how awful am I? I *enjoyed* it. It felt incredible. I will never forget it. I want to say how much the pleasure set my senses singing but at the same time how it's all mixed up with the sick guilt that made that guy so ugly as he inducted me into the Hall of Shame. *That I am probably a homosexual.*

But I don't know how to say all that, so it stays unsaid. I push it down with the hot memory and stumble through the meeting with my teacher as part of my brain tries to sort out how something so squalid could feel so good.

Styles raises the subject of masturbation. I guess he knows it is something sexual that is bothering me. He assures me it's quite normal, but then almost boasts that it's not something that has ever bothered him, so I can't tell how he would take much worse news than mere onanism.

Later, my mother notices my reluctance to go back to that place for petrol and her concern nuzzles at me to find out why. But I deflect her enquiries in muttered monosyllables. Our dirty secret is safe with me.

When I graduate to using my father's car, I drive to lover's lane one night with my girlfriend, near the former swampland down by the river, and we fumble awkwardly with one other. As we test out our desire we push on, beyond kissing. I have slid my hand down her panties and, impatient with my groping, she shoves my finger right up into her wetness. When she grabs my dick, I am shocked that a girl would do such a thing.

But when I suggest we could get into the back seat, she wants to know: 'What do you want to do?'

Isn't it obvious? I pull out the condom a more experienced schoolmate has given me, as if that will explain everything, and now it's her turn to be shocked. 'No, that's only when we're married,' she demurs, leaving me highly stimulated, with no place to go.

Later, when my brother finds the still wrapped condom in the pocket of the jacket I borrowed, I can see my stocks go up in his eyes. David doesn't know that behind my opportunistic forays with my girlfriend I see myself as a dirty little homo in hiding. Guys would be risking their reputation if they were found to have fooled around with other guys, and girls have so much to lose, too. (We're barely out of the '60s.) The upshot is that there's no one left to play with.

Ejaculation ergo sum! Masturbation becomes a regular occurrence. I am dismayed how little control I have over the impulse. In private, *eros* fixates my desire exclusively on men. I try to shag a piece of raw steak but its unresponsiveness fails to satisfy. Sometimes a face in a magazine will do: Alain Delon is hot, and who is this Tab Hunter, in Hollywood? Some of those swimming champions are photographed in brief bathing suits with chests so heavy and proud, unlike my own.

It's already a full-on compulsion. I practise different strokes, using soap, then cooking oil, and beat my meat to the point of depression. I promise myself not to do it more than X times a week but I always fail. I feel dispirited to be defeated so easily by a drive that is stronger than my puny will, for this visceral pull of sex doesn't fit with my prissy sense of self. Shocked to hear that a school mate has actually had sex with a woman, at the same time I have to recognise I would be more than ready to play up with anyone who would show me his penis, so my peace of mind is challenged by my own hypocrisy and I wonder: which part of all these contradictory impulses is really me?

I continue to seek out the imagery that might feed my fantasies. Occasional shots of models in clothing ads are paltry nourishment, but pictures of sportsmen in the newspaper sometimes offer more actual skin and muscle to admire. So I am deeply disappointed when the writer

Randolph Stowe plays the wowser, with a letter to the morning paper in which he chides the editors for including pictures of half-dressed footballers in the locker rooms after the game. Little does Stowe know that he has shut down one of the few sources of visual titillation available to this teenage poofter.

seek wisdom

Nothingness lies coiled in the heart of being—like a worm
—Jean-Paul Sartre

1963. 'Seek Wisdom' advises the motto, and it quickens my pulse. The university crest promises to answer the question that has festered in my psyche ever since the school motto planted its dud seed. Perhaps this is the place where my Great Quest for Meaning can bear fruit.

If a biography is the record of how a person came to be who he is, in my case it cannot be just a record of facts: meeting people, going places; all the so-called significant events. 'Events' would have to include the heady encounter with ideas that fitfully fuel my enthusiasm.

I have crossed the river, making it from Applecross to Nedlands, and joined the very 'Neddy boys' my brother used to sneer at. People speak posh here, like they do on the ABC, and among the lecturers it's hard to tell the Poms from the natives. The cultural cringe is alive and well on the benign banks of the lazy Swan River, at Crawley.

I am thrilled, if a little overawed, by this setting. During high school I failed to engage with most classes, but I squeaked through matriculation with the minimum marks required. I spend a week at the teachers' training college but when I hear of the opportunity to transfer to full-time university studies, I leap for the bait and fill out the required paperwork, behaving well enough in an interview to get the approval to enrol at university under the aegis of the Education Department. Problem solved … for the time being.

I am supposed to be preparing to teach in high schools, like the one I have only just left, but that's a bridge I won't cross for another four years, and about as real at this point as a man walking on the moon might be. As long as the subjects I choose can be tied recognisably to courses that I might eventually teach in high school, I am permitted to pursue the fields that interest me, instead of doing what I am told, and the Department keeps me on a loose rein, requiring me only to participate in teaching practice before the academic year gears up, and again after its close. No more stumbling through maths and sciences: I opt for English, French, German and Ancient History as my first-year units of study.

The University of Western Australia was founded on a Classics department and the civilising influence of the ancients is inscribed on all sides of this mellow campus. Sculpted philosophers' busts gaze eyelessly across smooth green courtyards, with tantalising quotations in Greek displayed on plinths beneath them. Chiseled into a large stone bench by the reflection pool in front of Winthrop Hall are the words: 'Verily by beauty it is we come to wisdom' and, carved into the wall of the walkway which connects the Arts faculty building to the central library, the motto exhorts me: 'Know Thyself', in letters three-feet high. As an incipient manic depressive, I do need inspiration to fuel my quest, so the promise that here I may seek wisdom AND find out what it means to know my self is extraordinarily inspiring. The boredom of high school is replaced by a sense of wonder and discovery. Briefly.

My minders at the Education Department do not permit me to take philosophy on the grounds that it isn't taught in the high schools but even the literature courses throw up some unsettling interrogatories. When Jean-Paul Sartre proclaims that *L'existence précède l'essence*, I am inclined to listen, even if I don't really grasp the full implications of what *le philosophe* is suggesting. Some of his ideas are already in general circulation, notions such as acting in 'bad faith' (*mauvaise foi*) and a model of personal 'authenticity' derived, not from the given meanings stamped with the imprimatur of received tradition, but rather from the daunting predicament of the human being proceeding courageously alone in a meaningless, God-free universe.

If I find that strangely inspirational, I find Sartre's weighty tome *l'Etre et le Néant* (*Being and Nothingness*) more daunting, especially if I try to do the 'authentic' thing and read it in the original French. Aside from the sheer bulk of the book, 'being' in the context of 'nothingness' seems a chilly proposition, even if I find myself disinclined to cling to notions of an antique 'God'.

I am also rather impressed by Pascal; not so much with *le pari* (the bet, or wager), which I read as a weak rationale for Christianity. If we don't know whether God exists then we should play it safe by betting that He does, rather than risk being sorry later. Then, if it turns out that the *Uber* Patriarch had in fact existed all that time, you win. God exists/God doesn't exist? The debate fails to engage me. Is this the only way to think about Meaning? I am more intrigued by Pascal's concept of *les divertissements*: the thousand things a man will do to avoid being alone, having to face the yawning void within himself, by himself.

So, rather than taking up a religious defence against the naked encounter with being, I try to read my own situation from the point of view of this heroic, French form of existentialism, which has an emotional, rather than intellectual appeal for me. (Perhaps I *should* have taken philosophy!)

Given my deep personal uncertainties about where I belong in the greater scheme of things, the universe does seem 'absurd'. Abandoned by meaning, neither the daunting Jewish Yahweh figure nor the Christian cult of Jesus holds out much promise in terms that resonate for me. I accept that without a 'God' concept—an omnipotent creator/designer to supply me with a pre-ordained purpose—it must be up to me as an individual to choose the life I think best. That feels right, but as inspiration, Existentialism can be a bit of a downer. If God is dead, a human is *condemned* to be free, they say, which leaves me faced with the challenge of making conscious, empirical choices at every turn. Little is 'given', especially in the form of authorised, pre-determined meaning; life is not driven by 'destiny'. Unable to defer responsibility either to a divine being, or to some essentialist notion such as 'human nature', one simply cannot make excuses. To do that would be a form of self-deception, or 'bad-faith'. Rather than creating us, perhaps 'God' itself is a human conception and in that sense, *we* created 'God'. We are not created in 'His' image, 'He' is created in ours, a very human projection. So, one is responsible for one's own choices. Your life is what you make it.

I make a couple of attempts to read the Bible from cover to cover but again, the trials and tribulations of the troubled tribe that laid waste to Canaan don't resonate for me. Also, according to some of the early chapters, my desires are an abomination, and I should be stoned to death, along with those who work on the Sabbath, or eat shellfish. I wince at the inglorious history of the Crusades and what I hear about the Spanish Inquisition. Instinctively I know I could easily be the target of moralistic inquisitions. It appears that whole apparatus is an exclusivist club to which I will never belong, so how can I take any of this as my personal heritage?

As for my family, my parents are not part of that class who still look to England as the 'Old Country' and who only endure life in 'the colonies' *faute de mieux*. My antecedents clearly come from somewhere else. If anything, I prefer to be descended from those rebel Yankees, at least on my mother's side, who threw off the Imperial yoke rather than linger in a neo-colonial twilight.

Even though I was born in this land, I am not Aboriginal. (Now, that would be authentic, at least to a romantic imagination.) I lack the louche glamour, too, that might derive from being descended from convicts and so far have found the ethos of larrikin Aussie mateship decidedly unattractive. I am too sensitive to its overpoweringly conformist subtexts to be able to relax into its embrace. Its boozy bonhomie is still so closely associated with alcoholism, in my experience, that I can't retrieve a sense of authentic kinship there. And 'mates' just don't want to get matey the way I yearn to.

I am a man without a tribe.

In second year I take on a full-year unit in anthropology and discover the concept of ethnocentrism. Obviously the way people have understood themselves, and the principles they have valued highly, are not configured the same way in different cultures and at different periods in history. Decades before Foucault, anthropology demonstrates for me that things might be differently conceived and valued in different cultural and historical contexts. Context is everything, culture determines values. Meaning is relative and cannot be assigned universally. So where am I to be situated? This is not idle speculation; I take on ideas emotionally and, while these encounters are stimulating, they also feed my growing unease.

I discover that to know the 'self' was the advice meeting all enquirers at the shrine of the Delphic oracle, yet I come across a provocative quote from a 17th century French philosopher, Diderot, which suggests that the self is a bit of an illusion, merely a series of moments contiguously related in time. I catch just a hint of the instability implied in this *aperçu* and postpone that line of enquiry indefinitely, for I am grappling already with what could politely be called an unstable subjectivity. Later, I pick up on the discussion among English philosophers around the time of Locke and Hume who questioned the nature of the uniting principle that supposedly constitutes a person. I tend to assume (like Hume, I suppose) that such a principle exists, but I am groping to find it. If Locke defined personal identity as a thinking, intelligent being that has reason and reflection, and who can consider itself the *same* thinking thing in different times and places, this seems too Cartesian for me. Am I really just this thing constructed out of ideas? And there is an implicit suggestion here that there might in fact be no 'self' at all, only a collection of moments of consciousness, many of which might each be contradictory to the other. An assemblage of entities posing as 'I'. That seems to match my state of mind.

If I can accept the suggestion of a complexity of selves, I tend to baulk at some of the other implications. If I still equate consciousness with thinking, my own thought processes are inconsistent, often incoherent and tainted by feeling, which blurs the crisp picture proffered by reason. I can certainly relate to the implication that one lacks substance because one isn't the same person from one moment to the next, but I fail to take the next step, which would be to inquire into the nature of consciousness itself and re-contextualise the notion of a personal self within that field. What tools would I use to explore that? More and more ideas?

I am really groping to find a narrative of selfhood that will satisfy my thirst for meaning, a coherent and continuous identity that is not only philosophically defensible but psychologically re-assuring, too. Everyone here seems too readily satisfied with the formula: 'I think, therefore I am'. But thinking is only a part of my turgid inner world and the comfort offered by Descartes' nostrum doesn't touch me, let alone alleviate my insecurities. I don't know yet that thinking is only one function of consciousness; that there might be another way of knowing, one that satisfies the whole person. So I rush around *doing* more and more, actively avoiding the naked encounter with being, just as Pascal said men tend to do.

The artsy life of the campus theatre scene calls to me and I wonder: is it as flagrant as ballroom dancing, and do I care? With several theatre companies active on and around campus there's a lot of production afoot and leaving my previous sporting activities to the jocks, I dive right in. The English department has a strong theatre component, and some of the lecturers encourage me to cultivate my thespian persona. Through this doorway I encounter a host of stimulating grownups whose mastery of the theatre arts bespeaks an apparent freedom from the kind of insecurities that eat away at me and, on stage—albeit briefly—working through well-rehearsed lines and movement, I can play at being a stable, coherent character.

In first year alone I am involved in six different shows, with small parts in productions of Sheridan and O'Casey, as well as in sketches for an international revue, where I meet students from Cambodia, Thailand, New Guinea, Malaysia and Indonesia. During the summer Festival of Arts I get small but paid parts in Shakespearean dramas staged in the New Fortune, a theatre built into the courtyard of the Arts Faculty building, which follows the ground plan of a theatre on London's south bank, from Elizabethan times. I play Paris in *Romeo and Juliet* and the Player King in *Hamlet*. In second year I get the lead in Ben Jonson's *The Alchemist*, under the direction of the incomparable Jeanna Bradley, although one reviewer feels that my playing of the lead role, Subtle, the alchemist, is perhaps too subtle.

Not so subtle is my performance in *Everyman*, the mediaeval morality play once used by the churches to instruct the faithful. I play Death. Working with the inspirational director Ray Omodei quickens my budding aestheticism. Omodei mounts a powerful production of the play in St. George's Cathedral in the city.

'Where art thou Death, my mighty messenger?' booms 'God', and I, clad in black robes, with stark face make-up shaded to make my head look like a skull, come padding down the central aisle of the cathedral, back-lit, my shadow looming into the nave. It's really quite spooky. But when the production moves into the small Dolphin Theatre on campus I fail to scale down my performance and get panned, in *The Critic*, for overacting. A year later, *Everyman* gets another staged reading in the Dolphin. This time, most of the actors work from texts in their hands but I remember my lines from the previous year. Edgar Metcalfe, the director of the commercial Playhouse downtown, plays Everyman.

This time, having taken the earlier review to heart, I revel in striking fear into the poor man's eyes with a chilling, underplayed delivery:

> *See thou make thee ready shortly*
> *For thou mayest say this is the day*
> *That no man living may scape away.*

Acting provides its own insecurities but, occasionally, playing a role gives me the chance to try on confidence for size. If Mr Balzan's demise caught me existentially unprepared, now, borrowing certainty from the character of Death itself, I enjoy turning the tables.

When we prepare to take Marlowe's *Dr. Faustus* to an intervarsity drama festival in Melbourne, under the highly creative direction of Joan Pope and Phillip Parsons, I play Mephistopheles, and thrill at the contrast between the ecclesiastical didacticism of *Everyman*, the morality play, and the hints of modernism in Marlowe. When Faustus wants to send Mephistopheles back to Hell, his preceptor in the black arts comes back with the line: 'Why Faustus, this *is* hell, nor are we out of it.' To a budding existentialist, heaven and hell must surely be here now, equally creations of the human mind.

The campus snuggles close where the Swan River takes a slow bend at Crawley. Feverish hours in the library in search of the answer to the oracle's injunction to self-knowledge mingle with idle periods lying on the riverbank or simply gazing in reverie across the verdant quadrangle. Virginia creeper splashes its extravagant palette against the weather-stained limestone of Winthrop Hall. Terracotta roof tiles stack up in earthy contrast against cloudless, bleached-blue skies.

At the end of second year, with the approaching threat of having to go back into training for the high schools, I opt for Honours, which will extend my studies into a fourth year. As I am still choosing subjects that ostensibly could be taught in the schools, the Education Department grants the necessary permissions.

I centre my Honours thesis in the plays of Samuel Beckett, part of an earnest study of the Theatre of the Absurd. I enjoy the bleak humour of the Irishman, who can pun in French as well as English, and who mocks the effort of trying to 'eff the ineffable', in *Watt*. Beckett's dry nihilism is an astringent tonic for my own enthusiasms.

Far from being an 'escape' (from the Department, at least), Honours brings on its own anxieties and, as the final year unfolds, I start avoiding classes, spending much time at the beach. Faced with the inevitable return, once my studies are completed, to the classroom as a reluctant high school teacher, even before Honours is up I quixotically apply for a post-graduate scholarship, in the hope of staving off the fateful day. By the time graduation comes around I have won the scholarship and gained a further reprieve from indentured servitude.

Tishie and Frank attend the graduation ceremony. Here's a shot of us: I am sporting a goatee and gazing through heavy-framed glasses at the scroll. While my parents look impressed, I am thinking: 'Is that all there is?' I have got a First, due in part to the aforementioned therapeutic resort to the beach but also, doubtless, to the happy coincidence of the manic phase of my incipient bi-polarity with the two weeks of the final exams. An inspired burst had carried me through the six or so three-hour exams, where I wrote furious, inspired raves for each paper.

After the ceremony I sip tea with mum and dad, nibbling inert white-bread sandwiches, cut in dainty triangles with their crusts trimmed off. I smile for the photographs, but this is a performance, too. I don't trust my own responses. All I have are questions, not answers. I have read the books, written the papers, taken the exams, yet even standing here clutching my hollow scroll—documentary evidence that I now 'know' something—I have this nagging feeling that my prey has eluded me. I have learned to play the game and ended up not only fooling the examiners but in the process have I fooled myself? My sister Val, who has followed me into university, is already having doubts and preparing to drop out.

Frank mutters his own doubts: 'When are you going to repay your debt to society?' he asks. Fair enough. But how can I go back into school and teach another generation of kids when I, the apparently successful product of the education system—primary, secondary, now tertiary, *with Honours, First Class, no less!*—haven't yet found out what I really want to know? My father's challenge is more an accusation than a question, and brings me no relief. For Frank, a degree is a utilitarian project that is meant to fit you out for employment. But are they seriously intending to let me loose into the system? I still see myself as a student, one who hasn't yet learned how to frame the important questions. A student in search of a teacher, if only I knew it. Now I have the scholarship to go on to a research Master's degree. Perhaps if I stay here longer I will find out what I seem to have missed the first time around.

I am sketching out an idea for a thesis situated somewhere among the playwrights of the Absurd—Beckett, Ionesco, Genet *et al*—and I sit in the library forcing my brain to come up with original insights into *Endgame,*

The Bald Prima Donna or *The Screens*. As I look along the stacks, my train of thought goes off the rails. Row after row of books, stretching along the entire floor; several floors in all. If I were to start with the shelf in front of me and read that row and then the next one, and the next after that, completing that whole section, how long would it take me to read all the books on this floor?

This is only one subject area. There are other, entire disciplines, shelved on other floors. How many thousands of volumes, just in this one library? Could I ever read them all? This is one of several libraries on campus. Even if I were to read non-stop, to play catch up, there are thousands of people out there, maybe hundreds of thousands, scribbling away right now, writing, writing; ever more books to fill more library stacks. If this is the way to knowledge, how will I ever know?

I gaze out across the quadrangle at the scarlet creeper cascading down the limestone. It's better to sit at a window with a view, trying to catch some calm, than to have a view only of books, books, books. But if I space out like this, how will I ever finish my thesis?

What *is* my thesis?

The more I try to crack the code with my head, a pain tightens in my chest.

I undertake a weekly theatre column in a Sunday paper—fifteen dollars a throw—and inscribe my confusion, my anger, my disappointment and my increasing aesthetic snobbery in print, in the process arousing resentment among theatre workers and becoming rather unpopular. I hope, ardently, that Art has the power to transform society and I cannot understand why theatre, at least in its present manifestations, should be so impoverished.

Walking the streets, I stare into people's eyes, seeking some reflection, a knowing look back at me, a confirmation that someone might have found the answer. Is it possible they don't even know the question? Are they bothered? Am I the only person who can't find meaning, simply, among the activities of everyday life? Is study making me stupid? Where is the borderline between inspiration, obsessed with the burning questions of existence, and sheer madness?

After a year of footling around, I settle on the French post-surrealist and theatre visionary Antonin Artaud as the centrepiece of my dissertation. Artaud ingested peyote with the Tarahumaras Indians of

Mexico and spent most of the last decade of his life in an asylum for the insane. Somehow this recommends him all the more, as I puzzle out what the post-surrealist means by a 'theatre of cruelty' and the 'poetry of space'.

midnight in the dorm

1966. My heart pounds against my ribs, my back pressing into the cold tiles of the shower recess. It's midnight and I am trapped, naked, in the bathroom of a boarding-school dormitory. Desperate that the man who is cleaning his teeth at the basin so close by should not catch me here, I try to suppress even the smallest flicker of presence, hoping that by sheer force of will I can eliminate any stray emanation that might disturb the space between us and alert him that I, an interloper, am here.

At the same time, that could be my boyfriend there at the washbasin and I have to restrain myself from jumping out to tickle his waist. Some better sense, more cautious, holds me back as I consider the possibility that it's probably not Helm but the other housemaster performing his ablutions.

Only a minute ago I had crept into the bathroom to clean up after making love and when I heard someone approaching I pressed my body into hiding, willing myself into virtual invisibility, back up against the wall. There is only a small frame at one edge of the shower, otherwise the room is bare, but the door to the bathroom, when open and pushed back against the shower stall, as now, gives some temporary cover. While it is only a partial baffle, sufficient to conceal me from a sidelong glance, it also makes it impossible for me to confirm if it is my lover or the other master. If I peer out to check, I could give the whole game away. I didn't switch on the light when I came in; he did. He has no clue that I might be here unless I make a sound. If he turns to his right to leave, he will almost certainly see me naked, pressed up against the wall. If he turns left to go, I might escape his gaze. Did I make a noise as I crept past his door to get here? Is he dopey from sleep, or is he wide awake? He is doing the rounds of the boys' dorm rooms, and he has taken a piss stop en route.

My lover teaches at this school and lives in as a housemaster. Helm is back at university, part-time, completing his degree, and this private school gig, with free accommodation in exchange for housemaster duties, supports him in his final years of studying.

We have been lovers for a year but have never lived together. When we first started going out Helm had an apartment, and I would tear myself from his bed to drive home across town, bleary-eyed, to my parents' house, where I still live, rent-free, while finishing my own penurious days as an Honours student. If my mother knows what's up, she isn't letting on. My toothbrush has not yet been relocated across town and I have my own key to let myself in to the family home. Traditionally, the ritual handing over of the key to the front door would occur on one's twenty-first birthday but I am involved in a lot of theatre so, for practical purposes, I have been granted privileges early.

'Is that you, Vic?' She stirs, no matter what the hour.

'Yes, Mum, don't worry, just go back to sleep,' I whisper through gritted teeth. On one hand I'm irritated that no movement is quiet enough to escape her vigilance, on the other, touched by her predictable but unwavering care. I start to avoid the front door and slide in through a door off the back verandah, making sure I am there before the family awakens.

'What took you so long?' Helm says, smiling. His dimples deepen and his huge brown eyes blink sleepily.

'That wasn't you ...', I hiss, *sotto voce*, '... in the bathroom?'

'WHY ... ARE ... YOU ... WHISPERING?' He breathes in a hammy stage voice as he grabs me and pulls me onto the bed.

'That wasn't you?'

'What do you mean?'

I have to make him understand how close I was to exposing us both: 'You didn't come into the bathroom? It *was* the other guy, wasn't it?'

'No, I was here all the time. I heard him go out. Where were you?'

'I was in the bathroom, dummy, have you been asleep? He came in and switched on the light. Oh, God, I nearly jumped out and tickled him, and I'm stark naked!'

'Wow. Let's be careful, eh?' We laugh and hug quietly on the bed.

Helm van Kemenade is five years older than me. He is strong, reliable and handsome. European—Belgian—and his first language is Flemish. The family migrated to Australia when he was twelve. He speaks good colloquial English (the Aussie variety) with a slight thickness in the tongue, and a guttural timbre that he makes effective use of when he's on stage in one of the theatre productions we are both involved in. Well-built and physically vigorous, with a broad, hairy chest and distinctly real pecs, he has a confident smile, full lips and these large brown eyes ('just like a damn cow,' he protests). False teeth already, even though he is only in his mid-twenties (nutrition must have been an issue in post-war Europe). His brown hair has gold highlights from the bright, relentless sunlight on the west coast where we live.

His family name, 'Van Kemenade', sounds noble, but such pretensions are not typical in Australia. Kids at his school called him 'lemonade'. The dignified 'Kem-en-aaah-de' is downgraded, according to the age-old Aussie imperative that reduces anything foreign to mind-numbing conformity; 'multiculturalism' is an ideal that won't be born for decades. I am glad I knew those other migrants—my neighbours the Balzans—and I feel protective towards Helm, wishing in retrospect that I could have shielded him from the gross insensitivity of my compatriots. But Helm doesn't need my sentimentality. The Flemish have their own kind of bluntness, he explains, and it is obvious that he can hold his own against the rednecks of his adopted land. Helm draws real strength from his sometimes fractious family. Even though he gets angry with his father, the ties have been strong enough to buffer them from the harsher aspects of their adopted milieu.

We met a couple of years back, during the summer Festival of Arts. Helm was teaching high school and finishing a university degree part-time, so we ran into each other only when cast in the same productions. I hadn't yet emerged from my sexual closet. When I heard the word 'camp' I didn't identify with it, and it certainly didn't seem to apply to Helm, who was too masculine to fit the stereotype. I admired his strength, his confident smile, and the muscles, all of which proved a baffle for my antenna.

Our paths crossed decisively at a rundown theatre, downtown, while rehearsing *King Lear*. Helm played Edmund to my good brother Edgar. One evening we sat side by side in the stalls, watching rehearsals. After two years of circling around each other Helm suddenly became direct:

'Would you like to go out?'

'Oh … Yes. Um … What did you have in mind?'

'I thought we could go to the drive-in.'

Hope flew up like a flustered dove thrown from a magician's hat.

'Why errr, yes, I would! When?'

Next evening, as I got ready, my excitement rose visibly. In the bathroom mirror my skin seemed to have more colour. Body temperature rises in the evenings, they say, but perhaps this was something more. Even as I grabbed for the car keys, I was trying to avoid thinking about the possibilities. I am twenty. I have never had real sex, let alone a boyfriend.

As I hurtled down the freeway towards my first-ever date, the question started to poke its head out of hiding:

'Does this mean …? No, he *couldn't* be … he's so strong!'

For the first time in the two years I had known this admirable man, I allowed myself to wonder if Helm might have the same feelings of attraction. Why else would he ask me out? Perhaps he just wants to be friends. It's probably nothing. Better not get your hopes up. As the car sped on over the Narrows Bridge towards Helm's city apartment, my feelings raced ahead and, for the first time, I didn't bother to rein them back in.

We didn't see much of the movie. In the privacy of the car, between a splurge of tears, we blurted out our mutual confessions; years of dammed-up hope and shame relieved in an embrace which promised a kind of comfort, and a recognition I had never before felt. Helm said that he found it hard making the first move. The women in the cast had assured him that I was almost certainly 'camp', and that he ought to take the plunge. Such a strong-looking guy and *he* had doubts?

Outside the Uni library I am talking to a girl from my French class. We have been out together once or twice, and I have tried to nail her on the floor of the living room of her parents' house in Nedlands. Like every 'girlfriend' I have ever had, right through high school, she was willing to pash on but, when it came to the crunch, she wouldn't come across, and I have given up on her.

She asks me how I am doing, what's the news. I'm in love, never felt it before and tell her so. She's glad that I have found someone and the pressure is off her, and she asks me: 'Who is she?' But when I tell her: 'Oh no, it's a … Um. It's a guy. I'm in love with a guy, you know?' she is speechless and can't quite pull out the words to say she's glad for me. I have never 'outed' myself to anyone. It's Western Australia, it's 1966. The phrase does not yet exist.

Love quickly becomes a physical fact and the feelings it releases are too strong to deny. I go through a bewildering flux of emotional states in a matter of days. I drop in to visit him and stay late on several nights. Rumours fly on campus. One of my former high-school classmates (the one who challenged me 'Aren't you a Christian?') notices my car parked outside Helm's place. I wonder why they all should be so interested, but somehow the word is out. I couldn't care less. My mix of friends has changed, the longer I have been on campus. Perhaps this kind of thing is expected of people in the theatre.

After all the yearning years of adolescence I am in bed with a man; a strong, handsome man, and he is willing. In my few earlier groping experiments I had never had the chance to let go and enjoy the sex without inhibition. Helm is a little more experienced, and makes fun of my tentativeness, encouraging me to explore our sensuality with less restraint. I can't believe my luck.

He has returned to university to finish his degree at nights, while I finish my final year of Honours and, after a few months, to save on rent, he gives up the flat to take the position as a housemaster in the private boys' school. It makes sense financially, but it has put a crimp in our love-making.

'I guess I'd better be going then,' I yawn.

'Just give it a few more minutes. He'll start to snore before too long and he won't notice you leaving.'

I'm getting sick of these surreptitious episodes, so, after almost a year of this paranoia, we finally decide to live together, renting a small, two-bedroom flat near the university; damn the gossip. Besides, it's not uncommon for students to share housing. The move is rationalised thus to my parents: It's just around the corner from the campus. As it's so close by, I won't have so many late nights coming home from the campus theatres. I won't need the car, so Tishie can have sole use.

In our new digs we keep beds prepped in separate bedrooms to maintain appearances, in case my parents ever visit, but Helm's mum is not playing the *faux naïve*. Ah, the Europeans. She gives us an oversized double bed. The mattress is so big it requires special sheets, which she also supplies. In the other room, the lonely single bed is always made, like stage dressing in a play called 'Separate Lives', perhaps. If Helm's mother is in on the subterfuge, it's clear from his father's eyes that he doesn't need to say anything to acknowledge what is going on. I'm in love with his handsome son.

Helm nudges me: 'Hey, are you still there?'

'Mmm.' We are lying side by side in the big bed after making love.

'You weren't breathing.' (He's been listening for it.) Sometimes when feeling peaceful I slip into that space between waking and sleeping and my breath kind of peters out. I re-assure him that I am not dead and we snuggle in against each other. Helm likes me to lie with my head on his chest and I like that too, but there comes a point when, in order to really release into a deeper sleep, one of us has to roll over. I hold off from doing so for the longest time because I hate to turn my back on him and I try to keep a backward hand or arm or leg entangled for as long as I am conscious.

Helm has to get up early for work, and I am supposed to make his breakfast. I am at a loss. I have never had to cook for myself, so he demonstrates. I grumble about having to get up early, still half asleep as I make his food, and he gets the same meal every morning: two fried eggs, sausages and bacon with a thick slice of *lekkerbrot* toast and a cup of strong tea. Occasionally I make him porridge, with walnuts; again following his tuition.

'Breakfast's ready!' I call out, yawning, across the landing through the window to the bathroom where Helm is shaving. Do the neighbours find it strange that a man should make breakfast for another man like this? Surely there can't be many people awake at this hour.

I sit sleepily with my lover as he eats and then, as the front door closes, go back to bed. I am in my final year of Honours and I'm usually late for my first class at 11 am. When I lived at home my mum would come through my door to rouse me around 10 am with a cup of tea, which I found tough on an empty stomach but Tishie was aware that if she didn't wake me, I would probably sleep all day. My life has swung around to the late shift, and when I am performing in a theatre piece my days are lazy preparations for the evenings when, on stage, I come alive.

Helm and I are virtually adopted by a pair of older men: Neville, a lecturer in the English Department and his long-term lover, Keir. With them as role models for long-term coupledom, we cling together in the hope that neither of us will ever end up solo as a lonely, tragic old queen.

We are repelled by the image of Aschenbach, from the movie of Thomas Mann's *Death in Venice*. The shot of Dirk Bogarde sitting and sweating pathetically, with the dye that he had applied to his hair to make him look younger trickling down his forehead, sends shudders through me. 'That'll never be us', we agree.

But even that wish is not enough to prevent us from separating, after living together for only a year. The sex is great, and a huge relief, but still I am driven to find the answer to a puzzle that I can barely articulate. I am frustrated that the theatre isn't coughing up the kind of transcendental vision that could transform society and I have been complaining about the local theatre scene through my weekly newspaper column. Expressing my frustration has brought anger and resentment on my head, which contributes to a growing depression and paranoia that the relationship does not alleviate.

After reading my way aimlessly through the field of modern French theatre, my constipated dissertation finally gets the kind of stimulus it needs from the incendiary writings of the visionary Antonin Artaud. However, Australia's only published scholar on the mad genius teaches in the French Department at the University of New South Wales. I find I can get my scholarship transferred to Sydney and I have to choose whether to stay on in Perth with Helm, or follow my star east. I opt for the latter, leaving the possibility of maintaining a long-distance relationship dangling, unresolved. My head-trip overrides my need for intimacy. We both know that it's probably over, and tears are shed.

Artaud saw theatre as too dominated by language. Influenced by surrealism, he challenged the conventions of the civilised mind, and he wanted to replace the artificiality of the well-made, 'realist' play with the evocative 'language of space': utilising untapped powers of sound and light, even the kinaesthetic impact of the actor's breath itself, on the nervous systems of the audience, to shift spectators into new states of awareness—nothing less. 'The actor,' Artaud wrote, 'is like a martyr, burning at the stake, signalling through the flames'. Finally, someone with the kind of intensity that can match my own inchoate aspirations.

All fired up again, I go to Sydney, taking up residence in student housing on campus. The post-graduate accommodation is across the road from the racecourse at Randwick, in a hut behind The Old Tote Theatre. I have moved closer to the centre of the 'action' but, as a know-nothing hayseed from Perth, restrained by feelings of inferiority, I find it hard to make connections in big city Sydney. On campus I form one friendship that I will carry forward for decades: Bob Beaver, an undergraduate living in nearby Baxter College. Otherwise, loneliness prevails.

I am courted briefly by an exciting man named Phillip George, who works in advertising, directing commercials for the J. Walter Thompson agency, but Phil has recently had his heart broken. Subdued by medication for depression, he is even less able to perform in bed than he is to commit to a new relationship and, almost before it has begun, our liaison recedes into a rueful, distant friendship. I leave a club in tears when George dances with another man. I left Helm behind; now I know something of how it feels to have my own heart broken.

The scholarship pays for full board on campus and not much else. If I want to get out to the only camp bar I know about, I have to walk to Oxford Street, Paddington, to save on fares. At Chez Ivy, I nurse one drink all night, and wonder why everyone ignores me, this intense young intellectual in glasses. An advertising slogan advises that: 'Men don't make passes at girls who wear glasses'; does that apply? Surely no one could be that shallow.

Sometimes, on the return walk to Randwick I detour down Bayswater Road, behind King's Cross, to a notorious 'beat', where nocturnal prowling is too ridden with anxiety to be enjoyable. Hardcore sex activists can mock the domesticity of two lovers sleeping together, but the adrenaline thrill of sex out in the open, with the ever-present danger of being caught in a police entrapment, proves less than satisfying. Nothing can replace the intimacy I have had with Helm, but as painful as it is, I feel there's a perverse poetic justice at work here. I ought to be prepared to 'go without' for the cause of Truth in Art.

One night I go home with someone I meet, who is too embarrassed to see me again, knowing he has given me crabs. Some people *are* shallow.

I slug away at the thesis, painfully developing chapters on each playwright whom I claim can be read from an Artaudian perspective. During lonely nights in my monk's cell in student housing I locate a laid-back late night jazz program on the radio, and I take refuge in that. Morgana King's thin, high angst perfectly suits my mood.

I hear my first work by Palestrina. The austere purity of the vocal line is like cool water being poured across my fevered brain, and out of some sense of visceral relief that I don't understand, I weep. What do people like Palestrina find in religion? Well, I can take comfort in their music—at least, this early stuff. The massed choirs of a Bach oratorio overwhelm me, crushing me with their strident confidence.

funeral suite, revisited

December 1968. 'Phone for you. It's long distance.'

There is just one telephone, for a dozen rooms, at the end of the hall. I hurry down the corridor. They wouldn't be calling from Perth just to say hello.

'I've got some bad news.' My father's voice. 'It's your brother.'

'What's happened?' Tell me the worst.

'Well, he had a rejection episode, the doctors said. He was going real well but the kidney started to reject and they couldn't get the drugs right'.

'Oh God. Is he … Is he.. Did he..?'

'We lost him last night.'

In failing health, David had the first kidney transplant in the West, and has been on drugs to suppress the natural reaction of his body to reject the new organ. After years on dialysis, chronic kidney disease had nearly done him in. But after the operation it really looked like he was thriving.

'How's Mum taking it?' Horrible how matter-of-fact it all feels.

'Well, she says she'll be right. The doctor wants to put her on sedatives … What do you reckon?' I don't know.

'Look, the funeral is on Thursday. Do you think you could make it back?'

'Yes, of course.' What to say? 'He was doing so well after the transplant and all.'

'Yeah. Well, he was their first one. Had his picture in the paper. He was working in Fremantle, first time he'd been able to work in more than five years … He was a real little battler. Looked like he was going so well, too.' Is this the longest conversation I have ever had with my father?

'How are Jan and the kids?'

'I dunno. Haven't spoken to them … Well, try and get over. Let us know your flight. We'll get Val to pick you up at the airport.'

I hang up and trudge back to my room. I have been living on campus for ten months, and made some progress on the thesis, but it's far from finished. I borrow money from Phillip George, the commercials director, pack my meagre possessions, and fly back to Perth.

I watch in ringing silence as they lower the box into the ground. I am in a daze. As a child, I had fears of being buried alive and now, as they throw cruel clods of clay into the pit, an impenetrable puzzle is thrown back at me.

I walk back to the funeral director's black limousine and finally let loose a howl. The sound comes from a place I have rarely been in touch with. Tish has said very little, but after hearing me cry she smiles quietly as if that confirms for her that I do love my brother after all. She has been concerned about that. Frank has sided with the doctors who wanted to put her on sedatives, but her calm dignity in grief outflanks their concerns.

I have been plucked out of a long, aesthetic dream at university and hit cold with this experience, which is well outside the frame of all my theoretical reckoning. If you were to ask me what am I grieving for I wouldn't be able to tell you. For the loss of a brother I hardly knew, dead at twenty-six?

David was three years older than me and it seemed to be his job to teach me that life was cruel and unfair and you could cry all you liked but a set of hard knuckles and a pair of strong fists would stand you in better stead. Here's that photo again, taken in primary school. David is the dark-haired one, slightly pudgy; the other, sandy-haired one with the gap between his new front teeth, deferring to his big brother's confidence; he's the one who goes by my name.

I pick over the memories: the monkey bars, two broken arms, my brother's confidence in the contact sports from which I could only recoil. 'That's S-T-U-G spelt backwards', proud uncle Bill penned on the congratulatory card that still sits on the mantelpiece at home, next to my brother's football trophies.

David the hero was the one who had taken me to the narrow lane beside the house in Howick Street to break the news about Father Christmas. He liked to tease me, his slight, younger brother, to test his own strength. One time around the dinner table, when I was five, he pushed me too far with his relentless aggravations and I flung a soup-spoon at him. Dave dodged. The spoon sailed past his head and connected with the glass-fronted door of a kitchen cabinet and it was me, not David, who got into trouble.

Just a couple of years before his operation, we played a round of golf together. Oblivious to his physical condition, I pushed on rapidly from fairway to fairway, forgetting his diminished state. At one green he had to stop to vomit from over-exertion. That snapped me out of my ignorance, and now the memory churns painfully in my heart.

I have never seen a lifeless body before. They have a viewing, with an open casket, before the interment. I see the face that once smiled with life, now silent; the body breathless; the skin like vellum; eyeballs sunken back into their sockets. Perhaps you could say it resembles him but, clearly, that utterly inert form is not my brother. Whatever he was, is gone; 'disappeared', as the French say. If 'he' was not something physical, what was he, what *is* he? What other spaces exist beyond the senses? If that form is here, in front of my eyes, but *he*—the energetic person, David—is not, have I ever really known who or what he was? What was I relating to, when I saw my brother smile, heard him talk? Staring at the body in the coffin, my brain can pluck no meaning from this rude encounter.

panic stations

1970. Back on campus, I stumble on through graduate school. 'Know Thyself' mocks me from the limestone walls. I only have a single chapter to finish on my Master's dissertation. My supervisor in Sydney likes the material I have submitted, but the longer I spend on it, the further its completion recedes into the distance. Something more urgent is calling for my attention yet I don't know what that is. I am beginning to crack up, but my dogged attempt to focus on Genet's *The Screens* intensifies my confusion. If the meandering questions of the unfinished thesis fitfully occupy my conscious thought, somewhere deeper the enigma of my brother's empty body drives into my unconscious to work away unseen.

1942—1968. His life just a dash between the coming and the going. He had kids. And he died.

In the library I suffer one of a series of panic attacks. For two months I have been waiting for the latest issue of a theatre journal from Europe. In an earlier issue the editors promised an article about Samuel Beckett directing one of his own plays, and it seems crucially important for my argument to read that article. But when the issue arrives, it carries no such piece and no reference is made to where it might be found. It's very important to me, because it was to be an account of the playwright's rehearsal techniques and would help explicate Beckett's approach to time. I go back and check the earlier issue. Yes, I was not mistaken, the notice is there, so where is the promised article? I check the page numbers; perhaps someone has removed it. The more I check, the more frantic I become. The reference desk assistant can't understand why the absence of a mere article should precipitate such speechless, wild-eyed terror.

Time is running out. The Education Department will soon call in their markers and put me finally into harness as a teacher. Meanwhile, a visiting professor from Santa Barbara mounts *Waiting for Godot* in the Octagon Theatre and casts me as 'Lucky', a character who has little to do during the first act, except for an impenetrable five-page outburst when prodded into action by his 'master', Pozzo. In the second act he is totally mute. Lucky's speech—an incoherent flotsam and jetsam of *non sequiturs*—is seen by critics as Beckett's bleak satire on the state of Western thought.

How appropriate, that I should play this wreck of a man. Man without meaning; all of Western thought scrambled into this garbled incoherency.

I visit a kindly psychiatrist in West Perth who is more familiar with young men panicking at the prospect of being called up to be sent to Vietnam. She puts me on Valium and orders an evaluation from a psychologist, who administers the Rorschach blot tests and deduces that I am overwhelmed by my mother.

I hate the dragging feeling that the pills induce. I feed on inspiration, I need to feel 'up', not 'down'. I ask the psychiatrist what approach she uses: is she a Freudian or a Jungian? She says she finds the question threatening, gives me the psychologist's report to take away and advises me to seek out an existential analyst. When I ask for a referral she says there are only two in the world, both in Scotland.

A swami comes to give a lecture at the University. When I look into the eyes of the Indian monk there is a certainty, an almost mocking humour there. Swamiji doesn't reveal any startling secrets but, after addressing us all as 'ladies and gentlemen', he has some fun deconstructing the word 'gentleman'. 'Be a gentle man', he advises.

It's not enough.

I hear stories from other graduate students about an unorthodox therapist, Jim Coventry, a psychologist rumoured to have been influenced by Zen, or an Indian *guru*. The details are unclear. My desperate improvisations are running out, and so are the scholarship funds. I get an appointment and walk to the psychologist's rooms, near the university.

None of the magazines in the waiting room has anything of interest. Where is he? Off the Valium, I am restless, I want to get down to business.

Coventry appears in the doorway. He indicates that we should go upstairs and I stride past him, taking two steps at a time. Coventry is walking slowly. I don't know whether to wait, or go ahead. Isn't the aim to get up to his room, so we can get started? The counselor proceeds, one step at a time, his very calm posing a challenge.

He has me read a section from a book on Vedanta that lists four doctrines derived from something called the 'Perennial Philosophy' that speaks of an eternal Self. All phenomena as part of the Divine Ground of Being. A way of knowing by direct intuition rather than discursive reasoning. It makes little impression on me. I barely notice the author's name, or the title of the work. Years later I track it down. It's from Aldous Huxley's introduction to an edition of the *Bhagavad Gita*, translated by Christopher Isherwood and his guru, Swami Prabhavananda, of the Ramakrishna Vedanta Order of monks in Southern California.[2]

I can scarcely grasp what is being expressed in the text, but it seems like something I should recognise, like a wisp of smoke rising up out of the depths of … what? In Sydney, Phillip George had shown me a frustrating book on Zen Buddhism. The stories hinted at a state of clarity that seemed highly desirable but their riddling paradoxes eluded me. George played recordings of Indian classical music and the *ragas* carried me away into a dreamless, sleep-like state.

Before I leave, Coventry shows me a pine cone he has collected on the way to work. He points to one of the seeds, with its single, transparent wing. The wind can catch it up and carry it away to another place. I recall the lovely image from the French publishing house, Larousse, with its trademark figure blowing seeds into the wind: *Je sème a tous vents*, it says. ('I sow to all the winds'.)

A week later I return to see him again. I try to walk more slowly up the stairs, matching his slow, deliberate demeanour but I can't restrain my speedier tempo. This time I am carrying a book for *him* to read but it fails to rouse his interest. He turns it around, and asks:

'What is this?'

He's more elusive than the book on Zen! Last week, he showed me a reading from a book, so I thought I would share one too. I try a clever riposte:

'A man's mind.'

'Simpler,' he advises.

I wish I could grasp the kind of knowing quietness this man embodies. We finally agree it is a tree.

'Look to the root of things'. Is that what he is saying? (Before it was the pages in a book, it was paper; before it was paper, it was a tree.) He doesn't spell it out for me, that's not his way.

Before I leave, Coventry tells me a story about a man at sea, swimming desperately, trying to reach landfall. No matter how long he swims,

---

[2] Huxley, Aldous. "Introduction." *The Song of God: Bhagavad Gita. The Hindu Epic Translated by Swami Prabhavananda and Christopher Isherwood.* New York: Mentor/New American Library, 1944.

despite all his efforts the land doesn't come into sight. He uses up every last scrap of energy and still there is no safety so finally, in his exhaustion, he gives up, prepared to drown. To his surprise, as he lets go, he finds that the water supports him. Instead of drowning, he floats; the currents move him where he needs to go, finally depositing him on a shore.

The water supports you and the currents take you where you want to go. This seems significant, even if I am not sure how it applies. I am sick of thrashing about and getting nowhere. Although I don't recognise it at the time, the psychologist is giving me a nudge in the right direction. It marks the beginning of a major shift in orientation which will take me in some weird, discomforting directions before it leads me where I really need to go.

Looking for accommodation near campus, I hook up with a couple from Melbourne, Patrick Howard and his wife Caroline, studying post-grad psychology. It's 1970 and the Vietnam moratorium movement is gaining strength. The Howards have brought an outspoken political activism with them and Caroline has been active in street theatre. Patrick and I go to the Perth Town Hall for a rally against Australia's involvement in the war where, in a graphic sketch piece, Caroline plays an Uncle Sam figure, tottering about on stilts, bombarding downtrodden Asians in their rice paddies.

After the performance, an articulate woman with long, lustrous hair gives a stirring speech urging men not to register for the draft. I admire her courage. For it is not only against the law for men of draft age to resist the conscription-by-lottery scheme, it is also illegal for this speaker to encourage their non-compliance. Patrick and Caroline know her already. Introductions are arranged and we hit it off.

She has been invited to a party by the son of a well-known artist, Guy Grey-Smith, at his house on the coast a few miles north of the city. As we drive, I rave, and find her an intelligent and receptive listener to my ideas about a visionary form of theatre that I hope could change the world.

The raven-haired activist has graduated top of her year, with first-class Honours, and she receives requests for copies of her research paper from all over the world. On a break before starting her post-graduate degree, this proper twin-set-and-pearls girl—former dux of a Catholic boarding school—goes to Rome to brush up her Italian, falls in with a bunch of students and professors who have closed down the university, and comes home radicalised. I have noticed her on campus, wearing colourful, ethnic dresses and long earrings.

I spend more and more time with her. We move into a shed in the backyard of a rented house in Swanbourne. The initial heady raves form the foundation of a stimulating friendship, but before too long, much to my surprise, and with the help of a marijuana 'joint' to get me past my inhibitions, it progresses into a physical relationship as well and for a brief period I will be her enthusiastic, if unskilled, lover.

She does not wish to be named in this memoir. She has her own life, and her own version of events, and out of an abiding respect for her, I do not intend to narrate her story, let alone account for her experience. There are people who will remember us together, or have read her interviews, for whom no disguise would work. For others, it is irrelevant and not a puzzle to be solved. I refer to her simply as my partner, and for a time we were together.

I meet up with a new group of people from off campus who have found another way to feed the search for meaning and, for the first time, my quest for intense experiences finds fuel in drugs. A gnomish figure from the counter-cultural underground has imported powerful 'Buddha sticks' from South East Asia. I spend hours lying on the banks of the river near the campus, tripping out on cloud formations massed over the Darling Ranges. Before long, I am introduced to LSD by a gimlet-eyed acid-head named Midge.

With the 'acid' comes a flood of new information; as well as mind-bending music and lurid new artforms from the UK and the US, blending 'op art' with Indian mandalas. A politics concerned with freedom for the mind mixes with vague sentiments about loving the Earth, now re-conceived as our Mother. The mythography of indigenous peoples suddenly seems relevant to our needs.

My diet shifts towards unprocessed 'whole' foods and soon, I stop eating meat.

My first trip on acid is a roller-coaster ride of expanded awareness, with episodes of fear gradually giving way into an exciting encounter with the myriad ins and outs of consciousness. Midge produces a 'tripping manual', an abridged edition of *The Tibetan Book of the Dead*, that in my radically altered state I am unable to follow. When Midge observes me anxiously teetering on the edge of freaking out, he mouths the mantra that will carry me away, much further than I could ever have planned:

'Let ... go'.

And, as simply as that, I am released, successfully, into the flow. A little death, then ... Nirvana, baby!

As I begin to journey the unknown seas of consciousness my thesis takes a back seat. I scarcely notice the link between the chemically-fuelled journeying and the endless delay in finishing. It seems less important to come to conclusions of any kind than to tap in to the flow of a moment-by-moment awakening. 'Be here now, man,' advises spiritual teacher Ram Dass. No time, no need, to build a memorial to my petty 'conclusions' about anything. What kind of an ego trip would that be? I have found the sphincter that is ego-self and learn how to release it, letting go of the angst of being me entirely. For as long as the trip lasts.

sydney *satori*

*The greatest blessings come to us through madness, when it is sent as a gift of the gods.
Heaven-sent madness is superior to man-made sanity.*
—Plato, in the *Phaedrus*

May 1971. My body tugs for attention. I have had nothing to eat for a
couple of days but the hunger that gnaws at me won't be appeased by
food. My feet spread out through the thin leather of my Jesus sandals,
gripping the pavement as the sinews in my legs pull the day towards me.
Thoughts are fragments, mere shards of consciousness cast up on an
empty shore. I love the experience of merging but I hate coming back to
everyday mind. Now, three or four days after my latest attempt to finally
blast off, the inevitable is happening. In place of the heaven states I have
been surfing, I am left with this restless, walking mania and an obsessive
collection of ragged little rituals acted out in place of meaning.

I count numbers on licence plates, reducing them numerologically to
single digits as my restless brain devours all data. I seek out mandala
patterns, matching every left with a right, trying to hold a centre firm.
What was effortless insight when the drugs were peaking is now
mimicked by these silly, empty rituals. People give me a wide berth as I
pad out my pilgrimage, parted warily by the bow-wave of intensity
emanating from my forehead. I haven't seen myself for days, but in their
looking back I catch a twisted reflection, in their stifled breath I feel the
loss of love.

I am looking for a house where I have stayed, a link back to my
ordinary life, a way home.

I wanted to drop enough acid this time so that the experience would
become permanent, instead of evaporating, like this, again, leaving me
scattered in a thousand pieces, like a jigsaw thrown aside by a petulant
child. When friends gave me several tabs for my birthday, I took them, all
of them, like some pseudo-sacrament, and full of high-octane God-fuel I
zoomed off into wonderland alone.

We were 'The Campus Guerrilla Theatre Troupe', a stoned-out band of radical actors with a vaguely political bent. With ample time to indulge quixotic quests we drove across the country to attend the first Aquarius Arts Festival in Canberra. My sensible partner stayed in Perth, working.

Fifteen hundred miles at least from Perth, via the Nullarbor, down to Adelaide, up through Swan Hill and Wagga Wagga to the Australian National University. Eleven of us, swinging through the countryside in a Ford Transit van. Our wardrobe was an eclectic tribute to imported ethnicity and every colour from the chemist's stocks of dye bled brightly through my electric clothing, each layer forming a counter-cultural rainbow waiting to be unveiled. (I soaked my underwear in the vats, too.)

We removed most of the seats in the van and replaced them with sleeping bags. Hundreds of miles passed in an easy haze as we rotated drivers. Bags of buddha sticks inspired the ride and whenever we spilled out the back of the van for a piss-stop, dopey earthy fumes clung to our hair and clothes.

Canberra in autumn was crisp. The trees were dancing maidens decked out in shades of Autumn. Hippies, students and sundry hangers-on gathered to celebrate the dawning of a New Age of peace and I greeted my brothers and sisters as fellows from the lost tribes returning to a new Jerusalem. Huxley's doors of perception were being blown right off their hinges. Stoned-out heads streamed through lecture halls, love-ins and impromptu songfests, mingling mind, body and spirit in easy familiarity. There could be no holding back against the swelling tide rising up on all sides; they flowed together in blissful unity as they were surely meant to do.

One evening, a young chamber orchestra from a university town in Germany gave a classical recital to a wild reception. Who was more surprised: they, at the ragged hippie enthusiasm, or the love children, at the musicians' brilliant discipline? While the Europeans were dressed in concert attire, all black and white precision, we were rainbow gypsies, feral folk to the Europeans perhaps but magical faeries to ourselves, especially on Sumatran 'buddha' grass. Music was a dazzling stream of sound, popping brain cells dizzy with scintillating allegretto measures, enchanting us with gracious gavottes and elegant, dancing minuets; every phrase, a cascade of waves surging through the senses, carrying us into higher states of delight.

It is 1971. Time to end the war in Vietnam. But when the politicos raised a call to action, to march on Parliament and stage a noisy protest, we Perthians resisted their street theatre training in favour of a gentler alternative: a sit-in on campus. Surely we should try to express the spirit of brotherhood in a new, non-confrontational mode more appropriate to what we were experiencing? We burned incense and sang wispy songs from The Incredible String Band. I didn't really know how to meditate, but I murmured made-up mantras, hoping they would somehow, passively, induce an Age of Peace into being. I chanted:

May the long time sun shine upon you
All love surround you
And the pure light within you
Guide your way home …

… over and over.

Years later, I will see a documentary clip from this event on television and recognise my former self on screen. I certainly look the part: I wear my hair down to my shoulders, under a dramatic black hat trimmed lavishly with a Thai silk headband. Stoned-out idealism blurred across my face; my lips are mumbling. But I remember how hollow I felt inside, how rootless that idealism was in me.

After the Aquarian lovefest, we trundled on the extra miles to Sydney and holed up at the house of friends in an inner suburb in the early stages of gentrification: Paddington, with its jumble of streets going this way and that, rows of terrace houses stacked up and down the hills, renovated by the score for upwardly-mobile professionals. We arrived at night, blissed-out emissaries of love and peace. I didn't pay attention to the street we stopped at, or the names of those there, I was still cruising on an experience of total trust. 'Let it be …'

The advice of the Zen psychologist had really taken root. I had given up the struggle, trying to release myself into the flow. Where university, theatre and radical politics had failed, spirituality was sure to provide. Samadhi, *moksha*, cosmic consciousness, call it what you like, I wanted nothing less than a blissful state of union with the Divine. I frequented the spiritual bookstores, fossicking among Vedanta, Sufism, Chinese Buddhism and Zen, month after month. One day I thought I had the key to enlightenment in my hands: '101 Zen koans, *with answers.*' Eureka! God in a book. The Way in words ...

Crushed to find that the answers were more difficult than the questions, I abandoned bookstores in disgust.

Fed up with theory, I was determined to grasp gnosis by direct experience. I had been to multiple screenings of *Woodstock*, on acid; chanted Hare Krishna with Alan Ginsberg in the Melbourne Town Hall; twisted into yoga postures atop a hill in the early mornings; gathered with the lost tribes in search of brotherhood. All without cornering my prey.

Drugs would be the way. What I hadn't found in books or churches I would capture with chemicals. Fuelled with acid, I crashed through the mundane barriers of everyday behaviour, hungry for union, as if in blowing my mind, permanently and irretrievably, the mind of God would be the only thing left.

So here I am, pacing restlessly through Paddington. I have been walking much in the past two days, criss-crossing the city. I am lost, and that very jumble of streets seems designed to drive me mad.

One morning in the early rush hour, tired of walking, I stop at an intersection on Anzac Parade, waiting for the traffic to clear. From four or five directions, several lanes circulate through an interchange as people travel to work, and I, this scruffy *saddhu*—he of no fixed address—having nothing better to do, pause to feel the hidden tide move all things.

In the middle of the broad intersection a traffic cop sits calmly on his horse. The reins are released, so the policeman's hands are free to direct traffic, and the horse is so in accord with its rider, that it needs no controlling. They are one.

I feel the breath moving the horse, the rider and the traffic, circulating everything in a smooth, effortless flow. I let myself dissolve into what is transpiring, knowing that this way of effortless being is always here to be accessed, easily, everything in one accord, and it's the most natural thing in the world to merge with it, this morning, this place, this horse, rider, traffic, park ... trees ... breath ... sky ...

I continue up Anzac Parade, all the way out to the Roundhouse at the University of New South Wales, strolling through the gates of the campus where I once lived. A man of leisure now, a tarot Fool, with no schedule to keep, no thesis to prove, no imperative pressing me into servitude. Just this thirst for something that theory can't slake.

It's race day at Randwick, across the road from the University. The horses' names seem significant, synchronised with my state of mind, and the track announcer's voice calling their names is calling me too. I slide in through a side entrance reserved for cars and follow the hustling swirl towards the inner circle. One of the horses is called 'Launching Pad' and it is perfectly apt that this should be the place where I will merge. Quit *maya* for good, disappear into Godhead.

As the world goes out of focus bodies press around and voices question: 'Is he alright?' 'What is it? His skin looks pretty blue.' They take me, by now senseless, into some kind of first-aid room.

'Are you alright? What do you need?' One face comes into focus, it's wearing a collar. They've brought a priest. He looks scared. I want to ask him: 'Do you know where God is?' But I can tell from his eyes that would make him feel worse.

'You'd better take him to the Prince of Wales.'

Now I'm in a hospital, still in clothes. An old lady with kind blue eyes looks into my face and says: 'You're going to be alright'. I wonder if she's an angel and she brings me some fish and boiled vegetables to eat.

The police are here to interview me as I come around. Detectives Smith and Smith, they say. It's like some cosmic joke. We enjoy it together, it feels like camaraderie, and I tell them everything they want to know. We are one, after all … 'Yes, LSD' somehow doesn't tell the whole story.

A night in the clink was not on my cosmic agenda.

'Come back to reality, have yer, son?' The crusty sergeant snarls as I empty my pockets outside the holding cell. I cringe at this crass intrusion and mutter defensively 'It's the same place,' to the older guy, with an enigmatic look intended to parry his thrust, back him off with mystificatory bluff. They take my sandals, a few coins, the belt made from a tie, and lock me in a cell.

I am vegetarian, so when they offer me food—takeaway chicken fried in an ersatz herb sauce—I decline graciously, preferring to continue my voluntary renunciations. The fish was an exception and, after all, it was probably a gift from an angel. (If the sergeant's an angel, he has become one with his terrestrial disguise.)

I lie on a wooden plank, comfortless, with a thin blanket barely keeping out the cold. In the middle of the night they tip a young guy into the holding cell with me. He's scared. He was drunk and someone complained when he pissed in their garden. The guy paces, worried, for the rest of the night, afraid of all the things he has heard that happen to you in jail.

I catch a flash of light in the darkness, and take hope from that, but in court next morning, when I face the judge, there is some truth to my words when I say I am glad to have been picked up. The sergeant's reality is an unfriendly zone.

When they release me from the courthouse, I literally don't know which way to turn. After days in heaven states, my synthetic *samadhi* has receded. How do I pick up the threads of a life that I have so eagerly thrown away? Where is that house I crashed in? I tried to fling myself into the arms of God, make Him catch me, and stay there, hugged into the bosom of Eternity. But I have merely done a pratfall. 'Eternity' is just a slogan written on the footpath. Rain spatters, a thousand feet walk over it, and the chalk fades into the bitumen.

Coming out of the court I don't know where I am, but I see a bus marked 'Circular Quay'. Maybe if I get on that I can get my bearings. When the conductor approaches me for the fare, I turn out my pockets and offer my nineteen cents.

'Um … How far will that get me?' The conductor takes a look at the get-up, the sea-green sweater, the grubby homemade pants, an Afghani sheepskin vest and Jesus sandals. I haven't shaved or so much as looked at my face or hair for days and there were no washing facilities in the cell. He shakes his head, 'It's alright,' and leaves me alone, so I sit back in the seat on the top floor, trying to recognise landmarks as the bus works its way towards the Quay.

I have left the court with some papers. I try to make sense of the legalese. Something to do with 'my own recognisance', whatever that means, and a court date. It seems important, but it's hard to keep the sentences in order.

Bustling ferries and sparkling water views can't hold my attention, either, when we reach the harbour-side terminus. Three days earlier, I would have been entranced by the play of light and movement but, where boundless bliss has been, a nagging urgency drags now in its wake. I have to find my way back to where I started, and that point is somewhere in the jumble of Paddo. Perhaps my friends will still be there with the Transit van and life can start again.

From the Quay I can find my way back through King's Cross to Paddington. I pull my jacket closer around me to keep me warm in the brisk autumn day and start to walk the two or three miles through the Botanic Gardens, across Hyde Park, up William Street, past Woolloomooloo and the Cross.

I notice a rainbow sticker—happy hippie logo—inside the window of a house in Crown Street, with its door right on the footpath. That seems like a lead. Perhaps they will recognise a fellow traveller. A woman comes to the door.

'Do you know Midge? Um … Midge Freeman?' She's irritated by my vague request, and only reluctantly lets me scan a telephone directory.

'I don't know these people,' she grumbles, wanting me to go away. It's no use, he isn't listed anyway.

With the help of the legal papers, I manage to work out at least what day it is. We were all scheduled to drive back across the continent about now. Nineteen cents won't get me that far. My glasses were just one more thing to be let go of when I relinquished all earthly ties, and the necessity for reading street signs becomes a problem. Paddington's lay-out is not on a grid. I can't get my bearings among the twisting byways. Even roads that I do recognise, in part, turn up and down hills and change direction and I tend to end up back where I started.

On the first night of my release, exhaustion starts to get to me. Paper blows in gusts of wind, touts leer from the doorways of seedy clubs, spruiking lurid shows.

'Don't Worry. Be Happy,' Meher Baba glibly advises from a poster, as the seamy side of King's Cross pushes rudely in my face. I want to collect myself, find home base. I give up the hunt for a while, parking my skinny arse on a wooden bench in a square. Eyes closed, I sit cross-legged, trying to pull myself back in to release myself into the wide, clear space I have inhabited before. Push away the grossness. Dissolve into the softer breath of the ineffable inner realms. Try to be still, at least. 'Know that I am God'. Don't worry, be happy.

Dawn finds me wearily pacing deserted streets again, trying to find a place to settle. Feet on automatic, I just walk, no direction in mind, letting the contours of the land move my steps, one foot after the other:

'Help me God. Bring me home. I'll just close my eyes and let's say You find me.'

Finally, at the bottom of some hill, I come across a house with a light on in an upstairs room. It isn't a place I have been to before, but the front door is open and I am weary enough to take it as a sign. I find my way upstairs, where the light was. There's a room with a couch and I lie down and sleep briefly for the first time in several days, too zonked out to care where I have landed.

When I wake a half-hour later, I notice a mask propped against the wall across from the couch, one of those black Balinese demon faces from the great dance dramas, with large protruding teeth and bulging eyes. Paper tiger, I think, is that all you are? 'Do not be afraid, these are only the projections of your own mind forms,' it says in my tripping manual, *The Tibetan Book of the Dead*. After days of heaven states, have I been tortured now with their mirror-image, hell?

Now even this 'hell' lacks substance. Fears are phantasms, played out in the theatre of the mind.

I sit up. There's a radiator to one side and it has been switched on. Someone has left the morning paper on the floor near the couch and the front page headline reads 'Aussie actor dies', reporting on the death of the great Chips Rafferty, star of stage, screen and radio. I realise that whoever owns the house must have come in while I have been dozing and, for the first time retrieving some sense of social decorum, I bolt down the stairs, let myself out the back door, and dart through a short alley, without encountering anyone.

If heaven and hell have collapsed like a house of cards, boundless trust has slipped rather badly, too. In its place I grasp for shreds of fact, attempting to be more logical, pushing my mind to track back and pick up threads of the fabric I have been so intent on unraveling. I obsess over location, knowing that one of the places I visited was just one door off a main street that I can certainly identify: Oxford Street. It runs right through Paddington. On one side there's a continuous thread of shops and pubs, on the other a church, a park, an army barracks and some offices, not necessarily in that order.

There was a street, a narrow street that ran off Oxford Street among a section of shopfronts. I remember how the doorway to a one-storey was situated behind a fence that ran down that side street; that's where the house was. I slept there, was it three, four nights ago? In a room, behind a door in that narrow house, behind that fence that ran back behind the shop. But which shop?

Doggedly, I work my way back up the hills to Oxford Street. I criss-cross the area, discarding one possibility after another, until I come to a tight street next to a shop that seems to fit my tattered memory map. I check out the fence to be sure, and there's a gate, and there's a door behind the gate.

Yes, it's on the right side of the street, and the gate's about thirty feet back from the shops, and behind that gate, a door into the narrow house behind the storefront. Exactly the right lay-out. This must be it, at last.

I go to open the gate. It's locked. No matter. I climb the fence and drop down on the other side and try the door, heart pounding. No resistance; the door opens inwards. But the room is dark. With my right hand still on the doorknob pushing open the door, I reach back with my left to switch on the light, revealing the interior of the room.

It isn't my friend's house at all ...

It's a photographer's dark room.

There on the wall facing me, directly opposite the doorway, is a vertical strip of photographs, with the same image repeated, frame by frame, up and down before my eyes. It's the figure of a man, about my age (it could almost be me) and he is pointing back, his gaze intent, directly into camera.

back to earth

Unknown to me, a reporter combing through court records has plucked the story of the court appearance and it runs in the West Australian papers with the headline: 'Perth man faces Sydney court on drug charges'. Unaware that my family has been informed of my embarrassing encounter with the law, I carry on regardless while I await the court hearing, my oblivious letters home only exacerbating my family's distress. I decorate the letters with pretty drawings in the margins and quotes from the Beatles about how I'd love to turn them on.

I have been remanded to appear before the magistrate again in a couple of months, so I have to find a way to stay on in Sydney for the duration. I track down my friend from earlier days at the University of NSW. Bob Beaver is living with his mum and dad in Surry Hills. Once I retrieve the streets name from my addled memory I get an attendant in a service station to help me find the location in a directory and he gives me precise directions. Marshall Street. Without my glasses I have to walk right up to street signs to decipher them.

Bob's parents are dedicated to improving conditions for working people. His mother, a self-described Marxist feminist, is a shop steward in a pressed metal factory, organising to give migrant women workers a voice. Luckily for me, their political conscience extends pragmatically to anyone in need. They take me in without question, and help me make sense of the court documents.

I am glad to hook up with Bob again. When we were at UNSW we fired each other's idealism and we still have an unspoken pact to alert each other to any pointers to truth, and the fragments of inspiration we might come across. Bob isn't interested in drugs and I swear off them while waiting for my case to come up. I get some part-time work doing box office at a theatre in North Sydney.

Bob is one of the conscientious young men who have had to go underground when refusing to register for the draft. My birth-date was in the barrel for the first lottery but the angel of death passed over me. I feel a solidarity with those other young men who are reluctant to go 'all the way with LBJ'. Bob has written a letter informing the draft board that he doesn't intend to comply in any way with the process. Found guilty *in absentia*, the court has given him a two-year jail sentence and he has to move around frequently to avoid the federal police.

In a rare interaction, I have argued with my father about pacifism. With his gammy knee, Frank didn't see active service, he spent his war years in training camp in Northam, so as his son I feel that his jingoism lacks a little authenticity. Frank demands to know what I would do if a bunch of foreigners tried to rape my sister. I cannot accept that the downtrodden Vietnamese have any aggressive intentions towards Australia, let alone towards my sister, and I loathe the way that Bob Menzies and his successors have used the 'domino theory' and the racist threat of the 'yellow peril' to keep the electorate in fear, and in line. I feel my father has aligned himself with the worst aspects of a xenophobic politics, and hold little respect for his views. Frank is equally unimpressed by my position.

Before my court appearance I am supposed to see a psychiatrist and meet with a probation officer for a pre-trial evaluation. A civil liberties lawyer named Ken Horler is setting up a tiny theatre behind Kings Cross, in Nimrod Street, and through contacts I retain from Perth I get work as an assistant stage manager and things start to turn around. Ken offers to represent me *pro bono* in court.

Other help is on its way. After the newspaper reports back in Perth, my partner comes to Sydney to see what she can do, and she is with me for my meeting with the probation officer who is to evaluate my chances of becoming less of a scofflaw. She doesn't have a flamboyant personality, precise, intelligent analysis is more her style, but my partner is a convincing presence.

As an idealistic drug offender I carry a rather large chip on my shoulder. The probation officer probes my reasons for taking LSD and I launch into my anti-authoritarian, 'this is a victimless crime' rave; a jumble of: 'the government is corrupt; dedicated to the service of the military-industrial complex; democracy is a front for big business capital; we should be free to explore the possibilities of consciousness; drug offences are bogus, this is a victimless crime'; on and on it goes.

With her eye fixed on the probation officer, under the table my partner calmly places her foot on mine, and starts to press down. It takes a few false starts before I get her point: the probation office is actually quite sympathetic. He is a Christian and has the sense to recognise a search for 'God' when he sees one. Rather than being a representative of hostile forces, he is trying to help me find my way out of a jam, but his signals are muffled by my windy rationalisations. That my partner can see all of this when I don't have a clue, is an example of the relative clarity of our mental states and the effectiveness of our preferred applications of intelligent inquiry.

The Beavers welcome her into their home, too, until she and Bob and I rent a house together on Cleveland Street. She gets a new research assistant job at the University of New South Wales, and I track down the whereabouts of the court-appointed psychiatrist. LSD is officially still in experimental use in psychotherapy and the formal charge I face has to do with 'taking a drug: to wit, LSD, without the written permission of the State Director of Psychiatric Services'.

'What the hell are you doing here?' The psychiatrist demands to know when I walk through his door. I start to say something about the court order—didn't the bureaucracy send him some paperwork?—and the doctor says:

'Get out of here, you're as sane as I am!'

I have no idea what the shrink and the probation officer report to the Court—how do these things play out?—but with the help of Ken Horler, who presents me as a well-educated guy from a good family who has briefly gone off the rails, I cash in a lot of karma and am let off on a good behaviour bond, with no conviction recorded against me, as long as I continue to meet with the probation officer.

I continue to work at Nimrod Street during the run of their next show, which is based on an historical event: the assassination attempt by a deranged Irishman on the life of the Prince of Wales, on his visit to Australia in the 1890s. Bob Ellis and Michael Boddy are the writers. I play the mad would-be assassin (with an appalling Irish accent). My character is found guilty and hung for his crime, and each night, during the song and dance number that closes the show, I am left to swing by my neck from the rafters. The tiny theatre-in-the-round at Nimrod Street brings the audience into very close proximity to the action. They have rigged up a parachute harness to wear under my costume and the noose-rope conceals a toggle that rises up under the back of my collar to hook the harness up to the rafters when I am 'hung'.

Gough and Margaret Whitlam come to the opening night and at the after-party they loom large over me, concerned to inquire whether I was in any discomfort during the hanging. Having all my body weight dragging against the harness is indeed uncomfortable; the longer I hang there, the tighter it pulls at my groin, and I am relieved to be hoisted down before there is any serious insult to my manhood. At least I don't have to sing and dance in the closing number.

I am supposed to go to Melbourne to take up a longstanding offer of work with the Australian Performing Group at the Pram Factory theatre, but people I know are pulling together a theatre production at the Pitt Street Congregational Church, based on the transcript of a famous political trial in the US, so when I am cast in a small role I delay my departure south. Here they pay Equity rates!

The Trial of the Catonsville Nine is the record of the US government's attempt to charge a group of Jesuit and Josephite clergy with conspiracy, so it grabs my interest. In May 1968, nine priests and nuns removed hundreds of draft records from the Selective Service Offices in Catonsville, Maryland, using napalm to burn them in the car-park, in symbolic protest against the war. Among them were Daniel Berrigan, a Jesuit, and his brother Phillip, a Josephite priest. A year before the famous trial of the Chicago Seven, this was the US Government's first attempt to float a prosecution for conspiracy against a prominent group from the anti-war movement. Philip Berrigan had previously poured blood on draft records as part of the 'Baltimore Four', and was out on bail on those charges when he took part in the Catonsville protest.

The script for the play is based on the trial transcript. I am to play one of the priests, who has been active in Central America, and through this production I feel connected with a larger struggle.

After the production closes I have exhausted excuses to join the troupe at the Pram Factory in Carlton. Moving south means I will have to arrange for a transfer of my probationary supervision. In Melbourne, the new probation officer turns out to be an American. Furthermore, he is a plain-clothes Josephite priest doing pastoral work, who knows Phillip Berrigan. This is just one of a cascade of synchronicities which sparks inspiration for my personal search. The new probation officer, recognising my 'spiritual search', gives me a copy of the New Testament to read, and in turn I offer him a book of Cha'an Buddhist poetry.

My partner has been working temporarily at UNSW, and goes back to Perth briefly to tie up her affairs before taking a job at Melbourne University. I am hoping that the political commitment of the Performing Group will fill the void for me, and provide me with some avenues for political and creative expression.

A strong mutual attraction drew me and my partner together, and she helped me enormously in overcoming any imagined difficulties I might have had in approaching the so-called 'opposite sex'. I am hoping that this will help me get over my long-standing attraction towards men. After all, as I have been advised solicitously by an older woman in the English department at WA, this 'homo thing' is just a phase that many sensitive males go through, (with the implication that a good woman will sort me out soon enough). I recognise I have found one of the best of women, but as my perverse feelings for men do not dissipate, I find myself in an acute psychological dilemma. While I haven't been acting out my homoerotic desires, I do feel I am leading a kind of double life. Does existential 'authenticity' allow for ambivalence, or am I, indeed, living out the kind of bad faith that old Jean-Paul Sartre would abhor?

My partner knows about my past, and even knows Helm, but I don't know how to tell her what is happening to me. I consider making a clean break. Even though she has come from Perth to lend support at a crucial time, I feel it would be in bad faith to continue the relationship. Apart from the unresolved issue of my sexuality, the spiritual bug has bitten me hard. The itch is always there, niggling away underneath everything else. In spite of the debacle in Sydney, I feel I should throw it all in and dedicate myself one hundred per cent to my quest. I don't know what I am looking for, but I'll know it when I feel it. My partner is as reluctant to walk that path as she has been to follow me into drugs. But instead of making a clean break, I cave in, taking the lazy option, my resolve giving way into the (imperfect) comforts of relationship.

As I am getting set up in Carlton, she rings from Perth to tell me that, in spite of our attempts at contraception, she is pregnant. I take the news with mixed feelings: in some ways I am excited at the prospect, yet I worry that I could wreck this child's life with my erratic ways, my confused desires and my obvious dearth of wisdom. I fled the Education Department, protesting that I had not yet learned anything I could in all sincerity pass on to others, and now a child is looming on the horizon. I am even less ready to be anyone's father. Possibly many men feel this way at a similar point, but in my case the reluctance is indemnified by my sexual ambivalence, which makes a very poor basis for commitment.

My partner would never countenance a termination, but there is no way she wants to get married, either. I continue to take the line of least resistance and we continue living together.

As drugs have proved a treacherous pathway to enlightenment I refocus my devotions into earnest consultations with the *I Ching*, also known as 'The Book of Changes', a Chinese oracle used for divination. Underpinning the text's sometimes opaque symbolism is an ancient philosophical system based on the concept of the 'Tao', or the 'Way', a wisdom tradition that resonates for me where the Judaeo-Christian mythology hasn't. I am even more intrigued by the subtle insights of Lao-Tsu's *Tao Te Ching* and the simple confidence I hear in fragments of Taoist poetry, hinting of sublime states of awareness:

> *Unlimited chatter and mystical natter*
> *Had best be swept out of the way.*
> *Then the radiant orb of wisdom's moon*
> *Will emerge from behind the hill.* [3]

Carl Jung wrote an introduction to the weighty Wilhelm edition of the *I Ching*—the edition most widely available at the time—and I am deeply impressed by Jung's theory of synchronicity. The Swiss psychiatrist first broached the subject in the early 1950s, when he was searching for a way to explain significant 'coincidences' in his own, as well as his patients' lives. I can't help noticing the same kind of 'coincidences' happening in my own otherwise aimless life—like the strip of photos in the darkroom, and the probation officer who knew the Berrigans. This notion (and Jung's related ideas of the archetypes) energises my search. Rather than putting the face of a 'God' onto it, the hint of underlying connectedness seems more compelling and suggestive of meaning, really speaking to me, where 'creator god' mythologies have not.

---

[3] Cited in John Blofeld's *Taoism: The Quest for Immortality,* Mandala Books, 1979

Sometimes during my crazy attempts to tap into the awareness of this matrix I feel that I have been interacting with an energy, a force field, if you will (on acid you can actually *see* it!) It is the very basis of being, the field of consciousness itself, and it has shown signs of being responsive to me, albeit on its own terms. But in spite of the 'flashes' of synchronicity, I don't know how to align myself with it, nor do I know if it would be realistic to think of it as having 'a plan' for me, in particular; it seems too random and impersonal for that and, besides, just where do one's projections end, and where does 'reality' begin? To think of it as having a purpose—acting on my life, from outside of me—just shores up the sense of a separate 'ego self'. I question whether I am thinking about it using stale, wrong-headed ideas. Haunting the Adyar bookshop just seems to make it worse.

So I consult the *I Ching*, burn much incense, listen to motets by Palestrina to re-capture that feeling of cool water poured over my over-heated brain. My partner buys a recording of a Mass by Monteverdi, recorded in a medieval church and played on original instruments, with the players laid out as they would have been in early performances. I soak it up; it's fuel.

Someone suggests Transcendental Meditation (TM), a technique that is taking root in all major cities. I need something like a meditation practice to calm, rather than stimulate, my mind. Even though TM is derived from Indian yoga practice, it is marketed as an empirical, quasi-scientific technique for increasing peaceful brainwaves, and it has attracted famous adherents. I feel that something is missing in that approach, John Lennon and George Harrison notwithstanding. I need something more than a *mantra*, even if I don't know exactly what.

By now I am a committed vegetarian and we eat frequently at the Shakahari restaurant in Lygon Street, a block or two from the Pram Factory theatre. This restaurant is said to be owned by someone involved with TM, and the menu influenced by macrobiotics. Dishes have whimsical, spiritual names like 'arhat's delight', and 'satori soup'. If only it were as easy as eating.

My partner sees my increasing interest in spirituality as a kind of regression. Having cast off Catholicism, all religion must seem the same to her. She reads it as pre-Enlightenment superstition at best and, at worst, as sentimental hogwash that is no substitute for rational social policies founded on liberal humanitarian conceptions of social justice and equality. Our paths are diverging.

What kind of person do you become when you can't live your real self? I have severe and deep-seated doubts about my own authenticity as a man and can find neither a stable centre within myself nor a compelling motivation to live through my work. As idealistic as I may be about the potential of the theatre, and the Arts in general, to make a difference in society, I go into the Australian Performing Group doubting that the theatre can match my ontological needs, even when it is founded on a political platform, as it is at the Pram Factory.

Doubt assails me from every side. The gay liberation movement is a late starter in Australia, and I have withdrawn from that potential freedom. It would feel like a betrayal to my partner were I to go back to men, so I continue to stew in my own anxieties, facing the prospect of having a child with fear.

factory work

Late 1971. In Sydney, Martin Sharp's psychedelic covers for *Oz* magazine and the electrifying razzle-dazzle of the Yellow House are glowing totems of the new counter culture. Some sections of the movement seem intent on following Timothy Leary's advice to 'turn on, tune in and drop out'. Others, while happy to add the new drugs to the arsenal of mind-altering substances, are impatient for radical political engagement. That seems to be more the case with the committed crew I join in Melbourne's Carlton. A new emerging generation is no longer satisfied with the cultural cringe that would have them tugging a forelock in the direction of Britain. It is still a rarity to hear an Australian accent on the stage, where plummy voiced pseudo-Brits hold sway, and you have to sound like a Pom, and an upper-class one at that if you want to work at the toffy ABC, or a damned Yankee if you want to work in commercial radio.

As much a propagandist as a performance artist, with a sort of socio-politico-aesthetic snobbery that will not allow me to participate in crassly commercial theatre, I have painted myself into an ideological corner. In Perth, I used my theatre column to rail against the use of public arts funding to create museums: why squander precious funds on a national company to house a decadent 19th Century European form like classical ballet, for example? What are we doing to foster young Australian choreographers? What does all that have to do with Australia, a new country, rooted only shallowly in that bed of history, with dubious allegiances to its colonial past, on the cusp of a new century? Shouldn't we support a new generation of choreographers, writers and performers who speak to our own concerns, in our own voice, rather than importing British and American work? I heralded the arrival of the Australian Performing Group (APG), the resident company the Pram Factory), when it came to Perth to perform a set of original plays. Now I have a chance to participate in the further development of this home-grown alternative.

Playwright and ideologue Jack Hibberd calls for a uniquely Australian form of theatre. Graeme Blundell, the driving force at The Pram, tells me he wants it to be 'intelligent, radical and uncouth,' as well as 'rich, relevant and ribald'. Blundell and Kerry Dwyer are committed to a physical performance style that owes less to the text as a piece of literature and more to the kind of improvised material that actors can bring to the work. If the techniques are borrowed, the concerns are local. Most of those involved have started at Betty Burstall's tiny La Mama theatre around the corner, and have close links with Carlton's counter-culture community.

For me, a stint in an activist proletarian theatre collective is a bit of a long shot but I don't know where else I can work. I am twenty-six, have spent too many years in school, and nothing is good enough for my over-refined aesthetics. In Carlton I am on shaky ground; these are real radicals, not posturing aesthetes. As educated as they are, they sport a quasi working-class skepticism towards the pansy arts and their intellectualism is pragmatic, not theoretical. Political engagement is the *modus operandi*. Yet in spite of all my doubts, I hope that I can find roots for a new sense of personal authenticity through activism. Although an aesthete, I am prepared to become a bit of a mongrel. Attendance at football matches is *de rigueur.*

From the lofty heights of post-surrealist French theatre I find myself positioned as a 'factory worker' to re-inforce my pseudo-solidarity with the proletariat, and add to my crypto blue-collar qualifications with environmental plays, developed in partnership with Lorna Hannan and the writer Nancy Cato, at another 'factory'—The Jigsaw Factory, in Richmond.

The APG has made a name for itself with sharp satirical pieces against the Vietnam War, and in addition to the experimental performance style it is a hothouse for original writing. David Williamson is already approaching his early elevation to greatness, Jack Hibberd is out-doing Samuel Beckett, and John Romeril's *Chicago, Chicago* brings street theatre techniques onto the stage. The form that a play might take in performance is being radically re-thought. Wannabe filmmakers lurk on the sidelines; John Duigan broods on the fringes, arriving straight from school.

Run as a collective, the APG harbours as many different ideological affiliations as it has members. There'll be no navel-gazing here. Trostky-ites jostle with Maoists; women's libbers arm-wrestle with mere males; beer drinkers rail against dope heads; writers defend their ground against the inroads of the improvisationalist acting push, and a cell campaigning for educational reform, spearheaded by Bill Hannan, Lorna Hannan and Claire Dobbin, enlists the collective to stage a performance piece, *The Compulsory Century*.

Decisions as to which direction the Group should take are to be made as a collective, yet the group veers towards anarchy. Max Gillies ascends to Chairman status and all his native diplomacy is needed to steer rowdy meetings towards consensus as we thrash out how the resources should best be used, and the kind of pieces we will program. Some of the core workers double up in administration under John Timlin, concocting applications for funding from the very governments we so thoroughly revile, which continue to come to the aid of the party with funding grants.

Most of the women get together outside of the confines of the Pram Factory to raise their consciousness within the Carlton Women's Liberation Cell Group. While happy that the sexual revolution is reducing women's sexual inhibitions, some of the men grumble into their beer, disturbed that intimate details of their private lives—and their sexual performance—might be disclosed and raked over by a bunch of radical feminists.

'I don't want you talking about our relationship with other women,' one fellow complains—as if women haven't been doing that all along. 'Besides, if it's all about equal rights, why can't men come to your meetings?' Even the out-and-out larrikins can only mutter in private against the fearful feminists; if they want to get laid they have to learn new rules of engagement so as not to offend their increasingly demanding partners.

As they begin to demand equal rights to orgasm in the bedroom, the women start to seek equal access within the theatre group, too. They request rehearsal time to stage the first production by the Women's Theatre Group, newly-formed under the umbrella of the wider collective. As all the acknowledged writers in the Group so far are men—some of whom have not kept pace in consciousness raising—scripts are viewed potentially as part of a patriarchal plot, so *Betty Can Jump* is to be an improvised piece, with the performance material developed entirely by the cast in workshop-style rehearsals, under the direction of Kerry Dwyer.

For some reason I am the only male in the collective included in the cast. Several women would be more comfortable if no mere male were involved. My gendered attitudes would scarcely withstand a critical interrogation but as my partner is active in launching the Women's Electoral Lobby, I am given the benefit of the doubt. Kerry likes my physicalised approach to performance and I am cast to play all the male parts, whatever they will be.

Memorable material arises in improvisation, much of which makes it into the performances, but my personal favorite doesn't make the cut. It is a sprawling movement piece where I am 'born' out of a symbolic mass of writhing female bodies. It is an arduous process and, after much heaving and huffing, I emerge from the birth canal stammering 'SSSS ... SSSS ... SSMMMO-THER'! Perhaps it is too much a male point of view after all, or as Kerry tells me years later, perhaps it is going deeper into the darker aspect of the feminine than they are ready for.

As the token male, they have me running around sporting a *commedia dell'arte* prop cock and balls, with over-sized testicles made from the inflatable bladders of footballs, and twisted, blackened pipe cleaners as pubic hair. The schlonger itself is contrived from a sizeable length of salami, which, after several days of performance, starts to smell).

Meanwhile, Dennis Altman is emerging as an early spokesman for gay liberation and Kerry and Graeme invite him to address the collective. Altman's stirring book, *Homosexual: Oppression and Liberation,* has recently been published, but none of us has read it. Radical or not, the Group has shown little evidence of sensitivity to queer issues. My own sexuality is very much 'oppressed' rather than liberated and I would be loath to use 'queer' to describe myself. 'Homosexual' is fraught with negative medical associations and, in a collective so divided across strict and sometimes hostile gender boundaries, deviant affiliations get short shrift.

As he makes his presentation, Dennis looks a little nervous, unsure of his reception before this bunch of apparent heteros. Sitting at the rear, I admire Altman's courage; he's a real pioneer. It takes more self-acceptance than I could muster to confront such a group on this issue. Somewhere in the back of my mind, homosexuality is still something I am supposed to 'get over', so I fail to respond to Altman's implicit invitation to come out and join the party. The others see me in relationship with a woman and whatever doubts they might carry about the nature of my sexuality are tactfully suspended. Even though I had my breakthrough love affair with Helm in Perth, at this time I am still consciously trying to bring myself back from the extreme edge of the spectrum on the Kinsey scale of sexual orientation—if I were honest I would rate myself a Kinsey 6, a total homo—but my partner is pregnant. My 'experiment' with heterosexuality has confused the taxonomy.

Looking back, I am struck by the number of simultaneous poses I am trying to maintain: as an actor; as an Artaudian; as a politically committed activist; and as a heterosexual. Little gay boys are encouraged from an early age to hide their real impulses, not only from others—in the very closest circle, the family; at school, among one's peers—but from themselves, too. The coercive effects of shaming usually fix the denial into place in our psyches before we have any intellectual (or political) resources to consider other options. Growing up trying to please, I hid my feelings from those closest to me, in my own family. I have moved from one degree of inauthenticity on through another and into yet another. No wonder macho men look at me with a superior sneer. It isn't the sense that I would really prefer to have sex with men which raises their suspicions; I suspect it is the degree of hollowness they can sense in my character, and it is always that weakness that draws most scorn, I believe. It will take years for me to recognise that so-called 'straight' men can be quite at ease with a queer man who is comfortable with his own sexuality.

At this point, I don't know where 'real' me begins and ends. I am afraid that the phoniness might have deep roots. Entertaining others might just be a way of prolonging denial. When I get stoned, I do improvisations, dancing little psychodramas to a music track, say, or performing *ad lib* comic riffs in mime, much to friends' amusement. But when I try to come to rest, I don't have a centre. I'm still in exile. Restlessness rules. I am a 'human doing', with no secure core in 'human being', performing a self entirely in response to social and ideological expectations. The feeling of being me is almost entirely anxious.

I have lost the plot, the story of my own life. Years later I gasp with recognition when I read a snippet from Donald Winnicott, the British child psychoanalyst, in which he analyses what happens when an unformed personality is required to adapt entirely to the demands of the external environment. 'There is not even a resting-place for individual experience,' he writes:

and the result is a failure in the primary narcissistic state to evolve an individual. The 'individual' then develops as an extension of the shell rather than that of the core, and as an extension of the impinging environment. What there is left of a core is hidden away … The individual exists by not being found.[4]

'The individual exists by not being found': this could form a good working definition of 'the closet', which will become a central trope in gay liberation circles. Certainly, I exist outside of my own core self here in Melbourne, in 1971, developing as an extension of the shell. I am 'tap dancing as fast as I can', trying to perfect the roles I think I am supposed to play. What a cliché; and in a theatre, of all places! The *performance* of a self has overtaken the development of a genuine sense of self-identity. I don't feel like one of the *real* people who knows what his/her life is about. Whichever way you decorate it, the closet is a very unhealthy place.

Graeme Blundell is keen to 'up' the skills level of the performers. There is an abundance of young energy, and a lot of anger, but little insight that can answer my needs. I have no clarity to offer as an alternative, so as much as I support the improv. guys I also look to the articulate writers who seem to have something to say. Meanwhile, a gnawing feeling tells me that it's already over for me. The theatre will not be the way to discover what I need to locate. But I have no idea what else to do.

At home I am plunged further into doubt. The imminent arrival of a child turns the screws of doubt into a tight knot in my gut. A father is supposed to know how to guide a child. I have no answers. I am still full of questions, groping for a lost connection. I have tried to find it in the community of committed, creative people—the APG is the only theatre company left for which I have any respect—and I'm in a relationship with a brilliant woman, but the chasm of doubt just gets larger, like one of those sinkholes that gradually sucks everything above ground down into itself, as half a street, several cars, and a row of houses are swallowed up by the underground subsidence.

---

4 The extract is from 'Aggression in Relation to Emotional Development' in Winnicott's *Through Paediatrics to Psycho-Analysis*. (New York: Basic Books, 1975).

natural high—Lake Pedder

Early 1972. I'm enlisted to put together a performance piece with another actor, Jude Kuring, and a musician to protest the rape of the natural environment in Tasmania by the combined forces of government and big business.

For guerilla theatre, mobility is essential. Rough and ready productions untrammeled by elaborate scenery or too many props, portable enough so that cast members can move with lighting speed across town during a demonstration (say, alighting on unsuspecting street corners to transform them, briefly, into *ad hoc* performance spaces) and then to move on, away from the investigative noses of the police, or anonymous informants for ASIO whom I imagine might be watching. We explode here and there before startled passersby, or descend on worksites where men in blue overalls—real workers—eat their lunches, their meal breaks punctuated by vociferous outbursts of highly didactic theatre.

For this occasion we create a graphic performance piece on behalf of the 'Lake Pedder Action Committee', about the destruction of a magnificent lake, which is to be sacrificed by the state government's Hydro-Electric Commission, intent on building yet another dam to supply cheap electricity for the power-hungry industries they hope to attract to the island state. In the process they will back up the waters of a river or two, swamp flood plains and obliterate wilderness ecosystems and unique species of flora and fauna, willy-bloody-nilly. Pristine Lake Pedder with its unique ecosystem will be swallowed up forever.

Jude and I are assigned to paste something together with a writer and to perform the piece in a city square in Melbourne. The play—all broad gestures, shouted lines and punchy musical ditties—goes over well.

The gig includes a weekend trip to Hobart, to reprise our performance piece on a Saturday morning in Salamanca Place, where people gather for the weekly market. We commit to travelling with only sketchy details, and early one Saturday morning fly south to Hobart in a light plane arranged by the Action Committee.

With one eye out for the police we stage our brash and noisy performance with its crude gestures, props and snatches of song and are gone before officialdom has time to decide whether or not we need a permit. The performance creates quite a stir. We reprise it in another location, near a fountain, to a much smaller group of passersby. And then …? Then we are scheduled to spend the rest of the weekend out at the lake itself, joining a relay of people who have set up a protest camp at the site. Activists intend to stay either until the waters rise over their heads, or the offensive Act is repealed, whichever comes first.

Lake Pedder is a long way from town, off in a wilderness area. The Committee proposes to fly us there—to land on the quartz shore of the lake, two miles long and firm enough for a light plane. Plan B—in case the weather does not allow such an approach—is to bus us to a point where the roads cut out, and hike overland the rest of the way to camp at the lake. Exactly what this would entail has not been explained to us inner-city types.

The weather, as it turns out, doesn't allow the luxury of swooping in by aircraft, so if we want to get to the lake it is going to be the hard way. 'Want' to get to the lake? Doing my duty as a radical actor is one thing, but to get there *on foot* was never part of the deal. If my preparations for an overland hike have been negligible, so are my alternatives. I know no-one in Hobart with whom I can stay, and on my forty-dollar weekly salary can't consider a hotel. The musician has sensibly made alternative arrangements to wait in town in comfort, with friends, before the plane returns to the mainland.

The members of the Action Committee are kitted out in sensible survival gear, strapped efficiently to their sturdy backs. This leaves: one tall, gangly lesbian actress who appears to sustain herself largely on beer, cigarettes and a certain mocking stance (fine for Fitzroy, a little precarious in the wilderness) and one performance artist, male; more musical than muscular, better at striking attitudes than tents.

Through her thick glasses, Jude blinks at me, a quizzical crease in her forehead. She often looks at me this way, as if she is wondering 'Doesn't this bloke know he's gay?' Today we find ourselves in the same predicament, poorly dressed for two days in the wilderness, neither of us wearing the right footwear, and with quite a different notion of 'camping' than our comrades. We are dependent to a large degree on the kindness of these strangers, with no food of our own, and without the skills, experience or physical conditioning suitable for challenging excursions into wilderness areas. Someone has slung us a two-man tent, *en passant*, and suggested we might need thick socks and proper boots, but there is neither the time nor the money to purchase anything so appropriate. Jude is wearing tennis shoes and I borrowed boots that have a tendency to slip at the heels, the ramifications of which will soon become apparent. We have no resort but to suppose that these hiking sorts know what they are about, and will somehow carry us along for the ride. Personally, I would rather be on a tram in Melbourne, heading home.

If the weather has closed out the option of going to the lake by plane, it hasn't yet occurred to me that might be a good indicator of the kind of conditions we could encounter on foot. The bus ride to the starting point is uneventful but leaden skies have already begun to dim the daylight. After a couple of hours, we are tipped unwillingly out of the warm bus to be faced with a featureless, scrubby landscape and a miasma of slippery wet greenness on all sides. Rain falls steadily. The members of the party who know the way slog off, faces set, towards a place somewhere beyond the low hills. Their destination is estimated to be a few hours' trek away. We floundering thespians divide our makeshift gear and sling it about us, like children playing at a game, and start out behind the main party into the trackless wilderness.

Well not quite trackless. A thin, black, greasy pathway meanders through the scrub, up hills, along ridges, through rocky outcrops and down winding slopes. Muddy, wet and slippery, it goes on, and on and on, with the rain falling, sometimes heavier, sometimes just a drenching mist. Water trickles into every unprotected opening around my neck and wrist and ankles, areas that those more experienced types ahead have probably battened down.

Occasionally a clump of one or two hikers will double back and feed us an efficient bar of concentrated energy food, suggest that we are probably not properly clad, and pad back into the gloom.

Early along the winding way fatigue sets in. Several times we have to stop to re-arrange our poorly balanced loads. Deep blisters form on unprotected heels and wrenching pains in back and shoulders come and go. To continue, I am forced to summon up real effort from some depth I haven't plumbed before, and all the while the track continues, on and on, as the blisters burst and bleed, rubbed raw.

After a few hours the light fails and soon we are engulfed in intense darkness, with the rain still falling, and that black elusive track petering out before our eyes. In the dark, through our rain-splotched lenses, we strain for any glimmer of visual information. At times, as our anxious gaze picks out glimpses of torchlight from the groups ahead, only our feet can find their way forward. Occasionally someone comes back and rounds us up. Our floundering is slowing down the general progress. Someone lends Jude a flashlight, but she has sprained her ankle and is settling into a deep funk of mute rebellion.

There is no going back. The way forward is disappearing fast in the dark and we have no choice but to stagger on, by now getting just a trifle desperate. One of the small groups takes Jude in, relieves her of her load and before much longer I really am all alone, and the torch has gone ahead with Jude.

I am a scrap of life dragged unwillingly along by the fading impulse of an ersatz idealism, and my determination to reach this goddamned lake is ebbing like the light. I pause to look up from the black track and scan the dim contours of hills ahead, but no matter how far I trudge to reach those distant shapes, as I peer through the gloom I find only more stretches of indistinct hills. The glimmer of torches from the groups ahead moves on relentlessly.

Whole ranks of hills pass. Surely it will be over the next hill, that one that seemed so far away, was it an hour ago? And that hill is eventually reached, too, and passed. Hope lies abandoned in my slithering wake, to the point where I am just moving on, with no goal in sight. My body throws up wave after wave of pain, emanating in turn from my ankles, then my shoulders, then legs, and back, but I have no choice but to continue.

I shift into a strange state. If, in the foreground, mind and body are protesting and complaining, at the same time there is this feeling hiding away, behind the tribulation, that this struggle is somehow just as it should be. Even as the situation becomes desperate, a part of me recognises something almost appropriate about the hardship, as though it were good for my … character? But I don't want to think I'm actually in danger.

And still the miles unfold, unrelenting. Layer after layer of mind and effort are called up, only to be spent. How to get this failing body home? Home? Abandoned in the wilderness! My inner drama queen shrieks in protest, to no avail, and quits the stage. I am heading further and further into nothing, no 'home' out here—walking *away* from town and city and house and hearth and fire and food and friend—yet every moment requires that I continue further, into darkness.

By the time I stumble to the shore of the imperiled lake, in total darkness, there is no sign of the rest of the party, they have disappeared without a trace. My heels, ankles and toes are raw and bleeding, sinews strained, energy spent.

The beach is a dully luminous stretch of wet, crunchy quartz, a glowing presence even in the dark.

Here at last. Where is this? Is anybody else here? No voices, no camp. Nothing. All these hours and *nothing?* It is a grim joke but there is no one to hear me laugh.

Further down the beach, off in the distance, a light blinks—a tiny speck of life in the gloomy waste of night. I trudge off weakly, pain tearing at my heels. Trudge, trudge, crunch, crunch. But that light has gone again. I try walking at the water's edge to find a line to follow.

Delirium takes hold and I wander into the shallow waters of the lake. Then, as the cold water snaps me back to attention I head back along the shoreline, all purpose evaporating. Nothing nothing trudge trudge trudge. Just that promise of a light ahead that beckoned and then was gone.

I stumble to a halt. The beach is cleft by a broad creek that feeds into the lake and all further progress is barred. Even if I could find the strength I simply cannot go any further. That light must have been somewhere on the other side of this creek but I can't find a way to cross it in the darkness. I am spent, splat knackered, puffed, with my spirit rent, my mind a vacant space, my body light, my bones all turned to water.

I want to just to give up, as if I could just snap out of this nightmare, and I start to weep bitter tears. My broken sobs bring forth a gruff, inquiring voice. A bearded man emerges from the darkness and, faced with the sight of this male form racked with tears, mutters:

'There are women here.'

Shelter is a piece of plastic sheeting against the black night and a cup of billy tea. One or two faces poke out from tents. There are four or five people here but they aren't the group with whom I trekked out. They must be some advance party, and they've already established a camp. Their tents are fully occupied and, as my own is in some other place with Jude, I pull out my sleeping bag, already wet in places, and try to cover either the bag, or my head, never both at once, with the square of plastic.

For the remainder of the darkness hours, with this group snugly ensconced in their all-weather tents, I twist and turn, trying different ways to make the intractable geometries of shape—my form, the sleeping bag, and this not quite adequate piece of plastic—come together in comfort. Day dawns and the wilderness reveals itself in pristine splendour. The beach is a glistening brilliance, some very special experiment in quartz, with serrations that scallop sharply into the waters for two miles along its edge, like the teeth of a giant white saw laid out on an alabaster bench. The waters of the lake are the colour of marmalade (a small plant growing throughout the catchment valley somehow dyes it so). A corona of mountains reaches up to the sky, encircling the scene and, snagged around the upper reaches of the hills, scads of clouds cascade like spirit forms, spilling down the hillsides.

The air is limpid, crystal, sparkling. All sense of 'inside' and 'outside' has evaporated, all organic sense of lungs and body long since gone, sacrificed on the altar of last night's initiation, dissolving back into the waiting earth. I am bloody and bruised, beyond exhaustion, having snatched no sleep at all from the night's bitter effort, and scarcely any of my usual receptors remain to gather in this scene. Yet some primal alertness peaks, stripped of all sophistication, to witness the brilliant purity all around; one single eye agape. Diaphanous, no longer 'I', rendered transparent, beaten into such thin foil that only light shines through as wonder, quiet joy and humbled appreciation emerge from my crushed and beaten self. The bubble of being softly pops and spills, each element returning to its source; gases rejoin the air, blood to water, breath to wind, body to earth—and everywhere this swelling pulse of energy pressing in, stretching, poking, pulling at the fabric of sensory reality.

Later that morning, my fellow campers set up a memorial at the lake in honour of Truganini, regarded as the last of the indigenous Aboriginals on Tasmania. They turn to me to say a few words as dedication, but I have little to offer in the way of words. I'm the actor, not a writer. I remember when I was sixteen I liked to listen to the poignant, piercing tones of Joan Baez, and her plaintive lament for acid rain—or was it fallout?—in the song 'What have they done to the rain?'

Just a little rain, falling all around
The grass lifts its head to the heavenly sound
Just a little rain, just a little rain
What have they done to the rain?

I don't know that the Tasmanian wilderness will become the battleground for a constitutional struggle between the federal and state governments, nor how photographers will capture some of the beauty of the natural world and inspire a new generation of environmental awareness. Typically, I have been an observer, performing as an activist, even though I work with a political theatre collective. But the naïve and often unfocused idealism of my generation plants the seed for an emotional defense of the natural world against the predations of industry. For people like me, before the analytical work by people like Noam Chomsky, or even the alarming reports by Rachel Carson, the ground for cynicism towards big business was laid by the folk singers.

Among the political hotheads, the environment is still regarded as a little soft as an issue, so it is a natural thing for a 'soft' male from the political collective to take up this protest. But the request for a simple dedication catches me by surprise and throws me back into characteristic self-doubt. I wish I had been able to say what I felt at Lake Pedder over that weekend: 'I feel like I have been put back in touch with something profound here. It would be a terrible thing to lose this place. And even more terrible, not to be able to feel an appreciation raw enough to bring me the humility through which I can learn what it has to teach us. Unmediated by human constructions this magnificence cleanses my perceptions and returns me to a state of wonder.'

the age of iron

Back in Melbourne, the grimy streets of the inner suburbs seem slightly unreal, as if my perceptions have shifted unalterably but, after just a few days, the familiar dullness comes back to wrap itself around me. Trams grind heavy iron wheels on metal tracks, dinning out their horrid chorus. My rapture is short-lived.

Somehow I have to gather my energy to cope with the basic demands of living. The Pram Factory is proving stressful and I need something practical to stay focused. After all the spiritual theories I have been reading, I am no more interested in going to another bookstore than in smoking another joint. I must do something tangible to refresh myself and keep my heart alive. I take up a regular yoga class at a school in St. Kilda and over ensuing weeks build a morning routine, using the simple exercises to pull my body into alignment and—through a listening practice—start to learn about letting go, without the use of drugs. First: letting go of noises, allowing them simply to be, then progressing to letting thoughts go the same way, I try to become still, to release attention from all distractions and find a clarified state of awareness. A Taoist poet advises:

> To return to your original state of being, you must first become a master of stillness. Activity for health's sake, never carried to the point of strain, must alternate with perfect stillness. Sitting motionless as a rock, turn next to stillness of mind. Close the gates of the senses. Fix your mind upon one object, or even better, enter a state of objectless awareness. Turn the mind in on itself and contemplate the inner radiance.[5]

George Whaley, of the Melbourne Theatre Company, comes to the Pram Factory to give an acting workshop. He challenges me one day over lunch:

'Why the hell are you doing yoga?'

---

[5] John Blofeld, *ibid.*

'Uh … For peace? Trying to keep it together … peace of mind, I suppose'

'Peace of mind?' he snorts, incredulous. 'No actor wants peace. Acting comes from conflict! If you want to be an actor, you need to feed on conflict.'

Cowed, I peer across the gap and the realisation prods at my brain that maybe I don't want to be an actor after all. But I push that possibility away. What else can I do? I have dropped out of university, failing to submit my thesis for examination. Theatre has been the focus of my idealism. I have painted myself so far into this corner that to imagine myself without it is to be stripped naked again.

According to my makeshift personal aesthetics, performances at the Pram Factory express the Group's multiple conflicts and confusions; intensity substitutes for clarity, raw energy trumps the subtle exploration of ideas. There's a lot of anger, but little insight of the kind that can answer my metaphysical longing. What can I offer here? Again, I feel out of place. The theatre will not be the way to discover what I need. I have no idea what else to do, but I am coming to the end of my improvisations.

dream sequence. Lord of the jungle

Mid-1972. In the middle of the night a dream.

In a clearing in the jungle, a myriad animals are gathered—countless species, with endless variations of face and form. In the centre is a flat raised area, and rising up on this platform is a huge serpent, as thick as a tree trunk. Despite their differences, all the creatures of the jungle are rapt, absorbed in watching the snake, which commands attention not so much by its size but by the power of the unspoken communication that it emanates. Its head is huge and hooded and reminds me of poster art of the Hindu deity Vishnu, himself surrounded by a thousand hissing snakes.

A forest, a clearing, all the animals of the wild. And in the centre, this impressive figure, drawing the many different life forms into one accord, melding all thought into one vibration. The archetype has stirred from the deepest place inside, standing out in bold relief from the usual miasma of unrecalled dream activity and it is potent enough to wake me up, as if to make sure I don't miss its significance.

I feel its effects for days.

In Christian iconography the serpent from the Garden was cursed to move on its belly, ground underfoot, eating the dust, punished as the tempter who encouraged primal Eve and Adam to be cast out of Eden. The figure in this dream, on the other hand, rises up splendid, powerful, uncowed—the wise ruler of all species. I recognise it intuitively as the symbol of wisdom. This is an encounter with some deeper level of being which, rather than wanting me to sleep and dream, threatens an awakening of another kind. Instinctively I respond to the image as a positive sign.

I take the chance to chant Hare Krisna with Alan Ginsberg at the Melbourne Town Hall; continue to read my way anxiously around the shelves of the spiritual bookstores; try to still my mind; torture myself with Zen riddles. My fitful exploratory visits to church leave a bad taste—empty rituals, smug priests, sleek as capons, and appalling, dreary music. You don't hear much Palestrina around the draughty churches in Melbourne and the wimpy folk songs of the new evangelicals are scarcely more attractive than the earnest nineteenth century hymns in 4/4 time of the Protestants. Religion seems too confident, with all its answers lined up in a row, while for me the questions have yet to form. No disrespect intended, if it works for them, but they seem full of old people's answers to old people's inquiries. To use one of their own metaphors, I need new wine, in a new wineskin—empirical, first-hand experience, not the ready-made formulations of the past.

The desperate search for Cosmic Union has all but petered out. I am simply trying to cope with a rising feeling of despair that it seems I have always been keeping at bay.

I am left with the simple practices provided through the course in *hatha yoga*—no great mind-blowing results in expanding consciousness, but a simple way to integrate my energies and bring my head back in touch with my body.

'Is that all there is?' sings Peggy Lee. 'Is that all there is, my friend, then let's keep dancing'. For me the magical dance of life is becoming a heavy-hearted, slow step. Hope has been ebbing, I am crushed by the growing feeling that this is all that there will ever be—that the rest of my days, if I can survive them, will be like this: hauling myself from sleep to sleep, with little inspiration, world without end.

Philosophically, I am sleeping with strange bedfellows. After spending so much time reading about the Patriarchs of Zen, the early Chinese Buddhists, the life of Siddhartha Gautama—the Buddha—some Vedanta, and Paramhansa Yogananda's *The Autobiography of a Yogi*, I look at the Bible again, beginning to see these stories about Jesus in a different light, with less of the spin put on them by the Christianity that came after he left, less of the doctrine, theology and institutional politics.

I feel as though I'm looking back through history to a time when a man—an extraordinary man to be sure—wakes up to a profound realisation of his innate divinity, and tries to reach out to his peers as a teacher—in the same way that the Buddha awoke to his own wisdom nature, five hundred or so years before, and spent the remaining decades of his life helping others find their way to a similar realisation.

I read Jesus afresh, now, as one among many teachers who rise up at different times and places and renew the spiritual life of their peoples. But the elation gained by my revisionist reading quickly turns to disappointment as I realise that these great moments have all occurred in ages past. How fortunate would you have to be, to be there when a great teacher arises amidst the people? Not a demi-God come down from Olympus; not an alien from a space ship. But a man, like other men, who has awakened the fullest potential of being and demonstrates it in the service of others. A boddhisattva, perhaps. And further, to have the good fortune to meet such a guide. Moreover, rather than rising in opposition, to *recognise* him or her, accept the teachings, offer support?

When I consult the *I Ching*, it advises me to seek out the great man. Further, it recommends that if I do not have the power to be the leader myself, I should throw my support behind the one who does. I would gladly do as the oracle advises, but that possibility seems extremely unlikely. I am not looking for a revolutionary politician, but for a master of wisdom. If only I had the good fortune to be alive at the same time as one of those.

I crave inspiration. Disappointed when my 'urge to merge' wasn't fulfilled by drugs I tried to leave my body. Now I am being forced to slow down, turn around and face being here as I am, in an act of conscious acceptance, even in a world that seems unwilling to reveal beauty or perfection. Is this what the existentialists proposed? I read *Be Here Now*, the book by Baba Ram Das, one of the early LSD pioneers who went to India and hooked up with a guru of some kind, but, as intriguing as it is, it's secondhand for me.

The death throes of the drama queen seem too drawn out. The shocking natural high at Lake Pedder, combined with the prosaic daily yoga practices, have taken away the desire for drugs, but this new-found sobriety is not enough. If I can't shake up the world, I want something to shift me into a different state of knowing. In all my investigations I have been addicted to doing and find myself disappointed with simply being. To my manic self this slowing process feels like death. Always, there is the need to know from direct, first-hand experience.

Perhaps there is a process going on, however, that moves on a deeper and more reliable level than my frenetic searching. Patience *is* a virtue, after all. Will there ever be another phase, when I will go beyond searching, when the *finding* will finally engage me and I will learn just what it is that I have been preparing for?

panic stations 2

August 1972. It's around 10 pm and the contractions have started. My partner's pregnancy has been managed by a specialist and she has booked in to the Mercy Hospital on the edge of the city. We take a taxi to travel the short distance to the hospital.

In this setting, the doctor runs things as he sees fit. They allow me to be with her for the first stage, then the doctor banishes me to the waiting room, where I will sit for several hours, starved of news. See how compliant I am; for I feel at a disadvantage, my status undermined by not being married, and my own doubts rendering me passive. With no information to work with, I wait and worry alone. Hours pass. Starved of updates, fearful, my mind rehearses a series of woeful scenarios, searching my heart for an inventory of my faults. As the night deepens, so does my sense of doom.

By the time a nurse brings news I have convinced myself that the baby, or my partner, or both, have died; that this is my 'bad karma' coming home to roost; that I will have to deal with the grief and with the deep sense of my own unworthiness, alone.

Mercifully it is not all about me.

The terse-lipped doctor tells me that she has lost some blood. I am intimidated by his authority, unable to tell whether the older man disapproves of me, or our situation, or whether he is simply annoyed at the lateness of the hour (by now it's around 4 am). My partner tells me later that she was less than satisfied with the specialist and very disappointed that, for all his reputation, he played out the role of the patriarchal expert, pushing aside what her wishes might have been.

Finally they let me in to see her. In the delivery room the baby, an eight-pound boy, is tightly wrapped in a cotton sheet. His head, still smeared with blood and whatever else, seems huge, almost bullet-shaped; he is asleep but indeed alive, and his mother calm, if a little groggy, after her ordeal. I feel shut out of the whole process—something I am not qualified to experience, yet when I go home at around 5.30 am I enjoy a feeling of quiet elation and the world seems to have altered in some way.

This birth has little to do with 'karma', it is a gift, *the* gift of life itself, I reckon.

I return to the hospital later in the day and they have been transferred to a ward. She has refused to allow the boy to be circumcised, which is still standard practice, apparently. (She is always better informed about the options than I am.) I want to name the baby David (which means 'beloved of God'), after my brother, who died too young, and she readily agrees. The fact that we are not married seems to have caused some administrative consternation (it is a Catholic hospital) but she has calmly taken charge and I am glad that she lists me as the father on the birth certificate. We use both surnames.

I am thrilled that they are both doing well. I am awed by the very real presence of the child but soon all my doubts will be pushing to be felt as well. Perhaps most new fathers are consumed with self-doubt. My sexual ambivalence adds to my confusion, of course. Both her family and mine are in Perth, but if they were closer I would not be able to avoid the feeling of guilt that I have brought her into this situation. Yet she is critical of the marriage laws and when the subject has come up she has declined.

The first night back home, she lays the baby down in a bassinette at the foot of the bed. As in all things, she is immensely well-informed and completely capable, but neither of us can sleep more than fitfully. Quite suddenly, in the middle of the night, the strained atmosphere is relieved by the sound of a very loud and prolonged liquid fart—David has broken the ice himself. We burst into laughter, glad to find that his essential physiological systems seem to be working well.

Sitting up in bed a few nights later I see that this could be some kind of fulfillment; together we form a sort of perfect trinity. Mother, father, child. I could say of this template that 'This is God' and know, somehow, what that means. But I cannot follow through. I feel myself shrinking back from the biggest challenge that life and my own choices—or reluctance to make choices—have presented to me. For all the admiration I have for the mother of my child, I see myself as inadequate, conflicted, unworthy. I am overwhelmed by the feeling that I still haven't found the essential information about the meaning of the life into which our son is entering, and the baby's arrival deepens the doubt that is caving me away inside. I am about to do to my own son what Frank's father had done to him. In a panic, I presume that it would be better if I were to leave, and better to do this sooner rather than later so that the boy can't form an attachment to me and be disappointed. In a few months that is exactly what I will do.

return

the perseverance hotel

Liberty begins the other side of despair.
—Jean-Paul Sartre

September 1972. For the time being, I escape the daily infighting at the
Pram Factory to seek out the peaceful atmosphere of the vegetarian
restaurant nearby, where I slowly take in a lunch, trying to come back to
myself: to the simple feeling of being that I sometimes reach in my
morning yoga practice.

'Why do you eat so slowly?' asks a young feminist who joins me for
lunch one day. She handles wardrobes for shows. Her fresh naïve look—
she uses no make-up to cover the freckles scattered across her nose and
cheeks—is no foil for her probing intelligence and her wide eyes challenge
me through owlish round glasses. I find the personal question a little
unnerving but I like her rigorous idealism. These Melbourne women
(especially the Carlton and Fitzroy push) are direct. Perhaps it's not a
challenge at all, more a request for information on a choice I might have
made.

'Oh, I wasn't aware. I suppose I just feel that all this food—it's kind of
like a sacrament,' I say, surprising myself. 'You know, the sacrifice of one
life form to another, so that *we* may continue.' I've started to slow down
to mull things over, especially since my arduous trip to Lake Pedder.
Getting a lot done no longer seems as important as understanding
whatever it is I feel compelled to do. I remember my first acid trip, back
in Perth, when I was standing at the kitchen sink drinking from a glass of
water and I could taste the detergent from the last time the glass had been

washed. Or perhaps the detergent was in the water itself. My body was the earth and it was awash in chemicals.

On that trip we soon lost interest in food. A beef stew that someone prepared earlier, before the drugs came on, lingered for hours in the oven. That night, as we came back to 'normal' reality, a bowl of meat was a gross primeval swamp, dating from the time of dinosaurs. Since then, eating meat has seemed almost regressive, and the act of taking food on board a mystery to be understood by slowing down the act and paying close attention.

One day I spot a flyer pasted in the window at Shakahari. It carries a line-drawing of a blissful boy sitting in the clouds with a sunburst behind him, and a quote:

'I am just a humble servant, and I've brought this peace for you.'

One or two of the restaurant staff met a young guru in India and have returned to Melbourne to spread the word; they have settled on the vegie restaurant as a likely place to encounter likely 'seekers'. One of the waiters, Peter, is a perfect mirror for me. We have been experimenting with the New Testament given to me by my Christian probation officer, and trying to use it as an oracle, like the *I Ching*. We flip open its pages for randomised instances of synchronicity in response to our deep, metaphysical inquiries.

A week or so after seeing the poster in the window I am walking back along Drummond Street to the house in Fitzroy when a car full of people pulls up. Peter leaps out, breathlessly stuffs a leaflet into my hands and says 'You must come!' A talk by a visiting expert on the guru's teaching. I make a note of the date and wonder if I will be able to make it. Work at the theatre is pretty much a seven-days-a-week job, with rehearsals, workshops, the newsletter, stints in the office taking bookings, helping with grant applications; all this on top of performances, six nights a week. The seventh is usually taken up with a meeting of the whole collective to thrash out programming policy and future scheduling.

So when the night given on the flyer rolls around I am chuffed to realise that I will be free and I walk to the house in Cardigan Street, where a talk is to be given by a *mahatma*. That must be some kind of high guy: 'maha' means great; 'atman', soul. Gandhi was a 'Mahatma', but perhaps this is different; a swami of some sort, perhaps. I have listened to talks by various swamis and yogis in Perth and Sydney already. They are usually Indian.

'Time changed. 7pm, Melbourne University, Students Union, room 133', says the note on the door. Now I am running, because that location is several blocks further and the time has been brought forward. I reach the Uni and seek out the room. Shoes are piled around the doorway. I slip off my sandals and squeeze inside where the meeting is already under way.

A brown-skinned man with a bald head is seated on a cushion on the floor, beside a small altar ablaze with candles; there are flowers and a picture of the young guru. The room is crammed with people. The 'Mahatma' wears a light cotton saffron-coloured *dhoti* and *kurta*. It is hard to tell his age; his head is shaved rather than bald in the usual sense, and he glows—is it with health, or happiness, or both? He appears to be around forty, or younger, but it's hard to tell. His talk is warm, expansive, inviting. Indian, yes, but his English is fluent and easy to follow.

I don't notice who else is there, but as I tune in to the talk, something shifts from me, as though a dark cloud has lifted, disappearing to leave the sky clear. I find myself sucking in everything that the radiant monk has to say. A kind of clarified liquor seems to flow with the words—a long stream of parables, anecdotes and quotations from the sages—and, in place of my usual muddy confusion, it's as though I am drinking from a source of timeless wisdom, which somehow feels familiar.

'These eyes only look outside; what you are looking for is within you. So how to look within? You cannot see your own face without a mirror. My Guru Maharaji will show you how that is done. He is your mirror. Not the mirror for your face and your body, but for your heart and your soul. If you come to him without any cheat or deceit in your heart, he will show you your true self.'

An hour or so later, after the meeting finishes, I join a smaller group which adjourns to a room back at the house in Cardigan Street, where a curly-headed Oxford graduate with John Lennon glasses named David Lovejoy gives a rational exposition on the topic of Self-knowledge.

'I didn't surrender at the Lotus Feet of the Master,' he says. 'It was more a case of defeat.' David is a competitive chess buff and cheerfully recounts that after encountering the young guru, no matter which gambit he used to resist the Master's call in his life, all the moves he tried eventually led him to the same conclusion—that he should become the student of this absurdly young teacher. Checkmate, apparently.

While Lovejoy's style of presentation is different from the Indian mahatma—except that they both speak spontaneously, without notes— the feeling it engenders is somehow the same, and I am abuzz with excitement, welcoming a new, yet strangely familiar possibility. Knowledge of the self. I remember those early days on campus in WA, when I was virtually impaled by the dictum from Delphi: 'Know Thyself'. Previously I was inclined to interpret that inquiry intellectually, which led to a palpable choking sensation in my chest, and the same questions have continued to burn in me. So, whatever others make of the project, to me the pursuit of this kind of knowledge has become a fundamental necessity, nothing less than a strategy for survival. The sequence of events that drove me across the continent and into the arms of the police has worked to deposit me in a much better place than I could ever have arranged for myself. I recall Jim Coventry's story: 'the currents will take you where you need to go'.

There's a pragmatic wisdom here that satisfies the head *and* the heart. As questions queue up in my mind, they are handled without even being voiced, one after the other, in a seemingly endless sequence of parables and personal testimonials.

'If you're hungry, reading a cookbook won't satisfy you. If you're thirsty and I write the word "water" on a piece of paper and you read that, won't you still be thirsty? Reading spiritual books is like pursuing a mirage in the desert. What you need is living water, and that only comes from a living teacher.'

It is clear that these followers of the guru—they call themselves 'premies', from the Indian word for lover, or devotee—speak from their own experience, rather than from theory. They make frequent references to scriptures such as *The Bhagavad Gita*, and stories about Krishna and, while I've always preferred the radical simplicity of the Taoists, these folk do seem to know what they are talking about. And there is another quality I can't quite put my finger on. While they are obviously happy, there is a kind of detachment, too. They are calm where you might expect them to be evangelical. They do seem pleased that I am interested in their teaching but there is a lovely modesty in their simple explanations, and I find myself devising questions just to get them to talk, so that I can tap into the feeling that reliably accompanies the telling.

David Lovejoy returns to Sydney with the mahatma, but I discover that there are meetings every night of the week, and fortuitously, my schedule opens up, enabling me to attend.

The thirst-quenching feeling continues in these nightly *satsang* ('meetings' 'Satsang' is a Sanskrit term that translates as the 'company of truth', and even without the marvellous mahatma I find there is plenty of satisfaction in this fellowship). I haven't realised just how dry I have been. Gradually it reaches me: it's not just a matter of joining some kind of post-hippie glee club, there is a specific practice on offer here. The mahatma—this one is called Guru Charanand—is empowered to impart the method, or the practice, with the teacher's blessing. It appears to be based on ancient meditation techniques that facilitate a kind of 'tuning in' to a blissful inner world. If that experience is anything like the mood engendered among the 'company of truth', I want more of it.

The time for theory is over. Here is a practice I can implement, as pragmatic as the yoga I have been doing every morning for the past few months. I have to take on faith the relationship between the kind gent in saffron—himself charismatic enough, with his humorous, twinkling eyes and an endless fund of instructive stories to be the teacher, any day—and the child guru in the photos, whom they all point to as the source and exemplar of this teaching.

No matter who speaks at these meetings—they all have very different styles and stories to tell, some of them just a few shy sentences—there is a quiet satisfaction in their eyes; simplicity rather than smugness is their style, and I know that each is speaking from a degree of personal realisation. And they don't mention sin. Every chance I get to ask them, either at the restaurant, where they'll say a few words and disappear, giggling, back into the kitchen, or at the nightly *satsang*, they speak of 'the Knowledge' or method which they have been shown, and the gratitude towards the teacher who has brought it to them. Their testimony speaks directly to a part of me that I have not yet been able to bring into focus, a core of being which seems to bypass the personality and ego. Listening itself becomes part of the practice, attending deeply to the sincere testimony from the simplest level of the heart. The listening practice I've been doing in my morning yoga sessions has been an appropriate preparation.

My excitement rises; is this what Socrates was referring to?

I particularly enjoy listening to the local coordinator—a petite woman in her late twenties named Julie Collet. Julie has been a social worker but, in search of something more, she quit her career and went travelling. When in England, Julie heard about Maharaji on a visit to Glastonbury Tor. Later she visited the young guru's ashram in Hardwar, in the north of India. Julie has a natural authority that makes her an ideal coordinator and, like several of the women in this group, she is not afraid of taking charge. Obviously the Knowledge gives her confidence. Her sapphire blue eyes sparkle when she speaks, and her mop of gold blonde curls melds into a nimbus of light whenever she speaks of her personal journey.

How long have I been searching for this? It's a rare moment, when a seeker becomes a finder. At some level I know that I have come 'home', in a sense, and the anxiety that has gnawed away at me for as long as I can remember is noticeably ebbing. After the meetings, I go back to my other activities inspired and, at some level of being, stilled. But in the welter of doing, the hurly burly at the Pram Factory and the challenge of other people's doubts, the feeling tends to dissipate. I have to hurry back to the company of the *premies* at night for a refill.

'What you are experiencing is actually coming from within you. When you come here, you are being led back closer to your own simple heart. This Knowledge can show you how to centre yourself in that experience every day. But it takes practise,' they tell me.

Whatever it takes, I am ready to give all that and more. I just want to be shown how but, as one of the few English speakers doing the initiations in the West, the mahatma is in great demand. That first night in Cardigan Street I passed up an opportunity to be initiated. David Lovejoy, the John Lennon look-alike, wanted to know whether I had prepared myself properly to receive the gift. The issue of 'preparation' was not raised in the earlier talk by the mahatma but in a sense I felt that my entire life had prepared me for arrival at this point and I was eager to go full steam ahead; yet Lovejoy's interrogative was enough to give me pause. 'Easy come, easy go', that's the saying. This feels like something I should do properly. So, rather than rush into the session the next morning, when

I was told there would be other opportunities I decided to wait, and 'prepare'.

That first encounter was in September, soon after the birth of my son; but now we are moving into October and I am getting impatient. Mahatma ji is authorised to teach the specific practices for tuning in— four techniques in all which seem to operate like a set of coordinates for locating inner peace. Without having access to them, all I have to go on is the nightly talks … and hope. I urgently want to take the next step, to integrate the practice into my daily routine.

It's Saturday night, and there is to be a big public meeting. The Mahatma has come back into town and will be speaking in Fitzroy. After several weeks of waiting, the bliss is charged with the promise of more, and my impatience is starting to chafe. If I can 'receive Knowledge' as they put it, I will know, finally, how to re-connect with this calm, unchanging level of being that I have had only a taste of in their company.

Over the past few weeks I have dragged some of my other friends along, and they have shown varying degrees of interest—some are downright sceptical. I find out the address of the Sydney ashram and send a telegram to my friend Bob Beaver, in Sydney: 'Go to this address in Riley Street, Surry Hills. Do not stop, do not pass go.' Bob has had to go into hiding, underground, as a draft-resister. He goes on to receive Knowledge almost immediately at an ashram in Killarney Heights.

At the end of his talk the Mahatma announces that he has to return to Sydney the next day for a talk he is scheduled to give. He encourages everyone interested in receiving Knowledge to listen to more of the nightly talks and one day, very soon, he will return.

I am crushed. All of this time—these tantalising weeks of promise— just to be told to wait? I have found my way to the fount of knowledge and wisdom but they won't even turn on the tap! Actually, they seem quite ready to do that: those who have already been instructed, either in India, in the UK, or in Sydney, are ready to launch into more telling, but while their words have been pouring like balm over my sore heart, by now they only exacerbate my thirst. Why didn't I take that chance back in September? Why did I let that cunning David Lovejoy talk me out of it?

Crestfallen, I stagger down the stairs and into the street. The others are bubbling about the mahatma's talk, but from the moment the Indian saint said he would be going back to Sydney, I have felt flat. I want to go over to the ashram to beg him for instruction, but the inhabitants of that house say Mahatma Ji is tired and needs to rest. I wander off miserably, wondering what will become of me. Until something makes me look up.

On a corner opposite there is a sign over an entrance to a pub: 'The Perseverance Hotel'. Disappointed as I am, I get it in an instant. Every time I throw the coins for the Chinese oracle, the *I Ching*, the reading is 'Perseverance furthers'.

'Meet the great man,' the oracle advises. Yet no oracle can give me what the mahatma has to offer. The seeking is over. There will be no turning back. Now it is time for discovery.

the knowledge you don't get in college

Other aspects of my life are in turmoil. I am oblivious to how my quest might be stirring things up at home, where my enthusiasm has not been catching. People around me can't understand why I would want to give so much time to this. But the bottom has fallen out of the Pram Factory as far as I am concerned. George Whaley scorned my need for peace but his scepticism only exacerbates it.

A couple of weeks later the mahatma returns to Melbourne to do a program at a large hall rented for the occasion. My partner agrees to come along to hear him speak—we have the pram in tow—but her experience couldn't be more sharply differentiated from mine. I am eager to allow the feeling of contentment to spread more deeply through me. She approaches it analytically, intent on parsing the meaning of the words the Mahatma utters. She offers to buy me a ticket to India, to 'go and see just how many gurus there are, there.' But I don't feel the need to do that. India has come to me. While I have been dangling in despair, it is as if some director behind the scenes has been preparing my life, in pragmatic ways, to begin on this path. My morning yoga practice is now an hour long. Coincidentally, the meditation practice is supposed to take an hour, as well.

The mahatma sits alone at a microphone stand on the large platform, which is virtually unadorned save for a giant photo of the young teacher, and a large arrangement of fresh flowers. A spaced-out girl dances across the stage behind him, fawning theatrically around the photo. Her performance is just that—as much a display as an act of devotion. The spirit of the times draws in a wide range of people with diverse attitudes—from curiosity to genuine thirst for instruction—as well as this kind of performative spirituality. A year ago I could have been in her place. The arrival of gurus from the East is part of a 'consciousness revolution' and the whole phenomenon folds easily into the inchoate hopes of hippie idealism. Chanting, drugs, yoga: it's all the same. All roads lead to the top of the mountain. But I already have my doubts about the nostrum. This process feels entirely pragmatic, even empirical, in contrast.

At the end of the talk Julie Collet announces that anyone who wishes to receive Knowledge should gather the next day at the Cardigan Street centre. My partner's scepticism is palpable but there is no question that I will cancel everything else to be there. I don't know how to justify this to anybody, but I am ready and willing to follow through. I am on the brink of a new understanding and it is precious to me above all things, a matter of life over death.

The next morning—a Friday—the upstairs room at Cardigan Street is crammed with seekers, scrunched up together on the carpet. Among the early arrivals, the smart ones head for a place near the wall, where they can rest their backs. I am hoping to get initiation, but my expectations are soon dashed as the recent arrivals spew up all-too predictable questions, on issues that are no longer of interest to me. 'How can I possibly meditate? My mind is too restless,' says one. 'Is this the same as *kundalini*?' asks another. It goes on: 'When I take LSD, everything turns into patterns of light.' 'Will this cancel out my *karma*?' 'How will this stop the war in Vietnam?' 'Wouldn't it be better to feed the poor?' 'Isn't this just self-indulgence?' Endless questions, pulled from the ragbag of concepts we have all been stuffing for years; half-baked theories, fragments from eclectic reading lists: theosophy, re-incarnation, rumours of wondrous *shakti* powers; fears about the anti-Christ—every form of spiritual belief and superstition is regurgitated, madly, hour after hour.

The mahatma responds patiently and each question generates a perfect response; his understanding seems boundless. Just when it seems that there could be nothing left to ask, someone belches up another concept for commentary and explication. While I am exasperated by what seem to be little more than secondhand ideas, the mahatma treats every question with respect and, as he explains the basics, we are all drawn in to a state of deeper understanding that dissolves the irritation aroused in me.

By lunchtime, the questions show no sign of abating and Mahatma Ji shows no sign of hurrying.

The figure of Lucky, from *Waiting for Godot*, looms over the proceedings but, for all my distaste, I have to recognise myself in their questioning. Lucky's sole utterance in the play is in the first act: a crazed speech that meanders on for pages, stuffed with half-finished thoughts and fragmentary ideas. In the second act he is mute, spent. We seem like caricatures of seekers spewing up half-digested concepts. I am watching a home movie of myself from a former life, almost as though I need to review this stage before I proceed. With this teaching there is no rush, apparently. It is painstakingly thorough. Quite different from merely dropping a tab of acid.

'You are hungry and you are reading recipe books. Does that satisfy your hunger? You must cook the food and eat it!'

As the day progresses, it seems that the question and answer session could go on forever. A stream of premies, already in the know, shuffle in and out of the room from time to time, to listen respectfully, encouraging the new aspirants to pluck up the courage and ask for initiation. A young woman demurely refreshes the flowers on the altar. Some people leave but, even as they do, their places are taken by new arrivals. I want to heave them all out of the window, along with their questions, but that doesn't seem like a very spiritual response. Should I throw myself, like a beggar, at the mahatma's feet? Wouldn't that be a little demonstrative for an earnest Australian, with no cultural models to show him the appropriate forms of respect? And maybe it would be rude, to interrupt the process. So I let go of my frustration, bringing my attention back to what the Mahatma is saying, and the experience deepens. Each time he launches into another story, another part of me has to let go. Surrendering by listening. It hasn't come easily, but it serves as a kind of un-learning; in effect, a letting go of ideas and releasing urgency itself into a river of peace.

My need is a spasm, clutching like a sphincter; listening, on the other hand, is letting go. As simple and pragmatic as it is, the mahatma's discourse unfolds a wisdom greater than the ersatz collection of spiritual concepts we all carry. It doesn't matter, finally, what people ask; we are all being drawn beyond mere curiosity and the reactive mind and into a state of radiant simplicity. And, in the process, finding humility.

The time is up, it's five o'clock and apparently we still haven't arrived at a satisfactory place. Mahatma ji is to speak at another program in the evening and he has to eat before the evening's talk. It is obvious there will not be a Knowledge session today. We are invited to come and listen to him again at the evening program in the large meeting hall in Fitzroy.

Food seems like an irrelevance, but I take a small snack at Shakahari and walk to the hall in Brunswick Street, near the Perseverance Hotel.

That evening, listening to the mahatma, something breaks in me—releasing me from all sense of urgency, from: 'I want' and 'I want it *now*'. Even the begging—'I need'—melts away. Beyond the urgency, something has released inside my heart and I know that I can wait forever. That I am already blessed to have come to this source, which is deeply worthy of my trust. That my life will forever intersect with the depth of this moment. This state will nourish the part of me that has been so inexplicably hungry until now. I do want to get started with the practice yet I could wait until the end of time, for you could live lifetimes and never find this place. I haven't had to hit the hippie trail to Goa, or climb the heights to Kathmandu, track down a *saddhu* in a remote mountain cave, or practise austerities for years. Someone, or something, has heard the call of my heart and has come seeking me out.

The mahatma tells us that 'Truth' is sitting inside, not as a tottering structure of theological concepts but as an experience of simplest being. It is the 'home' self. To return to it is more a process of un-doing than doing, of a re-alignment with Being, rather than the intricate manipulation of a sticky skein of ideas; forgoing all obsessive mental scheming and unraveling a tangle of knots to uncover a state of sublime simplicity within a trusting heart.

I am grateful to discover that, unlike the one-shot deal of a Jesus, say, who was (is?) the 'only' way, Vedantists believe that an avatar will re-appear, again and again, to guide the weary seeker home. Krishna, for example, who is regarded by the Hindus as the supreme manifestation of the Lord Himself, says in the Gita:

> *When goodness grows weak*
> *When evil increases*
> *I make myself a body*
> *In every age I come back*
> (Chapter 4, verse 8; trans. Prabhavananda/Isherwood)

The next day dawns and I beat the now-familiar path back to the little house on Cardigan Street. The first time I came here, there was no electricity and the kitchen had no floor. Under Julie's leadership a steady stream of volunteers has transformed the place through 'selfless service' (an equal part of the practice) and, bare and simple though it is, it shines.

'All of your life, these senses have been dragging you out into the external world. Now you must learn how to tame these wild horses and bring them back inside,' Mahatma ji explains. 'By the grace of Guru Maharaj ji, these techniques will help you come back to yourself and go within, where you will discover there is an ocean of peace. We will start with the first technique. Now close your eyes and wait 'til I come to you.' The mahatma moves quietly around the room whispering instructions as he helps us, one by one, with the techniques.

'Listen to the unstruck sound, the *anaha-naad*, the self-sustaining music which permeates the Universe. Become absorbed in that and let it bring you back home.'

I sink easily into the feeling of peace that is released from deep within, yet somehow beyond, me, listening intently to a stream of sound deep within my brain. As I lose myself in the glistening harmonies, a cavernous, restful space opens up within me. 'Inside' is deeper, wider, further than what is outside. I could write 'inside my mind' but in any real sense one's mind doesn't contain this, for it is itself contained within this wider field of conscious awareness. I can't remember ever feeling this way before, not even on LSD, and yet it is the most natural feeling of all. I am reminded of that beach in Broome, where the tide goes out, literally for miles; but when that tide comes in, it is a force of nature.

Like a hen nursing a clutch of eggs, I settle comfortably with my breath. As I follow the gentle beat of the primal conductor, my mind is content to be utterly absorbed in inner space.

The final technique gently anchors me in this peculiar state: neither dreaming nor waking, some place neither in the body nor out of it; neither thinking nor not thinking; neither empty nor not empty; not sleeping, not doing; awake. Consciousness is a single eye floating calmly on the deep waters of a quiet, infinitely expanded awareness, each breath a sip of subtle nectar, and my insignificant little ego self is quenched by a feeling of exceptional gratitude.

Some people deride the practice of meditation as 'selfish', as part of a disastrous turn away from the sacrifice of the self for the greater good, towards personal satisfaction. Maybe some practices could be construed this way, but it soon becomes obvious to me that this process is not about indulging the personal self, or ego. Rather, it is a deeper re-alignment of the little 'me' with the Source of all being and consciousness. One self equally distributed among all.

After a couple of hours my knees are nagging but, in spite of the aching discomforts of the body, I am reluctant to leave this space that has opened up inside. The feeling is intimate, closer than breath itself. I have spent years growing away from my own centre.

We take a break for tea and toilet then the mahatma goes through the procedures again, patiently explaining the basics.

I start to wonder whether I am ever going to be able to go as deeply into this dimension of peace again, without the mahatma there to coach me. That will depend on a very clear desire to make my home there, and the determination to re-iterate this state of enhanced concentration within a diligent daily practice. To get the mind so focused, training it to follow the subtle thread all the way back to the source like this has taken quite some preparation; more than just the past few weeks, I realise. To open up this garden of delights when so many other things are likely to be competing for my attention, externally, is going to be quite a challenge. For, as intimate as it is, the source experience doesn't draw attention to itself. It is the basis of consciousness, the very essence of being; yet it is the first thing to be overlooked in all the doing, doing, doing. What a great mystery! The instructor explains that, just as the regular attendance at satsang has prepared me for this introduction, so now I will find that the same process of deep listening will help to calm the mind in preparation for the new practices. Satsang is as important a part of the practice as the meditation techniques. That's why the premies who have been initiated already come back regularly to hear more.

I dance down the street to the restaurant, ready to show off my joy to the devotees who are becoming my new friends.

'Isn't it wonderful?' I chortle.

'Aah, yes it is! But now you have to practise,' they enjoin.

At home, a cold war is being waged, an unspoken struggle of priorities. After quitting the religion of her upbringing, my partner is alarmed that I could be falling into the clutches of what she sees as a quasi-Hindu cult. I respect her opinion in all things, probably more than I trust my own diffident stances, and I have taken her along to meetings, hoping she would connect with the oceanic feeling of peace, but she has found the explanations offered in the satsang sadly lacking; naïve and intellectually unsophisticated. I don't know how to explain to her that, literally for the first time in my life, my heart is soaking in peace. The anxiety that has been gnawing at me is losing its teeth. The recurrent drowning dream has stopped, never to return.

Next morning I go back to the ashram to catch the mahatma's last talk before he leaves. 'Remember', he says, 'If you point the finger at someone to criticise, there are *three* fingers pointing back at you', and this advice will come in very handy.

Each day I practise the techniques at home, struggling to reach the deep well of peace inside. I am thirsty for experience but when I try to recollect it, using the techniques to focus myself within, my mind rebels in a hundred gross and subtle ways, alternating between attacking me with doubts and calling my attention away from that true centre with a proliferation of thoughts. Even with the help of the techniques, the bliss is elusive. The evening practice often just sends me to sleep. *Satsang* gives me a chance to release from the struggle and coast along with the current of feeling. I start to see that it's not so much a matter of stilling the mind as surrendering to the greater reality as it is revealed, within. The techniques help, but the ego drive—even its drive for satisfaction—takes me away from the source, which is always already there. To live a life in service would help to release the ego grip; and a new respect grows from the sharing of testimony in the company of others. Instead of puffing up the ego with grandiose claims of enlightenment, the heart opens to recognise that everyone has equal access to the source of life and consciousness, and equal status in truth. The young teacher says, 'When the sun shines, it shines for everyone.' This welcoming is not what I have felt from the churches, which have failed to instil their mythologies in my heart.

Friends deride my new-found interest as 'cultish'. It seems that every other rationale for being and doing is highly valued, even institutionalised, in normal social life. To take a different path confronts entrenched customs and beliefs, even in so-called easy-going, live-and-let-live Australia; and the alternative counter culture of Carlton seems too exclusively committed to political solutions to allow the spirit to breathe. Cynicism has never seemed so stale, or so wrong-headed.

'Religion' is part of the problem, not the solution, they say. At one level I agree with this analysis, but aren't they too ready to paint all varieties with the same brush? What I am engaged with does not depend on belief, it's an empirical process. I am impatient that everyone can't see what is so clear to me. 'World peace starts within. You can't stop a war, in Vietnam or anywhere else, if you haven't made peace within yourself,' I proffer. Yet to some of my friends and colleagues at the Pram Factory it seems that I have been brainwashed; either that, or they see my bliss as just another form of getting 'stoned'.

'What does your partner think of all this?' they ask suspiciously. They revile the Indian trappings surrounding the teaching as 'un-Australian', and mock the name the organisation has carried over from India: The Divine Light Mission (founded in 1960 by Shri Hans Maharaji and rapidly growing). Happy to have finally found my path, the criticisms don't deflect me. As far as I am concerned, I am not learning to be a pseudo-Hindu, I am exploring an inner topography, mapping consciousness itself, and the joy discovered in that terrain is palpable. I have found the well of peace and I have no intention ever to leave it in favour of seeking the approval of others. Their objections merely strengthen my resolve.

Slowly, as I persevere with the practices, I feel an attunement taking place, tweaking my being into a new cycle of growth and understanding. What a contrast this is with the jagged vibrations of my former, druggy highs and the wild clutching after my synthetic *samadhi* in Sydney.

The young guru—my teacher now, even though I have never met him—pays a brief visit to Sydney but I miss the chance to see him. The silent struggle at home, and a new production at the Pram Factory which requires me to be present at rehearsals, persuades me into a short-lived resurgence of duty; reluctantly, I stay put in Melbourne.

A Sydney newspaper carries a report of his entry at Kingsford Smith airport. In the arrivals hall the devotees have scattered flowers to make a pathway for him and, while the reporter is touched by their songs, she is irritated by the young guru himself, who seems to be ignoring the very folk gathered to greet him. All these blissed-out people singing his praises, yet as she describes it, he looks 'neither to the left nor to the right'.

Trapped in Melbourne, this strikes me, the new devotee, as significant, in spite of the reporter's obtuse take. 'Neither to the left, nor the right.'

Like the Buddha, he treads the Middle Way. Her report serves as a kind of symbolic reinforcement for me. I am delighted to be the student of someone who appears to be non-attached, pulled neither to one side or the other and I remember the decision I came to, coming down off acid in Sydney: that I had to find a middle path.

A television reporter goes to the house in Sydney's Killarney Heights where the young master is staying and asks, incredulously, how someone who is only fourteen can possibly teach others.

'It is the Knowledge that teaches them the Knowledge,' Maharaji explains with a smile. 'Fourteen years has got nothing to do with it. Fourteen years is fourteen years.'

exit stage

Each November there is a festival at the main ashram in India, in honour of the teacher's father, Shri Hans Ji Maharaj (my *'param* guru'), and while most of the devotees will attend, once again I am one of the few miserable creatures who stay behind. At the Pram Factory I am rehearsing for the first performance of a play by Katharine Susannah Pritchard, *Brumby Innes*, which, in spite of its age, has never been performed. Set in the north-west of Western Australia, it has a similar plot to her novel *Coonardoo*. I am to play a grazier, the uncle of a young woman visiting from Perth who has been drawn into a relationship with the cattle station proprietor, Brumby Innes. (Lynn Curran plays the niece, and Dennis Miller the 'brumby'.) My own character, the uncle, tries to protect his young niece's virtue from Brumby's attentions but, in a pivotal scene of confrontation, he loses both a bruising fight with Brumby and any loyalty he holds on the girl's familial sympathies. Brumby's earthy magnetism rules her, body and heart.

Rehearsals for the fight scene proceed over several days. In the theatre-in-the-round configuration of the Pram Factory it is hard to pull your punches so, instead of a stand-up boxing match, Dennis Miller and I do a lot of rolling around and kicking at each other. The rehearsal room floor is concrete and the set mocked up for rehearsals is made out of heavy wooden packing cases. Dennis injects an element of macho strength to bring out the weaker aspects of my character, the uncle, and though he is not careless, there are painful collisions as we block out the moves. Each day I go home with bruises and a deepening doubt about my thespian vocation. It seems further and further away from what I am experiencing among the premies.

The play is set on a cattle station. The opening scene takes place in the camp of the station hands—all Indigenous—and includes dance and chanting; a form of *corroboree*, if you will. A visiting troupe of Torres Strait Islander dancers has been cast for this scene. The leader of the group is tall and strikingly handsome, with long grey hair tied back from his forehead in a red bandana. One night, as I come off stage after the fight scene, his flashing smile grins at me through the darkness:

'You sure are a terrible actor!' He laughs as he claps me on the shoulder, sending me packing. Something in the way he says it—honest, yet so full of glee—liberates me. Rather than raising the hackles of ego, it is as though the Islander is giving me permission to drop this acting thing, to get on with my real life, wherever that might lead me. Having found my true path I just want to get into it as completely as I can. Here is something I can really commit myself to.

But the more I engage with the life of the Mission the more I find myself at odds with friends who do not share my enthusiasm, and I'm drawing further away from my partner.

Unpacking the different factors affecting my thinking at the time, it's clear that the pathways of our lives were moving on fundamentally different arcs: she into her career, me into … what? I can't say 'spirituality', because for me it is more about 'survival'. And it isn't only the deep unease that comes from trying to play it 'straight' that grates. The relationship with Helm, too, was a casualty of the same overriding quest. At twenty seven, I have been trying to squeeze into the costume of a false self that clearly doesn't fit. I hope that the next phase of my life could be a discovery of a more authentic self, come what may.

What would happen if I were to stay? My deviant sexual yearning has not been 'cured' by learning how to be with a woman. Would I find myself sneaking around behind her back, engaging in furtive sexual gropings with compliant, equally guilty males? What kind of damage would it do to her nascent career, the scandal of a 'bisexual' partner? This is what comes when you act against your own nature, trying to conform: you don't just mess up your own life, it affects other people, too, long term. I should have followed my instinct and broken it off in Sydney. To continue as I have done has been a big mistake and complicated two other lives. Cleaving to the false self, performing what I feel is expected of me could not, to my mind, improve the situation, it could only make things worse.

On the other hand, David is *not* a mistake. He is a fact, a living, breathing, *welcome* fact who side-stepped his father's ambivalence, snuck under our defences, thwarting contraception to claim his space. David is the irreducible hard rock I can't get around, and I wouldn't change that reality even if I could. It's easy to see now, looking back more than forty years, that I lacked the patience to realise that even if we were to break up, as painful as that would surely have been, we might yet have worked out a *modus vivendi* that would take care of the needs of each of us. But that would have taken a great deal more maturity than I had at the time.

But if I had stayed (I can ask myself now) would I have had the courage to come out of the shadows? Ashamed as I am that I did not stay to support her, and lend my son even an imperfect model of a father, I suspect I would have got back into drugs, become terminally depressed, contracted HIV ... In short, I would have killed myself, one way or another. And brought more pain and disgrace down on other lives.

If homophobia has done its job, you just don't feel like one of the 'real' people. In the eyes of experts, you're a 'biological error.' That's the basis of a toxic self-doubt that has worked itself deep into your psyche before you have the ideological defences to ward it off. This sorry sub-text produces an unconscious impulse to *fulfill* the script: you're not supposed to be here, you're faulty; *ergo*, you should rub yourself out, one way or another. I see that at work behind the self-destructive tendencies of many of my acquaintances today. 'Gay pride' only works to heal the alienation if individuals find an effective way to deal with that inner separation: the insidious alienation produced by shaming. With 'God' itself installed as the judge of our 'abomination', religion only serves to drive the wedge deeper. We feel like damaged goods and, by not dealing with the deeper pain, some of us do proceed to destroy ourselves in a perverse fulfillment of the curse.

I reckon I would have destroyed myself, too. But another impulse in me, to survive my own self-destructive impulses, drives me to try to understand my real nature, to seek out the healing that will bring me home. Now I have the remedy to deal with my deep-seated anxiety. I dream that one day I will be able to come back and re-connect with David and by that time I will have some answers. Big answers. After all, didn't the Buddha leave his home, his wife, his child, to seek Enlightenment? I fail to consider that in the case of Gautama, as the son of the king, their needs were to be taken care of by the king's retainers. My head is in the sky and I can't see what my feet are doing. Putting my needs first, I press on in trust and blindly hope that all will be well, present indications notwithstanding.

renunciation

After being bent, then trying to be 'straight', celibacy seems to be the perfect solution for me, and I plunge further into this new zone of experience. For, if I had hoped that a satisfying relationship with a woman would have 'cured' me of my homosexual urges, sadly that has not been the case. I ask to move into the ashram in Cardigan Street, leaving my house, my friends, my partner, my baby, the job—everything—to put all my chips on renunciation.

Julie reads me the rules from the ashram manual, which sound to me like a draft of the guidebook for Heaven on earth. Here is an opportunity to not deal with sexuality at all, a blessed relief just to put it on the shelf. Again, as I abandoned the relationship with Helm to travel east and pursue the star I hoped would give meaning to my life—through Artaud, and the 'poetry of space'—I rush now into the ashram, my own needs typically taking precedence over other considerations. I am hungry for peace. If that can be construed as a selfish drive, the rule of the ashram is 'selfless service'. Your life is given over to the greater cause, to bring the news of this method, and the charismatic young teacher, to the world. As far as I am concerned, it is either that or madness.

In the tightly-packed room where the 'brothers' sleep—on the floor, side by side, like loosely packed sardines—there is little space for personal belongings. They have no cupboard to store changes of clothing and I give away most of my own small pile to the jumble store that has been set up for fundraising, under the satsang hall in Brunswick Street. A humble Irish brother makes room for my socks in the rough and ready pinewood packing case that serves as makeshift shelving. With three pairs, I feel gross and greedy compared with others who have only one. It appears I talk too much, too—chit-chat is taboo here—and I am often hungry on the austere diet. Breakfast is a slice of melon and a cup of herbal tea, and even that is taken only after we have sung a long *arati*, done our meditation practice, and cleaned the ashram from top to bottom, inside and out. I get a part-time job as a waiter at Shakahari and top up on food while at work, allowing me to feel virtuous in the evenings, when I can decline a second helping of dinner back in the ashram.

I have little time to rest in my new ashramic cocoon. Almost immediately, I am to be transferred to Brisbane, to help staff a new centre there. Errol Vieth has gone ahead to establish a base and is calling for assistance. People from the two major cities, Sydney and Melbourne, are being used to seed newer centres and I am to leave Melbourne with Penny Allsop, whom I know from theatre in Perth—she was initiated into the practice the same day as me—to join Errol and another young fellow, Don Wilson, as the nucleus of a centre for propagation in Queensland.

Others have a different scenario in mind. One night, five days after moving from Moor Street to Cardigan Street, I am coming downstairs from the satsang hall, still enjoying the sweet feeling of abandonment induced by the two hours of music and blissful testimony, when I come face to face with Midge Freeman, my former 'acid guru', on the stairs. Midge was the one who had shown me through the doors of perception, using psychedelics, and told me just to 'let go'—which had been very good advice, in the circumstances. But Midge seems disgruntled that his former charge has journeyed beyond his teaching.

'What are you experiencing?' asks Midge, sizing me up.

'Mmm, peace … Incredible peace,' I breathe, presuming that Midge will catch the vibe. His antagonism has scarcely registered with me.

'Bah! That's not *God*!' he mutters, disgusted.

The peace I have been saturating myself in is not mere relief; peace like the aftermath of war, say, although there is something of that in it. It is bringing about a deep shift at the centre of being, displacing the chronic feeling of malaise that has characterised my inner life for as long as I can remember. But the combined practices of satsang, meditation and service have started to send down a tap root into another level of experience, into a deep and palpable force-field which is less the personal being, Victor, than of something like Being itself. The peace that comes from this deep re-connection nurtures me, in a mysterious but tangible way, and I want never to break the connection that is forming.

But even so, in the face of Midge's challenge, I find it difficult to articulate the difference.

People are streaming past us down the stairs. If Midge's initial assertion has snapped me to attention, the mood from the hall is not entirely dispelled, so Midge switches tactics, backing off from confrontation, and invites me to continue our chat out in the street, where his antique saloon car is parked. Discreet side curtains mask off the plush interior from passers-by.

'It's reeea-llly good to see you,' Midge purrs as the doors click shut, his words swirling around him like subtle smoke. 'Let's just bathe in your presence a while.' A skilful operator, Midge borrows some of the bliss I am feeling to begin to weave a spell, with the help of a little flattery.

'You look greeeaat. I can see this stuff is affecting you,' he continues, 'but really man, this is not where it's at.' He floats the doubt: 'There's something more real than this "peace" you're experiencing.' And pushes it home: 'Come and spend some time with us, just a little while, and you'll see.'

Always a mysterious character, Midge is full of surprises and I haven't seen him for more than a year. I assumed that he was still living in Sydney but he seems to have moved on from his previous interests, and the invitation intrigues me. What new wonders has he come across?

There are others in the car, one of whom I do recall meeting before, and they tacitly support the promise. From this point on, Midge does all the talking. 'What you are doing is not cool, man. You should find out how to penetrate the illusion, once and for all.' Trading on the vestiges of loyalty from the acid sub-culture, and holding out the lure of even more secret knowledge, Midge leads me away from the hall and we drive off into the night.

'But what about the ashram? The people in Cardigan Street will wonder where I've gone …'

'You can send them a telegram if you're concerned. Don't worry, you'll be safe.'

These days, well-intentioned friends and relatives would be better organised to attempt to 'de-program' a person from what they construe as the indoctrinations of a malignant cult but, as amateurish as these my former associates are, what is originally supposed to be a conversation in the back of a car leads to a very long drive somewhere out into the countryside, with the implicit promise of a great awakening dangling like a carrot in front of this doubting donkey's nose.

Of course, I don't feel I have been 'programmed', or indoctrinated, at all. The process that I have entered into seems to be more about *un*-conditioning, especially when it comes to the meditation practice, where I am learning to back away from the tighter knots of the mind's all-too-familiar concerns and find release into a deeper experience of conscious awareness than that mediated by thinking. But Midge's conviction is enough to knock me off my newfound centre. I feel a little uneasy but, having cast myself adrift, I go along for the ride, which eventually deposits us at a house in the countryside, somewhere near Canberra, where others are waiting—quite benignly, it seems. Perhaps they have already entered Midge's promised zone.

One young woman reads to me from New Age books, including one called *The Aquarian Gospel of Jesus the Christ*, which held my attention briefly a year or so before. There have been apocryphal stories going around that the ritual of the Christian sacrament in the Mass, and its re-enactment of a 'last' supper at the Passover, is a ceremonial re-enactment of Jesus sharing a hallucinogenic mushroom—the red-topped *amanita muscaria*, perhaps—or some other psychotropic intoxicant, to recover awareness of the sacred dimensions of life.

Midge's method—what little he bothers to explain of it—has something to do with fasting from dawn to dusk whilst sitting out in the bush (possibly on acid, mushrooms, or mescaline; it is not clear) and the great revelation, whatever it is, will somehow manifest spontaneously. At least, I presume that is what he is getting at, but sleek-eyed Midge is the master of the oblique and subtle implication, and leaves you to fill in the blanks yourself. But I am not really interested in 'doing a Thoreau'—sitting in the woods to find out who I am and how I fit into the greater scheme of things. Perhaps there's nothing to this method at all, and Midge's real intention has been simply to lever me out of the community of devotees.

Soon, my own experience begins to re-assert itself. I feel, instinctively, that with Maharaji's practice I have already found gold. I miss satsang. And I miss the formal meditation practice. The 'Aquarian Gospel' seems like a step backward. Haven't I moved on from this?

So, what to do? I sit and wait to see what my next move should be.

The next day they watch me closely; they don't want me to meditate, apparently. Is it that they don't want me to fall back into the delusion from which I have been suffering? No-one spells it out. But neither has Midge's implicit claim to a superior way made any sense to me.

My passivity seems to lull them. They start to relax their supervision, and resume smoking dope. Meanwhile, what they don't know is that, while some of the techniques are best practised in private, it is possible to practise others even in company and they don't notice me making the subtle connection with what I have been shown, inside.

That afternoon, as their guard droops behind a haze of smoke, I find myself praying silently for guidance. By now it appears that they have nothing to offer me. What am I doing here, really? The location may be different, with different cast members, but it's the same blurred vibration that I've hung out in before. After the arduous path I have traveled I am impatient not to waste any more time. I rue how easily I have been lured away. 'Should I stay with them, should I try to bring them round?' I wonder. 'Is that my "service" in this situation? They seem contented; why should I be the evangelist? Should I just leave them to their dope and get on with my own journey? Should I leave, or should I stay?' I am silently, confident that, in spite of the situation I have got myself into, I will be answered.

Something lands on my leg. I brush it away, still intent on trying to divine an answer.

'Please, I need to know *now*,' I reiterate, mutely. 'Should I stay here and try to make them understand, or should I just cut and run? Please make it really clear somehow, and please let me know, *now*.'

Again, something lands on my leg, and again I brush it off inattentively, wondering how 'Spirit' could be so slow at responding to my urgent need. As I step back into my own inner truth, out in the middle of nowhere , with no money, and only the clothes on my back, I feel more free than at any other time in my life. But why is 'The Universe' not responding to my call?

Pay attention, Victor.

The third time I ask and the insect lands on my thigh, I pause to notice it. It's a flying ant. She's a queen. She is migrating, with wings grown to expedite her transfer. One nest has been broken up to establish another, and she will be the nucleus—I don't know the entomology to a degree that would satisfy a scientist but that's how I read the symbolism. I don't need to be dreaming to recognise this, it's a wide-awake reflection, analogous to my own situation with the ashram—being sent out from one nest to start another.

I may have been cut off from the supportive context of *satsang* and the community of premies, but the synchronicity of the message impresses itself quietly in my mind, and my heart leaps to know that, in fact, I *have* been heard. The one consciousness that moves all things is, indeed, close and attentive, the silent witness to my every whispered need.

That night, for the first time, they leave me unattended. I am free to do a full formal meditation, undisturbed. Before I settle down to sleep I pray to be woken up in time to meditate again in the morning before I make my escape.

At dawn, I am roused by a single thunderclap. I sit up, happy to meditate again, enjoying the sweetness and light wafting up from within. I fold up the jumper they have lent me and leave it on the bed, slipping out a side door to make my way up to a main road. It is just after dawn and a light rain is falling.

As a devotee, I have a lot to learn about commitment, it seems, but I am not about to waste any more time re-hashing the past. I don't know where I am but, even if there's very little traffic this early in the day, this looks like a major road. Perhaps it is the highway to Sydney. With no money, some unabashed hitching is in order. I take a guess as to which side of the road I should stand on. While I am wondering what to do, a car drives past. Damn! Really, there's nothing to ponder. Just trust and do it. I stick out my thumb and the very next car pulls up to give me a ride.

'Where're you heading?' the driver asks. He's about thirty, with an honest face, and he doesn't seem to find it odd that a guy should be hitching a ride so early in the day, carrying not so much as knapsack. His nonchalant mood chimes perfectly with his passenger's own sense of freedom.

'Well, I don't really know where I am, but I'm trying to get to Sydney.'

'Oh, good,' the guy says, 'I'm going across the Harbour Bridge. Does that suit you?'

'Suit me? That's great. I need to find Riley Street, in Surry Hills.' I remember the address of the ashram from the telegram I sent to Bob Beaver. Maybe I can get a shower and a feed there.

'Riley Street? I'm going through Surry Hills, right up Riley Street. Would you believe it?' he asks, as he switches on the car radio.

'Would I ever? You bet your life I would!' I crow to myself, sinking back into the seat. A ride in altogether another car but, this time listening to a chirpy country song from the radio, I really am back in the flow.

18 Edmondstone Street

February 1973. Just after 7 am I enter the front door of the Riley Street ashram.

David Lovejoy is coming downstairs from meditation. 'Ah, you've arrived,' he says. David is now the national coordinator of the Mission's activities. 'That's good, Penny arrived last night, you can go on together.' What a coincidence.

There is a pile of jumble in a front room waiting to be sorted for fundraising. I pick out a spare pair of pants and Penny, the young actress from Perth, and I head to Brisbane the same day, with a five-dollar float. 'I wondered where you'd got to,' says Penny, and she recounts seeing a luxury saloon car with curtained windows drive by when she was hitching out of Melbourne.

The journey takes two days, with long waits between rides. I tell her the story of the queen ant, flying out to start another nest, and we laugh. Maybe my entomology is a little off; queens don't fly, do they? Whatever … I am back onto the path and the trusting connection with the inner source is firmly re-established.

Errol is already active in Brisbane and has been driving taxis to raise funds. Compared to the expressive theatrical types he finds himself among, Errol is laconic, with a sense of something held in reserve that often appears as a wry, dimpled grin that sets his blue eyes twinkling. He and Don are in a house in Spring Hill, but we need something with a big living room where we hope people might gather for *satsang*. We look at a place in West End and Penny negotiates a low rent with the landlord, a local greengrocer whom she immediately befriends. 'West End' sounds reasonably posh to me but in early 1973 it's a little downtrodden.

Don has gentle eyes and a melting smile and he is fearless about telling people they ought to come along to hear about the Knowledge. In her role as 'housemother', Penny comes into her own. Her pert, enquiring face reminds me of the finches my aunt and uncle used to breed. With brown button eyes and a petite beak of a nose, her lively curiosity is irrepressible and engaging. Wherever she goes she talks constantly about Maharaji and his Knowledge, whether at work (a couple of afternoons a

week in a health food store), or on the way there (she walks to town to
save money), on the way back to the Centre (The Divine Light Mission
on Edmonstone Street), and all points in between. From Perth, I
remember her as shy, but that reserve was present only when she mixed
with the intellectual push. Being housemother liberates her from any
residual feelings of inferiority and she becomes the mainstay of the whole
operation. What's more, she has been to India and has first-hand
experience of ashram living as it ought to be conducted. When in doubt,
she pores over the 'Ashram Manual', which we refer to jokingly as the
'Maha-Ashrama-Gita', for guidance.

Pretty soon, people start trickling in to hear about the young teacher
and his Knowledge. While still green in the experience—in Melbourne we
were the newbies—now *we* are the insiders, the ones 'in the know'. Night
and day, blissed out or not, willing or not, we are called on to give people
a sense of what is on offer.

That is quite a responsibility so, before speaking, we do *pranam*,
bowing before the picture of our teacher to ask for help. Rather than
speaking from some personal store of wisdom, you must empty yourself,
in a sense, to make yourself available. A sincere *pranam* opens an inner
gate of receptivity and, mysteriously, you find that you're not on your
own. To speak about the path is a service, too, and somehow the words
always come through. For the listeners, perhaps, it is their own need that
draws down the grace, like kittens pawing at their mother cat's belly to
bring milk to the teat.

Whatever happens to be puzzling me at the time, new arrivals have the
unerring tendency to ask about just that. Usually, I don't know where the
answer will go, yet by the time I finish speaking, they understand and I do,
too. This is not quite 'ordinary' reality. You call on the grace and it
responds. 'The heart has its laws that reason knows not of'– we've all read
our Blaise Pascal.

Ashram life is frugal; even more so than in Melbourne, and inspiration
must stay high on extremely slender material resources. Yet the more
stripped back we are, the less we can depend on anything but a simple,
radical trust. No television or movies to distract us, no books or
magazines, unless we manage to obtain reprints of our young master's
talks, or copies of a British premie paper, *The Divine Times*. There's little
food for the intellect, even less for the affections; and, initially at least,

there is not much food for the body, either. We live mostly on brown rice and salad, or home-made bread and salad. Penny goes to the greengrocer—our landlord—buying only one or two things, and he fills up the rest of a carton with fruit and vegetables that are too bruised or spoiled to sell. Already vegetarian, the diet isn't a stretch for me. Guys with bigger appetites usually fill up when they go out to work to raise the money to support our 'missionary' activities. As more and more people come to listen, a trickle of donations supplements the outworkers' hard-won funds. I eventually get a job in a downtown bookstore, selling educational books.

The first major service project for me is painting the old, capacious weatherboard house white, inside and out and this project continues as long as we can afford to buy paint and find willing hands to volunteer. I instigate a stylistic change from the regulation white and royal blue that has become the standard décor in other centres. 'Blue is for devotion,' explains Faith Day, a kind of *über*-housemother who rules from Sydney. Faith is a former fashion model who has changed her name to mark a change in values. She gave up her career and moved into an ashram in Goa to care for a charismatic mahatma. On Edmonstone Street we top the fresh white house with a sky blue roof. That makes quite a statement in West End at the time, but I feel the lighter colour is appropriate for sun-bleached Queensland.

We collect jumble, hoping to start a second-hand shop like our brothers and sisters in Sydney and Melbourne, but raising the additional rent for a shop-front and finding someone to manage it is beyond us initially, so one Saturday we advertise a free 'sale' at a church hall in the main street and give away everything we have collected to people in need. It becomes obvious that we should have a better manager for our funds. Eddie Corrigan, an expatriate Irishman with freckles, a ready smile and twinkling blue eyes, turns up to listen to *satsang* one night. Ed is inspired to stay on, and takes on the service of treasurer.

What we are attempting in one of the seedier suburbs of Brisbane, and in Cardigan Street and Brunswick Street in Melbourne, and Riley Street and Balmain in Sydney, is also being undertaken by devotees in other parts of the country, (Adelaide, Perth, and Hobart soon follow) and in Europe, Scandinavia, North and South America, Japan and Hong Kong.

Our daily routine has us up at 5.30 am, assembling in the living room to chant our *arati*:

Protector of the weary and the weak
You bring the death of attachment
Save us from the ocean deep
Jai Dev, Jai Satgurudev.

This is followed by the first formal meditation practice of the day. Evening meetings run for two to three hours. The deep listening practice of *satsang* is the best preparation for going within, for meditation is a form of listening, too. So, after an evening *arati*, we settle into the final formal meditation practice to bookend the day, putting aside all theory and listening deeply to the silence of the inner heart.

With this schedule, it is a struggle to get to sleep before midnight, and we are up again at 5.30. No matter how late it is, Penny will always continue working. I wonder some nights if she has slept at all, and feel guilty going to bed while she is still finding service to do. We sleep on the floor—the carpet is literally threadbare—and take comfort in bliss rather than mattresses.

One day Penny and I get into a disagreement but our argument is interrupted by the sound of two doves fighting under the mango tree in the back yard, which sends us into peals of laughter. This bizarre sight calls for more *satsang*, and the reason for our petty disagreement evaporates.

If our privations are blissful, they soon become more tightly wound. Across the road, where an old house sits on an elevated site, workers begin preparing for the construction of a hotel. It will be a large complex, featuring a drive-through bottle shop. The first job they tackle is to tear down the house, then they level the hill on which it has been sitting, and they take even more time excavating space for a basement, too. They begin work at dawn, six days a week, and continue well into the evening, often in overtime shifts. All these stages of preparation require the presence of an endless stream of tip-trucks, which line up from dawn at the kerb along the front fence of the ashram. The trucks wait their turn with engines idling, belching fumes. Chugging bulldozers noisily dislodge the earth into piles. Front-end loaders rattle incessantly, clanking heavy metal contact with the trucks receiving the rubble and excavated soil.

If I have imagined a cloistered life of quiet retreat, the busy sphere of mundane action presses up insistently against my naïve expectations of a life of sublime contemplation. When it comes to precious meditation time I learn the hard way where my focus needs to sit. If you want to become aware of the sweet sound of the Divine Harmony within your own being, it is less a matter of shutting out the world than it is about where you direct your attention. I need to go deeper. Rather than resisting the distraction, fighting against what is beyond my control, a kind of letting go serves to bring one closer, inside. Moreover, the cacophonous din proves gross and relatively easy to ignore, compared to the sly manoeuvres of one's own endlessly distractible mind, which is what I really have to confront. It will be many months later, when all shreds of resistance and resentment have been chipped away, the hotel is complete and the trucks departed, that I feel the work going on in the so-called 'external' world perfectly matches an 'inner' process.

the distillate of peace

Drink the sweet honey that steeps the petals of the lotus of the heart.
—Kabirdas

One morning, the ashram is clear of people by 8am. I have nothing else to do until 10am, when I have arranged to meet some associates in town— premies who are travelling with the touring cast of the musical *Hair*. Because of the show's performance schedule, they find it difficult to hook up with the nightly meetings and they are glad to meet with fellow devotees whenever the chance presents.

I go back into the meditation room, returning to a process that I am by now often reluctant to leave.

The room is spartan. There are no chairs. The only decoration is a small, low altar covered with a plain white cloth. A spray of flowers sits in a jar next to my teacher's image. I close the door, pull up a cushion from the pile in the corner and settle in for another session. But first, I do pranam before the photo. It's a gesture of submission. However it might look to an observer, this formal practice of deference helps me to locate, among the myriad possible responses, a simple sincerity within my heart; stripped of sophistication, irony and ego; simple enough to ask for help.

I double up the cushion under my rump, pull my legs into a lazy half-lotus posture and drape a light shawl over my head and shoulders. It's like going into my private cave. I use the techniques to bring my attention back home, as I have done a hundred times before, finding myself slipping into a more comfortable accommodation with deep inner space. When I am busy *doing*, this inner space all but disappears, but when I stop doing and pay attention, *being* may begin to reveal its depths.

The first technique slows me down considerably, my physiology shifting into a quieter gear. The second technique opens me into a cavernous, ringing void so profound that it is pure freedom to just breathe, relaxing the little sphincter of self into the infinite darkness. Webs of sound glisten and spin, drawing me away from the need to think. A quiet pearly glow suffuses the darkness.

Each successive cycle of breath invites me into a state of deeper trust and, through that trust, into a gradual surrender of my entire being to what is welling up within. One after another, subtle knots unravel, and with each little letting go I am carried further into the expansive centre of being, floating loose on sweet eddies of breath. My deep thirst for peace is being quenched, and gratitude deepens the absorption.

Usually it is thought and its attendant complexes of feeling that suck up all the available energy, holding attention locked outside the profound peace secreted at the core of being. Today, I find it easy to leave the little self behind—knitted together as it is with little obsessions, clutched close with fear. Now, when thoughts come knocking for attention, it is as if there is no one home to answer.

Sitting through the final technique, the whole experience coalesces into a deep stillness that flows out to permeate every part of being. It would be more of an effort to move away than to have to bring my focus back. Inside, outside—it's all the same. No place. Infinite space. A peace beyond all understanding.

An hour later, I bow in gratitude to the photo of my teacher, fold the shawl and place the cushion back in the corner. I call out to Penny:

'I'm going to see the guys at the theatre.'

'Here, take them some *prasad*.' Penny wraps treats offered at the altar from the previous night. 'Give Lindsay my *jai satchitanand*, won't you.' One of the men in the cast, Lindsay Field, a handsome musician from New Zealand, was initiated the same day as we were, and there is an almost sibling bond among the three of us.

I find a pair of shoes to slip on, click shut the door and begin the walk into town. The stillness stays with me all the way to the theatre. I am a deep ocean of peace that nothing can disperse.

Reaching the theatre I enter through the stage door, but the cast are still working through part of a rehearsal. Lindsay grabs a moment to come over and asks if I wouldn't mind waiting. With nothing else to do, as the rehearsal continues, I close my eyes, sitting in the darkened stalls, happy to ride the waves of breath back home.

Gradually I become aware of a thick, beautiful taste collecting in my mouth and throat and, as I swallow, I wonder what I might have eaten this morning that could have left such a lingering sweetness. Did Penny add some of her stash of dates to the muesli? But this is nothing I have ever eaten. The more I stay with the stillness, the more the sensation thickens. It's as though the entire experience of peace has distilled itself into a subtle liquid that emanates not so much from my physiology—it collects within my mouth, for sure, and I can swallow it, but it is not something I have tasted before—the essence of the bliss realm itself. 'Surely it will go away,' I assume, and continue with the practice. But it doesn't, it is a constant. Even as I chatter with Lindsay and the others after they break from the rehearsal, whether I am talking or listening it is there. Rather than me clutching after it, the experience itself holds me in its embrace.

I walk back to the ashram, and all along the route I continue to enjoy the intensely blissful sensation. When I begin the evening meal I think, 'Surely it will stop now,' but it doesn't. It is present with me all through the evening meeting and when I wake the next morning, it's still there, holding me close to joy.

If you have 'an experience' on the path, you're supposed to keep it to yourself. It's considered bad form to talk about it, especially if it sounds like boasting. More than that, 'states' are transitory affairs and yesterday's experience in meditation doesn't help today's practice—you must always begin at the beginning. The important thing for me at this stage was to notice that whenever I put a sustained brake on endless doing, then being herself might start to reveal her hidden treasures. How did I—*why* did I ?—before this time, construct a life so completely away from this perfectly natural centre? And what happens to a society that insists on living in willful ignorance of these deeper, quieter blessings?

holy company

Soon we get news of a mahatma's impending arrival in Brisbane. Aspirants who have been waiting months for initiation have provided much of the voluntary people-power to keep things running, and with their dedicated assistance we have opened centres in other towns in Queensland and northern New South Wales.

Our teacher has sent out a young monk in saffron robes to supervise activities Down Under. We all travel to Adelaide to meet him at our first national gathering: a celebratory 'Guru Puja' festival, in July 1973. Mahatma Ji (the 'ji' is respectful) as we call him, is like a junior brother to the blissful Charananand who initiated me in Melbourne. The new arrival is known as Padarthanand (they all have the 'anand'—meaning 'bliss'— appended to their titles).

The young monk gets off an international flight in Sydney and David Lovejoy immediately hauls him off to a press conference, before boarding a connecting flight to Adelaide the same day. With little sleep, the new mahatma is plunged into a round of public talks, questions and answers, and meetings with the dozens of aspirants who have gathered from the different centres around the country. At first, his English is limited and strongly accented, but it is a relief for us to listen to testimony from someone who has been with Maharaji and has been given the *agya*, or authorisation, to speak on his behalf. The premies listen to his talks just as eagerly as the new arrivals, drinking up the inspiration.

It doesn't take long for Mahatma Ji to start bending his second language to his needs. As he travels from centre to centre, housemother Faith Day—a stalwart devotee trained in the Indian manner—travels ahead of him to set up kitchens and train the local housemothers (some of whom are men) in the proper procedures of Indian cuisine, and strictly implements the codes of cleaning and caring for the holy man. As national coordinator, David Lovejoy usually accompanies him.

'Wherever I go, Faith travels before, and Love and Joy follow on behind,' the mahatma says, as pleased as we are with his play on words.

In Brisbane, we are trying to get ready to host a visit on our own. We need a thousand dollars and a car. The money is for hall hire, audio-visual equipment, newspaper advertising for his talks, and so on. We also need to fix a broken-down toilet in the ashram. If we could get a car we would use it not only to take him to events in hired halls in Brisbane, but out to the centres we have founded at Coolangatta on the Gold Coast, Nambour on the Sunshine Coast, and in northern New South Wales, in the 'tidy town' of Mullumbimby.

'Oh, don't worry about fixing the toilet for the mahatma,' one newcomer advises, 'he's Indian. Don't you know how primitive conditions are over there?' But Penny has too much love and respect for the Master's representative to settle for the lowest common denominator. His tireless representative never demands anything for himself but we feel it a privilege to provide for him that which, sometimes, we have not supplied for our own needs. Tapping in to the source of peace inside, you realise how little, in a material sense, you really need to be happy. 'Plain living and high thinking' becomes one of the first mottos we pick up from our new instructor. Anyhow, most of the early arrivals are unreconstructed hippies, so the ideologies tend to mesh.

'How do you pay for things?' is the first question many people ask. Everything is funded by a combination of money raised from outside jobs, and voluntary donations from people who attend the evening meetings and want to help. There is no charge for initiation, unlike the Transcendental Meditation technique on offer, for a fee, and we are rather proud of that.

Just when the need for more money becomes evident, a Canadian chap walks in the front door, sits down to listen, likes what he hears and decides to stay. He asks if there is anything he can do to help. He tells Eddie Corrigan that he has just received an insurance payout of a thousand dollars and has been wondering what to do with it. Would that be of any help? It fits the budget, exactly. A Dutch auto mechanic who fixes broken-down vehicles in his spare time, arrives the next night. Suddenly, we have the car to ferry the Mahatma around, as well as the cash we need to host his visit.

Mahatma Padarthanand is a handsome young man with a University degree, a slightly limited command of English but an astonishing capacity to learn, and ready to share what he knows. He soon wins our respect and admiration. If I thought that enlightenment was a transcendental, other-worldly experience, Mahatma Ji is pre-eminently practical. Rather than teaching us to become neo–Hindus, he has the knack of always focusing his understanding on the situation at hand. 'Everything according to time, place and situation,' he recommends.

He is soon making more puns in his second tongue. 'Are you a saint?' one young woman wants to know. 'No, I am not a cent, I am a dollar,' he explains with a straight face. While we ponder whether or not he is a realised soul, he gives practical advice on everything—from washing the kitchen floor and preparing food, to advertising and setting up the events. He shows young mothers how to massage their babies, Indian-style, winning his way into the hearts of people all over Australia.

When Padarthanand does Knowledge sessions, as the local coordinator I am often allowed to sit in. Since my initiation with Charananand I have had nothing to go on but my own practice and it is fascinating to watch and participate in the instruction as the mahatma's assistant. At first it's simple: Padarthanand has me read out extracts he has collected from the scriptures, which refer specifically to each of the techniques, but before long he demands more of me. He asks me to recommend the people whom I think are 'ready' for initiation. 'You know these people,' he says. 'You've seen them longer than I have, what do you think? If they receive Knowledge, will they practise?'

Not wanting to arouse resentment, I don't really want the responsibility of making a selection, giving some the green light and asking others to wait. Mahatma Ji invariably melts at the first sign of a tear, and tends to initiate them, anyway, regardless of my recommendations. When I complain about this, Padarthanand tells me: 'What can I do? Maharaji has made my heart like butter.' And I melt, too.

So we develop this 'good cop, bad cop' routine. I offer my considered opinion, based on whatever logic seems appropriate—how long have they been listening to *satsang*? Do they still smoke dope? Are they here just out of curiosity, or do they have a genuine thirst?—and the mahatma decides, leaving me to cop the flak.

It is not that we intend to refuse anyone the opportunity of initiation, but it does seem important that new arrivals be given a chance to listen for a while and understand what kind of commitment might be involved with continuing a long-term daily practice. I had waited several weeks before I received initiation in Melbourne and many of the newcomers are in the same situation that I was, expecting the instant results you'd get from dropping a tab of LSD, or ingesting magic mushrooms. Some have a head full of ideas from Theosophy, or want to argue theology. The disciplined inner focusing requires sustained attention over time, as well as a lifestyle that will support and focus the practice and, as they're not all going to want to move into an ashram, it seems doubly important that they understand what kind of effort is required.

If the mahatma instructs someone too soon, we local devotees are the ones who have to live with the consequences. Some want to smoke dope in *satsang*, others can barely wait to set up shop as teachers themselves, even before they have learned to be students. Still, I am reluctant to be seen evaluating another's sincerity. In the preparatory satsangs we tend to use the parable from Jesus about what happens to a farmer's seed that falls by the wayside, or on stony ground. Only the seed that falls on ground that has been prepared properly by the farmer—cleared of the proverbial rocks and weeds—will find the conditions it needs for growth.

'What did Jesus say? "The kingdom of heaven is like a tiny mustard seed." This Knowledge is just a seed. You must plant it and water it with your practice, protect it with your dedication and bring it to life with your faith, and then it will bring you such gifts as you can only dream of,' the mahatma explains with his customary quiet assurance.

If Padarthanand spots a failing in me, he isn't averse to bringing it to my attention. In the Indian fashion, he doesn't pronounce the English 'V' sound clearly; it tends to come out softer; usually as a 'W'; so my name becomes 'Wik' instead of 'Vic'.

'*Wii-iik,*' he calls out, playing with the diphthong. '*Wii-iik* … Are you *weaaak*, or are you *strong!*'

He asks the meaning of my name. 'Victor' isn't hard to explicate, but it takes a little longer to describe the meaning of the family name, which is basically a 'swamp'. Padarthanand smiles as though I have revealed the secret code that unlocks my personal *dharma*.

'You see,' he says, 'the roots of the lotus are in the mud, but its flower blooms above the muddy water. Victory. Your higher nature conquers your lower nature.' QED. But Mahatma Ji knows, better than anyone, that real growth takes time. I am intensely aware of falling short of that kind of 'victory' and wriggle with discomfort as the Mahatma puts his finger on my dilemma. I'm too aware of the *weak*ness. If the ashram is a supportive environment, it is not a guarantee against the 'lower nature'. Even here you have to be clear about your goal and make the choice, every day, to go towards it, or other interests can take you away. The opportunities for service and the constant *satsang* keep me at the task and protect me from the lazier options on offer, like smoking dope, dropping mushrooms, sleeping around. The ashram shelters me by keeping these grosser options at bay.

'It's like a science experiment,' I explain to a newcomer. 'In an experiment you are trying to concentrate on a particular process. To really focus on that, you have to eliminate the variables. That's how this lifestyle helps me. I can put these things on hold, not out of some wowser morality—after all, I have always done whatever I wanted—but to bring a deeper experience into focus. This is always a voluntary process. It's not the ashram rules that keep me here—I could leave tomorrow. But I have tasted so much already that I would be a fool to turn away now.'

aquarius redux

May 1973. We travel south into New South Wales, to Nimbin, for the second Aquarius Festival. Nimbin will soon be famous as the locus of experimental, commune-style living and create a stir in the lush farming country in the hinterland, out past the conservative country town of Lismore. For our temporary abode we erect two geodesic domes, clad in yellow canvas—one for the evening *satsang* and another as our sleeping quarters. As a service project, we help dig latrines for the use of all comers. We also take the chance to tell as many people as we can get to listen that there is a young Master alive on the planet today and he can show 'The Way'.

Onstage, under a fat full moon, Kim O'Leary sings:

Our soul is like a white bird of freedom
Its genesis was long before the Garden of Eden
But it's trapped inside these man-made walls
Of ego separation
Singing to our tired minds
The song of liberation.
Oh, how this bird longs to fly
Its wingspan would cover the sky
Please let these walls tumble down
Please let this white bird be found …

I have come a long way from the first Aquarius Festival in Canberra, just two years ago, when I thought that psychedelics were *The Way*. In the lush pasturelands of northern New South Wales, potent weed is on offer and, in the farmers' fields surrounding the festival site, magic mushrooms offer another frame of reference entirely, one that I left behind somewhere near Canberra. I find it easy to decline invitations to get back on that particular roller coaster, for I remember too well the lessons of 'coming down' to abandon the deep peace I have discovered within my own heart. My teacher speaks about two trains running alongside one another—both seem to be going in the same direction, but pretty soon, one track runs out. Which train do you want to be on? Someone defends his drug use saying, 'But this is how I came to you!' And he says to them: 'So you came to this hall in a car today, right? But did you try to bring the car inside?'

Yet not all is how I would wish it. I have been practising Knowledge for a year and, still, I have never seen my teacher in person, only an assortment of photographs. When a film with the title *Satguru Has Come*, including footage of him as a boy, tours through Brisbane, I watch it over and over, in tears.

To this point, my commitment to the practice is based on the peace I feel in *satsang* and the experiences that come up out of the deep stillness of the meditation practice. To work alongside this mahatma is another great encouragement—the monk's pragmatic wisdom inspires me in new ways on every visit. But Mahatma Ji's focus is on the Master, who is his inspiration, and even though by now I do feel allegiance to the same figure, I have had no direct personal experience of him.

One night I dream of his father, Shri Hans ji Maharaj. He is on top of a hill, playing with a bunch of saffron-robed mahatmas. He comes over to the side of the hill where I am perched and looks down into my face, gazing all the way into my heart. From him I feel the kind of love and acceptance I never felt with my own father.

'If you want to know who I am, you need to know who *you* are,' Maharaji has said, and it is true that to connect with this deep field of peace within does satisfy that quest. But I follow a living teacher and I wonder about being grateful to someone I haven't met.

Moves are afoot to remedy the situation, and it will be Padarthanand who is instrumental in facilitating my first face-to-face encounter with my golden boy guru.

first sight

November 1973. 'Send up the six Australians.' The security guy nods to us as the message crackles through his walkie-talkie. Padarthanand has gone ahead—he must have worked his magic to gain access for us, too. We're on the ground floor of the Astroworld Hotel in Houston, Texas. There's an outside elevator reserved exclusively for the 'Celestial Suite'— the ultra-VIP level of the hotel. Texans like to boast they have the biggest and therefore the best of everything, not just in the country, but the whole Universe, apparently. I know at least one person who will be enjoying the joke.

It's November 1973. The American devotees have hired a huge football stadium, the Astrodome, for a three-day celebration with Maharaji. A chartered planeload of Aussies has come to join the celebration. The 'Dome is the largest undercover stadium in the country, and the push has been on to fill it with people for the 'Millennium Festival', whatever that might be. A little early, perhaps, for the turn of the Ages but, to a generation who have seen the dawning of a new age of brother- and sister-hood, it's perfect timing.

Meanwhile, in the weeks leading up to the big event, a cascade of street parades—quixotically named 'Soul Rush'—has been moving from city to city, enjoining the locals to come to Houston. I am impressed to hear that Rennie Davis, one of my heroes, is attending. Davis, a member of the Chicago Seven—political activists whose protests during the 1968 Democratic National Convention in Chicago led to their 'trial for conspiracy to incite riot and protest'—is also a follower of Maharahji, and his presence as a spokesperson at the Millemium helps bring attention and wide media coverage to the event. The mood is abuzz with heady myth-making; rumours swirl. A comet named Kohoutek is about to appear in the skies over planet Earth and credulous, blissed-out premies speculate that the Astrodome itself could actually levitate, with all this cosmic energy brewing—'Kohoutek', in their reading, stands for **K.O., Hou**-ston, **Tek**-sas'.

Until now, we simple folk from 'Down Under', guided by our pragmatic elder brother, Padarthanand, have been far from the eye of the storm, with little exposure to the phenomenal energy emanating from the person of our young teacher. Our devotion is more rooted in actual meditation practice than in the kind of cosmic rumour-mongering we pick up on in these here parts. I've been practising assiduously for more than a year.

Beyond the premie bliss-field, America is reeling. The clash between the idealistic youth culture—its music, its politics, its drugs of choice—and those of the conservative Establishment has sent powerful shock waves across a divided nation, propelling a disillusioned yet idealistic generation into the same kind of search I have been on, yearning for a social, political and economic order which they could hold in more respect. Until then, they are withholding committing their energy wholeheartedly to the body politic. Vietnam is still a war zone, and Laos is being bombed (unofficially) to smithereens. The CIA has been involved in covert operations in Chile to bring down the democratically elected Allende government. Earlier, in San Francisco, protestors slipped flowers into the rifle barrels of the guards, urging them to 'Make Love, not War', but the love-in has soured after violence at a concert featuring the Rolling Stones where heavy dudes handling security go too far.

There is a sense of outrage among decent, law-abiding Americans who don't understand why these youngsters can't just do what they are told. But ostensibly peaceful protests have met with violence—members of the Ohio National Guard have shot dead students protesting at Kent State University, following President Nixon's authorisation to invade Cambodia. This led to a strike of more than a million students nationwide, trying to close universities. To the young, age is no longer simply a guarantee of wisdom, and to the old—the generation who fought in Europe and the Pacific to bring peace, during WWII—youth has traded its innocence and obedience for obnoxious protest. But what kind of peace is it that requires going to war with foreign countries that pose no threat?

Religions, too, have been under scrutiny, their moral teachings challenged by a new generation's embrace of the sexual revolution and, in an increasingly secularised society, getting high on drugs has substituted for access to a lost realm of mystical experience.

With the values of previous generations crumbling, perhaps these wise men from the East have something to say. Maharaji has been interviewed on television talk shows. But he isn't an old fellow, with white hair and a long grey beard—he is still a teenager.

Earlier today I found my way with a few other Aussies to a house where Maharaji's mother, Shri Mata Ji, is staying. The Holy Mother gave a stern talk about how it is her young son who has succeeded in getting a generation of young hippies off drugs, when the combined forces of parents, the police and the legislature have signally failed. That's not exactly how she put it, but I get the message (in translation) and in my case, it's certainly true.

The ever-resourceful Carol Page has commandeered a car and a driver to get us across town from our meeting with Mata Ji to this big hotel near the stadium in the hope we might get to meet Maharaji in person. And Padarthanand has been trying to wrangle an opportunity for this random band of Aussies to meet him in a much more intimate setting than the cavernous expanse of the Astrodome.

Already a throng of devotees is camped out in the hotel lobby after news leaked that the young teacher is in residence here. 'No one else has been allowed up all day, not even the President of the Mission,' the security guard says, shaking his head, when we arrive with Padarthanand. But, of all the fervent requests made to go up to the suite, it is our small band who get the nod. It's not as if I have plotted or planned for this, others have made all the moves; it is a matter of being in the right place at the right time. Coincidence.

We emerge from the elevator on the penthouse level of the hotel where a stream of music is flowing along the hallway towards us. We follow the sound into a sitting room where the young Master turns to welcome us from his piano stool—he was the source of the music we followed. We settle on the carpet, eyes fixed on the figure at the piano. He is just a few weeks short of his sixteenth birthday.

He is the one who has brought this potent meditation practice to the thirsty hearts of my generation of young seekers, but everything about him seems to be designed to turn the usual set of expectations on its head. There's nothing 'usual' about all this. When has it happened before? What in our parents' lives, or in our own cultural history, has prepared us for this unprecedented encounter; what expectations could have prefigured this event? He is an original, all-new phenomenon and he is too young even to grow a beard.

Photos have never captured the exact colour of his skin, which glows a pearly gold, a kind of blend of all the races. From the back of the group I stare, thirsty to drink in every second of his presence. (How can eyes be thirsty? drink?) I find myself relaxing into the sheer pleasure of being with him as I watch and listen to his interactions with the others. His every gesture, utterance and response is enlivened with a supple joy and at the same time, at his core there's a deep and powerful stillness.

When I look at him, there is the sheer beauty—the caramel smoothness of his skin, the deep black hair, the lustrous pink of his nails, the overall contours of form: how smooth the joints between hands, wrists and forearms are, and the almost geodesic roundness in the planes of his face. If I were to play that game: what kind of animal does he resemble? I always come to the same conclusion—he's a dolphin; a young, golden dolphin.

He plays with the other premies who know him well enough to be familiar with the interaction. David Lovejoy has known him for years; met him in India—was it 1970? I am mute. I feel an ineffable tenderness behind the banter, a deep, edgeless gentleness in his manner. But above all, at his centre, something or someone floats free, like a ship's compass floating in oil. And whether he's playing or still, he sees you, even when he's not, apparently, looking.

During the anxious days at University I used to search out the gaze of people walking towards me on the footpaths. I was probing for a pair of eyes that could look back with knowing. A thousand and one attitudes were returned, of course; everything from hostility to indifference; even confidence. Could I have described the response that would have answered my inchoate question, pin-pointed precisely which vibration would lock into the synaptic receptors of my dizzy brain to score the Eureka response that I was seeking? In the Freemasons Lodge my father rebuked me for that very tendency to probe the eyes of the other Masons, testing their experience. I wanted to know: 'Do they know the meaning of what they are saying … or are they just remembering their lines?' Although I was inclined to challenge authority, this was not merely impudent activity but it had become a reflex, automatic impulse. Some of the senior members—Past Masters who occupied seats in a section of the Lodge—could meet my gaze with impressive *gravitas*, but that wasn't what I was seeking. Did all the pomp and ceremony indicate a tradition that really held the secrets of being and knowing?

Perhaps if I had gone through a dozen more Lodge initiations I might have found my answer. Perhaps I hadn't discovered the one book at Adyar that would answer my relentless question, or rather, my existential need. Perhaps that priest at Randwick racecourse was having a bad day. Perhaps he was rattled by my manic intensity. Perhaps I was going too fast to receive the kind of help he could give. Here, with my young Master, I come to a full stop. His powerful, gentle love receives and absorbs my yearning intensity with ease, and returns my heart to me, quenched, instructed, profoundly satisfied and mysteriously energised. It's like the feeling of basking in the sun, but it's for the whole self.

Just to be with him, sitting quietly in a hotel suite somewhere in Texas, is the most exciting thing I could do in the whole world.

When it's time to go, I wait for the others to pay their respects; not used to the formal conventions, I need to watch for cues. Then, before leaving the suite, I stretch out my body before the young master, full-length along the floor, not even touching his feet. I know, in every cell of my being, that I want to find a way to be of service him. To bring this quality of deep, realised peace into people's lives would be a good cause to dedicate a life to; and it would be worth a life to help him. For the first time I feel I have made a real choice, from out of my authentic being, even if that is a paradox—that the choice is to surrender to a teacher.

I'm moving down the hallway towards the elevator. Padarthanand dances alongside, saying: 'You see? You see?' My feet are hundreds of miles below, supported by softly springing clouds. I blink at the mahatma as if to say, 'Yes, yes. Of *course* I see …' but I am inside too deep to be able, let alone to want to respond in words. Wherever it is he has put me, I want to stay there. This joy is complete fulfillment.

the eye at the centre

A sensible man prefers the inner to the outer eye
—*Tao Te Ching*

'If you find yourself pointing the finger at someone else, remember that there are three fingers pointing back at you', Mahatma Ji advised us. In this environment the reality of that simple piece of advice can became almost unbearably acute. Ashram life is crowded. As a kind of boot camp in consciousness, as basic training in right relationship, it is very thorough.

In order to get butter you have to churn milk. In these group houses you find yourself thrust together with people you might not otherwise have chosen to hang out with and, naturally, you can find some of them irritating. And if there is someone among the blissed-out *premies* who really gets your goat—it's uncanny—that very person will be the one you have to share a bedroom with, or work with on a service project, and it seems like you'll be pushed up against them until the irritation passes. And in this pressure cooker the very person who gives you the pip during the day will, inevitably, be asked to speak that night and share what is happening for them.

It's not as if anyone is meddling fiendishly behind the scenes to arrange these encounters; it is the inevitable result of a genuine stirring of consciousness. *Satsang*—the company of truth—forms the foundation for community in the wider sense and I am being forced to learn to listen with respect for the stories of each other's heart. Only in the heart zone do you find the point of unity, the space to feel together, breathe together, live together. If this were solely a path of meditation you might feel you were becoming enlightened and that could make you feel rather impressed with yourself. But all these others have been given access, too, even those you find obnoxious. These people are on hand to test your real progress every day, in every way. The only appropriate relationship is one of deep respect, until the sense of 'other' is more and more erased. Whether shy or confident, having to speak the truth of the heart's perspective becomes the great leveler and, as each recounts his or her story, you fall in love with love itself, as it is revealed through the first-hand testimony of devotion.

As other communities start to take root outside of Brisbane, I travel with Penny in a draughty Mini-Moke to share *satsang* with people gathering in the new centres. On a visit south to a rambling house in Coolangatta we spend an evening in *satsang* with some twenty folk there and on the next morning we continue south, towards Mullumbimby and Byron Bay. We stop *en route* for a break where the road crosses a creek, and clamber down to sit on flat ground that surrounds a rock-pool.

I settle comfortably into an impromptu practice, allowing my attention to fall back inside. The natural setting makes it easy to let go. Human 'doing' lets go, to recover 'human being'. Thinking is doing, too, and that, too, falls away. Instead of 'I am Victor' or 'I am meditating', all the predicates go, leaving just 'I am'. That, too, falls in turn, surrendering to the simplest essence underlying all. 'I' folds into 'am' and there is nobody home.

Before Victor was, this is.

After half an hour or so, as 'I' re-emerges, it is with the clear feeling that I could come back as that rock, or that tree, or the bird, or my fellow traveler, or the water; and this deeper level of awareness is the primal embrace which holds everything in love. Peace fills me with its nectar.

True, I don't always go so deep. But I know I am home when I make contact with this Self-beyond-self, where I hold no need to justify my life, or prove anything for anyone else's edification.

Padarthanand comes to town and is in great demand. I grab the chance to listen greedily as he fields questions during an all-day *satsang* for newcomers and aspirants. We are staying in a second ashram, in Hill End, one with a larger living room to accommodate the growing numbers. There's a small bedroom off the living room that is kept for the use of visiting instructors. At the end of the day, I bail up Padarthanand in his room, wanting to add my own needy question to the long list that he has been responding to all day. The young monk is always such a reliable source of wisdom and good sense.

I find him sitting on the end of the bed. He is visibly tired, but I press on with my question, regardless.

Doggedly practising the techniques twice daily, as required by the ashram routine, I have been troubled by a niggling doubt, fostered not so much about the obvious benefits that accrue but because of what I've heard about others' sensational experiences in meditation. I have started to feel that my own practice must be lacking in some important way. The Bhagavad Gita describes a light 'brighter than a thousand suns'. Is my so-called 'third' eye slow to open? I am often there to assist whenever the Mahatma instructs in the Knowledge sessions, so I have heard the basic instructions for the techniques over and over again, but I want some follow-up advice about my own personal practice.

'Why do you want to see light?' he inquires. That throws me.

'Well, I thought I was supposed to,' I could have replied but, instead, I grope for something that sounds worthier, holier perhaps than mere envy.

'Why, to … purify me?' That sounds like a reasonable proposition.

'Do you think that is what will make you pure, seeing the light?' The young monk pauses but the querulous seeker fails to come up with an answer. The monk rocks his head on his neck in that peculiarly Indian manner.

'Look around you,' Padarthanand continues, with a tilt of his nose indicating the very room where we are sitting. What? I don't get it.

'Do you remember what a big mess this place was in when you started fixing up the house?'

During the various stages of the renovation process we used this room to store all the tools, paint pots and debris, and it was the very last part of the house to be fixed.

'And how is it now?' The timber tongue and groove walls are painted a lovely, buttery cream, the door frames are trimmed in white; calico curtains soften the light and a thick carpet covers the floors. It isn't plush, it's simple, but the whole place glows as if the hours of work poured into it by volunteers have imbued it with love.

'It used to be a mess, right? And now it is so clean and beautiful; suitable for his devotees to gather and sing his praises … What was it that transformed this place, what made it so pure and beautiful?'

'Why … service,' I admit.

'That's right.'

The young monk hardly needs to spell out the lesson. I could go on practising the techniques for years, trying to train my mind into perfect, yogic, one-pointed stillness, as if using the fierce concentration of my 'inner eye' would bring the Divine into focus, by force of will. But even great yogis have had trouble doing it that way. 'Service is the accelerator on this path', I recall Maharaji saying.

Sometimes they call it 'selfless service' to make the lesson clear. Like 'karma yoga', the path of purifying action—action that, instead of perpetuating karma, works to erase it. I know from my own limited experience what it can achieve in taking me beyond my little self. And here is this dear man, who works all day and every night to inspire us all—a spaced-out bunch of former hippies, mostly—into a focused life. I am the one who should be helping him, and I am petulantly asking for more. Could it be selfish to crave enlightenment?

Padarthanand explains that we are accustomed to defining an 'ashram' as a 'shelter'; a place for weary souls to withdraw, to find rest: a kind of 'retreat', in a sense. He makes a telling distinction, unpacking the meaning of the root words that make up this term we use every day. In Sanskrit '*ā*' means 'come to', the monk expounds; '*sram*' means 'to make effort'. This is the place where you 'come and work hard'.

The real lesson is the Mahatma's own example.

So, I never really need to ask about the practice again. I have been trying to bring my mind into one-pointed focus as an act of the will, when it is in fact my entire being which is being harnessed and re-trained. The different aspects of the practice—the *satsang*, the service, and the meditation (with some meetings with the Master himself, if you're lucky)—conspire to weave the complex strands of human being together into one, overriding purpose. Eventually I will come to understand that the experience grows at its own pace as I patiently weed and water the garden. Along the way, there are 'highs' (or depths), to be sure—some of immeasurable, uncontainable bliss—but, most of all, the inner focusing brings up for review the real condition of one's mind from day to struggling day.

Somehow, these lessons come into intensely high relief whenever the mahatma comes to town.

a shock to the system

May 1974. News reaches us that Maharaji has married. He is still young—
a teenager—and he weds an American devotee from San Diego, named
Marolyn. This causes consternation in some circles. The press, for
example, finds it strange that the teacher should marry while many of the
devotees are renunciates.

This won't be the first time that he makes a change that shakes up our
expectations. Some of the devotees decide it is time to get married, too,
and leave. For them, the ashram has done its job and they move on to the
next stage of their individual lives. His own father was a householder, and
fulfilled his role perfectly. But his mother, Mataji, whom I heard speak in
Houston, is rumoured to be upset that her youngest son has not followed
tradition by marrying an Indian girl that she would select for him.

In Australia, I am far removed from such internecine squabbles, and I
don't find it more strange than anything else I have encountered. Even
from a distance, there is a lovely symmetry in the marriage for me: the
guru has married a devotee and, in that union, East and West have been
conjoined too. I note with delight that—across the International Date
Line—the wedding has taken place on May 20th. For that date in the US is
already May 21st in Oz, and that's my birthday! We don't take such
occasions too seriously in the ashram, but it's a symbolic personal
reinforcement.

For me, the ashram is still a wonderfully focused environment.
Looking on, others might call it 'disciplined', even austere, but being
saturated in peace a great deal of the time is quite a different order of
experience and I have no desire to throw aside the assistance that the
structured environment lends me. Were I to leave now, what would I get
into; and what would that imply about my choice to leave my partner and
baby? Other premies prefer a more pragmatic style and sometimes satirise
me as a 'gopi' (one of the milkmaids enchanted by Krishna's play). It's
obvious that devotion takes many varied forms. Looking around it seems
obvious that Maharaji is capable of working with students of very
different temperaments and styles and that he will often change gear in
taking us through unexpected changes. 'If you have had me up on a

pedestal,' he says, 'be aware that I've jumped off that and kicked it over.'
There are many such shifts to come and most will shake up some
unconscious expectations we have been carrying. He's not creating an
institution for the future, nor a particular set of doctrines; and the most
cherished of 'eternal verities' will be subject to scrutiny, one way or
another.

I have made my choice. This environment is still serving to take me
deeper. So I stay and enter wholeheartedly into the process of
transformation.

Late at night the ashram phone rings insistently until it drags me up from
sleep. Penny has already taken the call and calls me to the phone.

'Divine Light Mission … this is Vic,' I answer blearily.

'Hello Vic, this is David Lovejoy, in Sydney. I know it's late, but we
just had a call from the States. Marolyn is in labour and we have been
invited to be in meditation during the birth. People all over the world will
be joining in. A phone tree has swung into action. Will you call everyone
you can in Queensland and invite them to participate?'

I start rousing the others while Penny makes a few calls to pull the
phone tree into action in our region. Through the rest of the night we
meditate and the next day we hear that a daughter has been born and that
she has been named 'Premlata'. 'Prem' is the same root word for 'love'—
as in our teacher's own personal name—and 'lata' means 'vine'. The
Master has used the marriage and the family to symbolically enact his
relationship with his premies. He has married a devotee, and when it is
time for the birth of the child of their union, he has found a way for us all
to participate, bound together in conscious meditation, internationally, by
a 'vine of love'.

The press scratches its collective head and mocks the antics of the
controversial young guru, but my devotee heart is deeply touched.

In 1974, the city is inundated as the Brisbane River reclaims its flood
plains. Train services are cut and the airport is closed. We are lucky to be
trapped with Mahatma Padarthanand. People come to *satsang* nonetheless
and some of them volunteer for the citywide clean-up operations. The
mood of the city goes through distinct shifts and the release of service
energy among the people leads to a kind of elation as people volunteer to

clean out the mud from the houses of complete strangers. But the mood drops precipitously as homeowners return and it darkens as they start to negotiate with insurance companies, if they are covered at all. Some lose everything. Having very little is in itself a kind of protection. The highest point the flood reaches as it moves up Melbourne Street is the back fence of the ashram and we feel protected, in a very tangible way.

After two years in Brisbane I am transferred to Sydney, into a communications role on the national staff. In the intervening two years, as we have opened centres in several parts of Queensland, hundreds of people have 'received Knowledge', as it is called. The same has been happening in other states. There are centres in all of the major cities around Australia, all staffed by volunteers. There is also a national monthly newspaper. One of my jobs on the national staff is to start a service organisation, the World Welfare Association, to make use of the excess of service energy that we have tapped into from a thousand eager beavers in the various centres. People donate time to give guitar lessons in psychiatric hospitals, others arrange picnics at old folks' homes, cooking in soup kitchens, dances in half-way houses and even Knowledge sessions in prisons. The range of activities in any one centre depends on the skills and enthusiasm of the local community.

I am chuffed to find that the same job is being coordinated in the US by Rennie Davis, of the Chicago Seven, whose presence had boosted morale at the Millenium. So there are threads of continuity from my previous life even now.

The main Sydney ashram is now in Mosman. While we still sleep on the floor, we have more bedding, at least. A team of housemothers (including men) prepares sumptuous vegetarian meals. The wider community is a much more varied mix of householders and monastics, and some have gone into business. In Brisbane I worked for a while at a bookstore. In Sydney I work in a tiny makeshift factory near Central station, where they cast silver alloy jewelry for an alternative small business entrepreneur who has people selling the stuff out on the streets.

5.30 am on a typical day. Sleepy bodies stir from their cocoon of sleeping bags and blankets and shuffle towards the bathrooms. Within a quarter of an hour, all residents are gathered in the meditation room. One lights candles as others drag out songbooks and rudimentary instruments to accompany the morning *arati*. Not all the singers standing huddled in their meditation shawls have perfect pitch, so it's a relief when residents (or visitors) include a real musician or two, to hold a note. Otherwise the next fifteen minutes are as much an exercise in trying to find a way to sweeten the sound, merge your voice into the collective chorus and harmonise the disparate threads, as they are an exercise in devotion. Cymbals clatter, a drum scratches and thuds; bead-shakers rattle haphazardly as the chanting wakes us up and draws our attention together for meditation.

'Meditation begins in the form of the Master.' My teacher's face glows in candlelight.

Sometimes a flicker from a verse of the song flares into meaning in my heart and brings tears to my eyes. The words of this *arati* are like an 'Ur'-satsang; all the advice I ever need seems encoded therein. After the chanting we settle like tortoises into shells made up of warm blankets and shawls, and for the next hour or so the room becomes almost breathlessly still; a dozen minds drawn back into the stillness inside. Someone yawns, scratches, before moving on to the next technique. Occasionally, a body slumps awkwardly to the floor and straightens up again. Here in the sleepy suburbs a group of young Australians willingly submit to a gentle discipline to enter, and savour, the sacred silence.

By 8.00am, a draggle of bodies has rotated through the showers into the breakfast room, now dressed for a day of service.

Sunlight streams in through a window and frames the head of one of the men quietly taking his food. Tony Lunn is a brilliant young graphic designer who has counted among his clients large corporations in Europe. Here, he uses his skills to put together our little national newspaper. Wordsmith Michael McDonald is the editor.

There's no strict rule of silence in the ashram but we are expected not to 'chit-chat', and people are naturally inclined to stay close to the quiet they have absorbed in the practice, before going out to wrestle with the day. Some of the devotees head out to jobs—which serve as valuable source of funds, more than as careers—while others have full-time roles assigned within the organisation. Terry McKinnell is compiling a financial structure to coordinate logistics among the different centres; John Perry is researching different templates we might better use to operate as a legal entity—are we a charitable foundation, an educational institute, a church? What roots will connect us into a largely indifferent world?

And who is this person whom we might get to see, say, only once a year, yet who can inspire such dedication, among such diverse people, in different cultures halfway around the world? Part of the answer lies with the experience that he is helping us tune into, through the meditation practice and the growth of community; but there is also something in the personal qualities of the teacher that magnetises us, each for his or her own reasons. In addition to the intrinsic value of exploring the expanded inner world, a mysterious healing is taking place on other levels.

Marolyn gives birth to a second child. This time it is a son, named 'Hans' (for 'soul') and, once again I am moved as I catch a glimpse of that child's growth within this very special family. One of the US magazines carries a cover photo of Maharaji playing with the boy, and the image captures a moment of perfect trust. The father has tossed his son into the air, and his arms are reaching up to catch him. Hans's attention is fixed gleefully on his father's upturned face, whose own gaze is totally attentive to the child.

Perhaps this is what all kids are supposed to feel with their father, but it has an added poignancy for me. I compare the image with the memory of my own father's twisted teaching, forcing David to jump off the kitchen table, with the message that we weren't supposed to trust anyone. So, there are elements of psychological healing spinning off from this so-called 'spiritual' relationship, too.

In the words of a devotional song, the guru can be mother and father to you; and brother, lover, friend; these are all attributes of the relationship that develops between the teacher and the student. For, in addition to my own efforts to re-focus myself internally, another dimension of the experience comes through the unique kind of interpersonal relationship that unfolds with this kind (and vigorous) guide.

There's a special quality in the feeling of the experience, a certain awareness—to which I was previously insensible—that emerges from behind the relative dullness of everyday awareness. What noise does a camellia make as its petals unfold? How much more subtle, then, the opening of the heart.

Dormant sensors awaken to exquisite new wavelengths of joy. Not stamp-your-feet, wave-your-arms-and shout-out-loud kind of joy—there are other occasions for that—but quieter and quieter revelations; soft awakenings into subtle layers of love energy, as I learn to let go, inside. This experience is what I am designed for, ultimately, the *summum bonum* of my human existence.

From the first inducements offered when a mere baby to the powerful titillations that prompted me to drool after experiences on offer outside me, the senses had been conditioned to take me further and further *out*, always away from my own centre; a centre that is not in my 'personal' self, at all, but at the very root of being. Losing contact with that centre I learned to expect satisfaction where there was only more and more stimulation, hoping for love from other beggars as bereft as I am. 'Inside' became a miasma of emotional and mental confusion.

reflection

But Ariadne had given me a thread to find my way back from the labyrinth of desire. And it was entwined intimately within my breath, that primal energy which makes everything else possible. It's utterly fundamental, the *sine qua non* for my existence, and for every single action I make—from a thought, to a heartbeat, to digging in the garden, to dreaming, to writing a book. But as important as it is, it usually doesn't draw attention to itself … unless I do something to stress it.

If you ever got 'winded' in a football game you'll know what I mean. I did, a couple of times; I was knocked onto the ground, or shoved in the diaphragm, and had 'the wind' taken right out of me. Or maybe you have found yourself under water, struggling to get up to the surface for your next life-saving breath. You would have felt such a primal urge demanding that breath; everything else becomes insignificant. At those times that quiet, latent energy really does take over and shows its hand, as it were. Usually so quiet I could take it for granted, on such occasions it *demands* its due and it doesn't let up until the lungs open and things return to normal.

For breath isn't just air, or the movement of the lungs. If that urge that draws your breath ever were to leave you, there could be food in the stomach, nutrients in the bloodstream; but this old body's done, finished, dead, *finito, kaput!* Ready for the scrap heap.

So, if you were to get together with your breath, really pay attention—meet it on its own terms; not yanking it around, not forcing it to do your bidding (so that would exclude *pranayama*); just notice it and continue to stay with it—bringing your attention back continuously into its self-manifesting rhythm, letting the mind and attention settle there, absorbed—you might start to notice some simple facts about it, chief among which is that *it* causes *you*, rather than the other way around.

Sit with it. For months.

There are qualities of feeling in there that you're usually too busy to notice. Something shifts in your awareness. It's not a theory to be surrendered for analysis, nothing to build a philosophy upon; you have to get back in touch with it, to receive it and sense what it is, where it comes from, what it contains; its quietness conceals endless reservoirs of depth and power.

Follow the full pronunciation of each breath. Every cycle is unique. Sometimes it flat-lines, for God's sake. That's okay; calm down, it's still supporting you. It's doing its thing. It's not a single phenomenon unrelated to everything else, it is the underlying matrix of all things. *You* are one of its things. As you calm down, letting it set the pace, little 'you' gets in synch with it, and by doing that, with a whole lot more. Your centre shifts. 'Human doing' calms down as 'I' nestles into the womb of being.

This may be the beginning of knowing through feeling, a deeply felt research into the nature of being itself. Intelligence, *in the body*, recovered by simply hanging with your breath and letting it be your guide. Gradually, it coaches you in trust. You find little clumps of tightness release as you sense your way into a different relationship dynamic with inner space; you let go to a series of subtle shifts in gear; little knots untangle as each breath opens more gently into the next. Peace energy seeps into you, from deeper inside (within, yet beyond you). To allow this to manifest, you're virtually disappearing. From within this peace, the heart feels safe enough to open. Trust and gratitude emerge, and a healing connection is forged with a deeper stratum of being, of conscious awareness itself. That doesn't depend on you, you depend on it, utterly. The ultimate cause, our origin and our destination. You are that.

green banana curry

Tell the mind there is but One. He who divides the One wanders from death to death.
—Katha Upanishad.

'I always knew you were an ascetic,' an old friend tells me on a visit to what is one of the more comfortable ashrams, in the plush Melbourne suburb of Kew. She thinks I have 'renounced' everything but, inside, I'm flying. My heart luxuriates in an intense experience of love and she can only see what is happening with the externals. Where is the asceticism, exactly? In this house they've even got themselves off the floor and into real beds. There are chairs in the new *satsang* hall. But even in the early days, when I made do with a blanket on the floor (more than sufficient in sultry Brisbane), the spartan conditions were not the point.

The majority of people coming to receive Knowledge now don't opt for the ashram way of life—they aren't required to, in any case—and there are many changes over the years, as my teacher steps away from the Indian cultural trappings that marked the early waves of contact. As he takes his message into more and more countries in coming decades he will continue to pare back the inessentials. But even if the packaging is updated for new contexts, the techniques for tuning in, continue to reveal the essence of being. Lifestyles come and go. The need for peace is constant.

It's amusing, if a little disturbing, when people label us as being part of some sect. Many of us new arrivals are unreconstructed hippies, so the Asian origins haven't seemed at all strange to us. Our enthusiastic eclecticism travels hand in hand with the hope for a rich, multicultural society. Barriers and borders belong to the old civilisation that is dying, or at least being renewed with diverse influences that old-time colonialist prejudices have heretofore quarantined us against. I believe that all of us humans are hybrids: in our genes, in our thinking, and in our cultures. Looked at from the outside, the Indian flavour of the early years has probably been misleading, it must have seemed like a neo-Hinduism. For some people Christianity remains an upstart sect of Judaism. But here we are not required to study philosophy or learn to read Sanskrit, or Pali (or

Greek, Latin, Aramaic or Hebrew, for that matter) or pore over foreign scriptures. I tried to do all that before. This process is more direct, and the pulse of my heart's hope has scarcely skipped a beat.

1975. In Adelaide, one of the best chefs from the community has designed the menu for a new vegetarian restaurant. The invitees for the opening are a mixed bag: premies from the ashram and the broader community of householders mingle with friends of the investors, food writers, and sundry other young folk impressed by the chic décor of the new eatery.

I am chatting with a small group when a young woman suddenly drops out of the conversation, recoiling as she realises that many of those gathered here know each other.

'Oh, no ...' she murmurs in horror. 'You're all members of ...'

'Yes, it's called the human race,' I offer, my rejoinder less sarcastic than offended. I am puzzled by her hostility. Just what is it that we have done to alienate her? We have not been proselytising. The food is good, the company warm, yet in her eyes we have been rendered somehow 'other': aliens, another species—just plain weird. I try to explain that the experience that Maharaji guides one towards does not make you feel separate from other people. If anything, the deeper you go inside, the closer you come to the point of common unity with everyone, but maybe that's too paradoxical for her to grasp. There is no antagonism between 'self' realisation and respect for others. To honour the boundless source of one's being is to recognise the same possibility in others. That is the foundation of equality and a reliable, grounded basis for progress in understanding the principle of unity in diversity.

But she has already lost interest and wandered off.

One time my teacher described how, when people become a stranger to themselves, then everyone else becomes a stranger too. He told a story about two islands, set miles apart in an ocean, separated by a stretch of water they can't bridge. With no communication between them, save for futile, misinterpreted smoke signals and the occasional piece of flotsam or jetsam washed up on each other's shores, they puzzle about each other. With little real information, their thoughts run wild as they fantasise about their differences. Sometimes, in paranoia, one will suspect the other of having hostile intentions. But those two islands are not as separate as they appear. If you could follow the landmass of an island down below the water line, to the ocean bed, and if you were to continue along the ocean bed, it should come as no surprise to find that you would come up as that other island. The connection might not be visible on the surface, but in reality, these apparently separate entities are deeply connected.

I feel that Knowledge is that kind of connection: to dive deep into it is to recover the experience of the underlying matrix of being which unites all life. Rather than making me feel 'separate', in fact, it brings me into closer sympathy with others. On this occasion, the young woman has pulled out of the conversation and is not interested in re-joining us, no matter what I say. But if I take up her point of view, and look at my situation 'objectively', or at least from the outside, there are elements of the way I am living that could seem strange to an unsympathetic observer. Some of us have little or nothing to do with our families, after all. Those living in the ashram are celibate, or trying to be, and live in crowded group housing. Many go out to work and give over their income. There are no television sets; we don't read books or magazines, except those related to the Mission's activities; we never go to the cinema. In fact, we begin and end every day with a quiet meditation practice and every evening we gather in the same hall and talk about the same topic; and all of us—householders and renunciates alike—seem very attached, even devoted, to a young man whom we hardly ever see. Although it is a voluntary commitment, our participation in what must seem to be a very strict sect excludes much of what other people feel is necessary for a happy life, yet 'happy' is the very word we would use about our own existence.

As strange as it may seem to an 'outsider' , I am not any more uncomfortable with this outfit than I was when trying to fit into the costume I was supposedly born for as an Aussie male—stubbies, singlet and thongs; a clenched jaw and a firm grip on a can of cold beer. Here, the emphasis is on the meditation practice, on service and the company of other students in *satsang*. You could get together with other people to play bridge, watch a football match, even to talk about God but this has a different quality. '*Satsang* is when your heart sings and it comes out of your mouth,' is the way a premie child defines it. Without it, you might end up thinking that you were the only one being blessed, but here is a constant reminder that the same love resides in every heart. Rather than submerging you into narcissistic self-absorption, it is one aspect of a beautiful training in mutual respect. If you put your palms together in front of your heart, and bow your head to acknowledge the presence of the other, it's a profound recognition of that respect.

'Are you a … *follower* of this … chap?" they ask. Well not really, no, because he isn't *going* anywhere to *follow*. When I look to him, he's pointing back at me.

'What you are looking for is inside you,' he says, again and again.

a night at the opera house

In 1975, Maharaji visits Australia again, appearing at the Sydney Opera House. I travel up with the other devotees from the ashram in Adelaide, where I have been sent to coordinate activities. It's been a long time between drinks, and in spite of the focused lifestyle of the ashram, the twice daily formal practice of the techniques, the satsangs seven nights a week, I am yearning to see my teacher again. I want nothing less than to merge, really; to give up all separate existence; to dissolve into this experience and never come back. All of my devotion is focused on the teacher—the living embodiment of the experience that quenches my deepest needs. That urge to merge, which I acted out so floridly in Sydney—was it only five years ago?—has fixated very definitely on the person of my teacher.

The Opera House is filling up. I quickly find a seat in the centre of a row, not far from the front.

Inside, I am virtually begging to leave my body and merge with him, with what he has come to represent to me. But this yearning to merge (on the external plane, so to speak) is pushing me out and away from the centre within. I don't recognise the difference, but almost as soon as my teacher begins to speak, he addresses this very issue for me.

He launches into a story about a king and queen who were very rich. The king has given his queen a priceless necklace, which she cherishes as a gift from her beloved husband. One morning, before bathing, she takes off the necklace and hangs it on a peg. A crow flying overhead notices the brilliant gemstones and, being attracted to bright sparkly things, swoops down and carries it off. When the queen emerges and dries off, she is horrified to find that the necklace is missing. Has she misplaced it? How can it be lost? Has someone stolen it? She raises quite a commotion and commandeers everyone in the palace into finding the jewels. Suspects are interrogated, careers threatened, sinecures suspended as the queen's anxious search intensifies. The king tells her not to bother, he can have another made, equally beautiful. But the queen will not be calmed.

'No, I want that one! No other will do,' she complains. 'It was a gift from you, my loving husband, and it is precious to me.'

The king is so upset by the queen's distress he issues a proclamation that anyone finding the necklace and returning it to the palace will receive a great reward. Soon, the whole kingdom is out searching.

One day, out in the forest, a solitary woodcutter sees a beautiful necklace in a lake.

'Why, if that's the queen's necklace, I can get me a nice reward,' he mutters to himself, and he jumps in to retrieve the treasure. But the necklace disappears. He scratches his head and clambers back up onto the bank to see where it might have gone. Sure enough, there it is, twinkling away at him in the water. He jumps in again, certain that he has a better fix on its location, but once again, as his fingers search the bottom the necklace simply disappears.

Passersby are puzzled to see this man carrying on in such a fashion, jumping into the water with all his clothes on, then getting out only to do it all over again. He tries to shoo them away, determined that the reward will be his and his alone, but some of them catch a glimpse of what he is after too and before long, twenty or thirty people are shoving each other aside, leaping into the water, scrambling around and making one hell of a din.

Presently a sage happens by. He pauses to observe the goings on. After a while, having diagnosed the problem, he calls for their attention.

'Look: when the water is calm, you can see the necklace so clearly, but when you jump in, it seems to disappear, right?'

'Why state the bleedin' obvious?' They mutter.

'You are looking in the wrong direction,' he advises them.

The sage takes the woodcutter by the chin and, turning his head back to look up into the branches of a tree overhanging the pond, says 'Look there!'

'The necklace has always been behind you; what you have been chasing is only the reflection.'

Such a simple parable, but it is a powerful rebuttal for the outward focus of my yearning. In spite of years of practice, that pull which is drawing me to go out, even towards the teacher—the source—could be just another, powerful delusion. Clearly, I am to look within. The teacher's role is to be a mirror. The devotee has to make the connection firm, *from the inside*. The need for this will soon become clear.

At the same time, the incident also points up how invaluable the teacher's guidance is to me, in that very process. As a student I don't really know how to do this—this devotion thing—but if I persevere, the teacher is there to pop my delusions as they arise, and I will be the one who benefits. The Master is the one who is trying to set you free, even from your fondest delusions, not bind you to him. Once you have understood this, you can enjoy his presence free of the neurotic yearning.

'It just gets better,' he promises. And, slowly, experience teaches me that this is true.

Rather than pulling back and quitting what strangers take to be a 'cult', I decide to go even more deeply into the process.

hit the road, Vic

Wellington, New Zealand, early 1978.

I walk slowly down the broad staircase, pausing as my hand reaches towards the doorknob. On the other side of the door is a group of people—nineteen in all—waiting for instruction and I am the one they are waiting for, to do the job. Since October 1972, when I began, I can't say I have improved at the practice, but while one part of me wonders how in heaven's name I have got myself into such a situation, I can't deny how the preceding months—even years—have brought me precisely to this point.

I have been working with this group of aspirants for several days. Julie Collet, already an instructor, has been in New Zealand, too, and our paths have come together briefly over the past two weeks. But as I prepare my very first group of aspirants for a Knowledge session, Julie is called away to Fiji and now I am really on my own, with no one to check how I am going. The same feeling I have had ever since I was first required to 'give satsang', five or six years previously, is multiplied a thousand fold. I have to admit, I know I don't know how to do this and I pray silently, 'Make sure this unfolds as you would wish and … please make sure I don't confuse anyone!'

I am not talking to some mysterious God figure, but communing inwardly with my teacher, a connection I have learned to trust as a real-world, personal relationship. Everything I know, everything I have experienced, all the mistakes I have made—are all in play, and all feed into this process of instruction. I'm in the same situation as Padarthanand was and by now I know I couldn't be doing this under my own steam.

Several hours later, I feel like a nurse assistant clearing away after an operation. The doctor has left, the patient is doing well and I am merely taking care of logistical details. The session has unfolded simply, one step after the next; I demonstrated the techniques just as I have been shown recently by Maharaji himself. They practised; I answered their questions; averted one participant's minor asthma attack; and now they are launched. I haven't been required to be the universal expert, with the answers to everything; I have just had to help them begin.

After a three month training that began in Rome and continued in California, Maharaji has sent me on the road to work on his behalf as an instructor in the method and for the next six years or so I will have no fixed address, no income - just a suitcase and a ticket to the next place.

As I sum up, I emphasise that they are entering into a relationship with Maharaji as their teacher, rather than with me. Their relationship with him as their guide will develop as they put these recommendations into practice but they owe the initiator no loyalty or respect other than as a spiritual brother, a fellow traveller, a student of the same Teacher.

Buddha on the mountaintop

Waiting the word of the Master
watching the hidden light
listening to catch his orders
in the very midst of the fight.
—J. Krishnamurti, after El Morya

Tokyo. 1979.

My dreams of a Zen-inspired aesthetic have not prepared me for this real Japan. Perhaps I expected quiet, raked pebble gardens and the tranquil simplicity of the tea ceremony; instead I am confronted with a grey, polluted urban tangle. Narrow freeways stacked in shadowy layers fly between high-rise office buildings, windows pressed so close to the road you could almost reach in and swipe the paperwork from the clerks' desks—although this would be unseemly in the land of formal politesse.

Thickets of TV antennae sprout ragged from tightly packed, low-rise houses. Near railway stations, *pachinko* halls cluster, with large and gaudy crepe-paper rosettes rowdily declaring their presence. Enter into one of these brightly lit venues and you're immersed in a garish environment: row after crowded row of men, eyes glazed, playing at a kind of miniaturised vertical pinball machines. Small steel balls clatter through their gates—the din harangues the hearing—and bright lights dazzle your eyes. It's Las Vegas without the showgirls, or the high rollers, crammed tightly into graceless rooms.

I had expected a nation of austere Buddhist aesthetes contemplating brushstrokes on inscrutable scrolls featuring a single *kanji*, so I am disappointed that *sararimen* prefer getting drunk in tiny bars, postponing their return to their workers' dormitories, or long train journeys back to wives and families in the far-flung suburbs.

Still I am struck by the restraint. They're an intensely emotional people and there are so many of them—six times the population of Australia—crushed into such inadequate spaces. But the performance of extreme politeness civilises their intensity, grading levels of formality in language and in behaviour like the elaborate, layered dressing of a *kimono*, or a formal *kendo* fighting suit. Aggression is restrained, in various forms of martial arts, by the same refined earnestness and respect.

On railway platforms I watch, fascinated by the elaborate etiquette of an older generation, bowing again and again when leaving another's company. It seems that you should never be the last one to receive a bow, and the bobbing up and down continues in what becomes almost a caricature of proper protocol that appears preposterous to my easy-going Australian mindset. Such ritualised interaction is a way of masking the passionate nature of this potent race, an effective lubricant for the intensity of social intercourse among a very crowded population. In my home country, a relaxed, informal way of being with others is highly valued. But even my cultural blinkers don't prevent me from recognising the civilising influence of mutual respect that enacts the deepest principle properly guiding ethical behaviour.

With antimacassars on every headrest, the taxicabs are the cleanest in the world. Their drivers wear white gloves, as do hectoring politicians spruiking campaign slogans through raucous megaphones atop their mobile campaign vans. I wonder if the clean white gloves are a guarantee of freedom from graft and corruption, or whether it's merely an elaborate ritual masking human venality.

In the acutely overcrowded cities the spare aesthetic ideal starts to makes sense. The off-centred asperity of *ikebana*, the simplicity of the tea ceremony, the chilling austerity of ancient Noh—all speak of a yearning for space, for less where there is always more, to win back a little room in which to breathe. In the life of most families, the tiny living spaces mean that rooms may be used for two or three purposes throughout the day. At night everything is bundled into cupboards, clearing the floor for sleeping space, with *futons* laid out on the sweet smelling *tatami* matting. Room sizes are calculated not by the square yard or metre, but by the number of these mats configured into the floor. The futons are hung from windows for airing whenever weather permits and then rolled up to take their turn in the cupboards, until night calls them forth again. Amidst all that I feel too big where I should be self-effacing. Even my name, when transliterated into Japanese, changes meaning. Once again, that 'V' sound of English can't quite find a home in another tongue and I become 'Big' Marsh.

At the traffic lights outside Shibuya station I am stunned by the swarms of vehicles alternating with masses of dark clad folk crossing when the lights change. Too much stuff, too many people, too much coming and going, too much pressure to always be doing, with simple states of being sacrificed along the way. (I suppose that's why they treasure the quiet mood of tea ceremony and those raked, pebbled gardens.)

With so much competing for their attention, Zen Buddhist practice strikes most ordinary Japanese as remote, even austere, and I wonder how ordinary folk will take to the new (old) meditation practice I offer on behalf of my young master. Much interest, in fact, is coming from alternative types, such as the young musicians residing in enclaves like Kichijoji, where the brothers' ashram is located.

'The Japanese are afraid of three things,' an expat British professor, Piers, whose father sits in the House of Lords, explains to me on a visit to Okayama, 'earthquakes, their fathers, and big people.' Perhaps that explains their fascination with the super-sized fighters of *Osumo* wrestling. It's not long before I get interested in the sport, too. I watch, breath suspended, as *Wurufu*—the nickname for Chiyonofuji, leader of a new breed of *yokozuna*, with rippling muscles in place of sheer bulk—swiftly and easily dispatches bulkier wrestlers.

My beat now covers a dozen countries in east Asia and the Pacific Rim. In my first five years in the ashram, I lived in four cities. As an instructor, I now have no home base at all; I travel from community to community—seventy-two cities a year, and counting. In the past twelve months I have been through various Customs and Immigration checkpoints eighteen times. If I am lucky I might get a brief, if potent, boost of inspiration at an event with Maharaji, then I am sent back on the road. Wherever I go, people are thirsty to hear this message of inner peace. When my mother plaintively calls out to me: 'Come home, aren't you sad to be alone?' I explain 'Home is where the heart is, Ma!' Everywhere I go, I am anything but alone. I'm not being mean to my mother. My centre is within me, utterly portable.

Maharaji gives an example of a ship's compass, which floats in oil rather than being tethered to a rigid structure. Even as the ship tosses about in the waves, the compass keeps its bearings for the benefit of all aboard. As I go from place to place, many things change, and my over-stimulated mind is always bouncing about, but I get my bearings by turning within.

It's bewildering enough to find myself in a culture where I can't read any of the signposts, so when it comes to getting about I am happy to just go where I am led. In Tokyo, I pad obediently behind the local coordinator, Kato-san. I'm heading out to do a public event in a hired hall. In the more spacious environs of Australia, or the United States, these narrow streets would be classed as laneways; here they press right up to the entrances of houses built tightly close to each other, to make room for cars. But the quickest way to get around is by subway and train.

We reach the station and patter down crowded stairwells, threading along platforms jammed with people, ducking in and out of subway cars, changing trains not once but three times, to arrive breathless at some generic building I would never be able to identify alone.

None of these talks, not even a simple conversation, can take place without an interpreter. With everyday language—spoken, written, signposted—opaque to my brain, a kind of disorientation sets in. Even if I could read the simplest syllabary of *hiragana* and *katakana*, most of the street signs, the advertising, and the tangled noodle map that is the directory for the interconnecting subway and rail systems, are written in *kanji*, the characters derived from Chinese. Fifteen hundred kanji, learned one at a time, and I'd be literate enough to read the newspaper. But before I have a chance to get a handle on all of that, I am whisked off to Seoul where I go through the same struggle with Korean script, barely learning the obligatory verbal gestures of politesse (*anyong hashimnika, kamsamnidah*); only to be wrenched from there to move on through Hong Kong, say, and then Taiwan, where I repeat the whole rigmarole in Mandarin, with some of the local dialect thrown in for good measure.

In Tokyo I say '*Mina-san, komban-wa. Nihongo ga shabere nakutte. Gomen nasai*' to a round of titters.

In Taipei, I parrot like some linguistically challenged baby, in the sing-song Mandarin they patiently coach me in: '*Ge wei, wan an. Wo buhwei jiang jonguo hua. Duibuqui!*' 'Good evening everyone. Please excuse me, I don't speak your language,' I say in polite, carefully tutored cadences. That puerile attempt has them rolling in the aisles as I hand over to the interpreter to translate the rest of the talk; although in Japan hilarity in a public setting is more often expressed as a discreet titter behind a hand.

And everywhere, such masses of humanity! I go back to Australia for a brief tour and wonder where all the people have gone. Are they inside, watching the cricket? I muse. And why are their noses so big?

As I travel on through Malaysia, Singapore, Hong Kong, Taiwan, the Philippines, Fiji, Sri Lanka and so on, I abandon as too difficult the task of remembering a thousand new names, in quick succession, in too many new languages: Bahasa, Tamil, Malayalam, Hindi, Urdu, Gujerati, Cantonese, Mandarin, Taiwanese, Kek, Hokkien, Tagalog, Japanese, Korean. As I encounter a thousand new faces, subtle ethnic differences in facial features open a new aesthetic of beauty to my blinkered Western gaze. No matter which country I am in, satsang really proves itself to be the company of truth; in these different cultural settings I find hearts seeking the common thread; and words come second to feeling. The striking differences in culture, language and belief give way to the underlying matrix of unity. When separated, unconscious of that grounding, we yearn to belong, in a way that family, community and nation can only partially fulfil.

In Japan there is one thing I *can* read among the flashing neon. On a huge sign mounted above a city building, among the cacophony of neon signage, like leftovers from the set of the movie *Blade Runner*, there's one sign I read writ large in the *romaji* script: 'Victor'. That *is* my name, but is that my image? An electronics company uses the icon of the little dog sitting faithfully, listening at the speaker trumpet of an old Victrola, but here, instead of advertising for His Master's Voice, which is how I remember it back home, it's the corporate logo for JVC, the Japanese Victor Company—in advertising shorthand, simply 'Victor'. In the entire urban visual tangle, then, the only thing I can read is my own name, but it's me as a little dog listening attentively to his Master's voice. A reminder writ large, wherever I go, of what I most need to heed.

A group of devotees from the cities gathers for a retreat outside the metropolis, near the iconic Fujiyama. Members of the local community have taken a hiatus from the city's frantic pace to enjoy two days of quiet, folded in the presence of the fabled mountain. A half-dozen aspirants have collected, too, and it's time to initiate them into the practice.

Typically, each time I am to do such a session it's a daunting challenge and some part of me finds it confronting. I have been doing this for two or three years already, in many locations; you'd think I would have mastered it. But as I prepare the aspirants for the big day, I am forced to recognise that I too am being prepared. The quality of their sincerity tunes the satsang, and when the time comes to demonstrate the techniques, one by one, and practise them together, fewer and fewer words are necessary. The room becomes still, the silence thickens. The interpreter and I fall silent as we slip effortlessly into the glistening sound of the infinite. After days, sometimes months, all the telling finally resolves into this precise demonstration of grace, where a subtle presence, larger and smoother than anything I—its mere instrument—could say or do, draws us into one vibration, revealing itself perfectly, the deep centre of being located in each one's heart. Meditation is listening, inside.

While I play the role of 'instructor', this coming together is not orchestrated by me. Nor is it happening 'through' me, as some kind of 'channel'. You might say it happens around me, under me, above me, *in spite of me*; in fact, the less of 'me' there is, the better—that's why it is always confronting, clearing me out of the way in order for us all to tune in to this underlying presence, which is at one and the same time the most subtle and the most powerful reality. 'Being'—usually concealed by the everyday business of doing, with all its attendant preoccupations—steps forward and claims undivided attention. Working as its servant can be intense, but it is a rare privilege.

In Taipei, rampant capitalism is busily shoving up graceless high-rises. Crowded buses chuff diesel smoke as they nudge busily by rice paddies. Tiny red taxis, driven faster than gentility and safety would allow, surge through narrow roundabouts. Drivers use only one hand for steering; the other is positioned on the horn, sounded continuously to warn off the other vehicles, and everyone pushing to get into a space that hasn't yet opened up before them. With relentless blasts, we nudge through roundabouts, competing with private cars, buses; entire families piled onto bicycles, and the inter-weaving manoeuvres of a thousand scooters and rattletrap motorbikes. The Goddess of Mercy, Kuan Yin, is on active service in Taipei.

On steamy nights the local premies throw open the front windows of the ashram to welcome any moving breeze. The brothers sleep in the front room, with a standing fan positioned just inside the window to push air through the space. The room where I sleep is in a direct line with their window. Squadrons of large brown cockroaches ride the air and the fan assists their entrée, sweeping them straight past the brothers to land on me, and I awake to find myself hurling the dry little critters off my skin. I have to get up and close the door, despite the heat. I drop off to sleep again only to be awoken again with them crawling all over me. Dammit! They must have found their way underneath the door. I find some newspaper to stuff under the crack, hoping to stem the invasion, and the heat becomes stifling. I lie awake, listening to the sound of their bodies slapping into the door, and the scratch of them scrabbling to get past the paper barrier that I have wedged in place.

I don't have cash to buy food and even if I did I wouldn't recognise the culinary possibilities in the markets; so in each town I wait until an overworked fellow devotee has time to prepare a meal. All ashrams are vegetarian. Delicious as the meals are, unfailingly, (even the bitter melon), food offers no possibility of a pig-out to escape my relative austerities. And of course the local papers are inscrutable and there's no television in the ashram.

But it isn't all austerity.

Peering past the cultural barriers I find many delights. In each community I fall in love with the devotees, always delighted that Knowledge is reaching people in so many countries, cultural differences notwithstanding. A young husband-and-wife publishing team publish a newspaper cartoon series for children. It's called 'Mister Satsang', in Chinese, and they have fun turning some of the teaching stories into graphic fables. Ah-Mei and Ah-Min shine with enthusiasm.

Taiwan prides itself on being the repository of all the best aspects of traditional Chinese culture, rescued from what they sometimes see as the philistine rulers of *Da Loo*, the mainland, who have brutalised many treasured cultural traditions, even simplifying the written script. Religion is taken uncommonly seriously here. Intense Buddhist seekers, young and old, come to engage me in dharma battle. Such seekers of truth are eager to hear about the teachings of a young Master out of India and, after testing me in various ways, many stay to take instruction.

The need for an interpreter continues, of course, for every interaction, and the best English speaker usually ends up in round-the-clock service to facilitate the two-way exchange. One afternoon, I am hanging out in the ashram with a guy who has a car. 'Sam', a local fellow, is a householder, with his own responsibilities, but he's able to make time available for service. His job for the day is to take me, the instructor, anywhere I need to go. Sam has considerably more English than your average Taiwanese and as we chat, he tells me about a young woman working out of a teahouse in the middle of town who operates as a kind of Buddhist psychic.

Now, it could create quite a scandal for a person in my position to be going off to see a psychic. Serious Buddhists intent on Enlightenment look down their nose at the cultivation of lesser accomplishments, too. But curiosity gets the better of me—a Chinese, Buddhist clairvoyant is just too exotic a possibility to pass up and, besides, who will ever know?

'What's say we go and see her?' I ask Sam.

'I sorry. She very busy. Maybe wait two, three months for appointment. Sorry, I should not talk this.'

I am a little disappointed, but Sam suggests we could go to the teahouse and just wait, in the unlikely event an opportunity might arise. As I hardly ever go out, not even for meals, a visit to a teahouse will be an interesting event, so we head into town.

Sam parks the car in a side street and leads me down some steps to a pretty little basement café where we order some *oolong cha*. 'Oolong' is 'dragon' and the twisting dried tea leaves resemble the dragon's curling shapes.

We watch the young woman as she moves from table to table to read. She spends a long time in a back room where an entire family is gathered and she reads for each and every one of them. Content just to observe, I have given up on the chance of a reading. But after almost two hours she comes over, sits down and, without any ceremony—no incense, no deep breathing, no rolled-back eyes—announces:

'You come from the Buddha, and your work is to travel to the corners of the world, teaching people that the essence of all religions is one.' (Sam is interpreting.)

Crikey! You could knock me over with a paper fan. How could she possibly know what work I do? She certainly didn't know I would be coming in and, from all appearances, I should be an American student, studying Mandarin, say. That would account for at least 50% of the Westerners my age in the city. Others might be businessmen, and perhaps

40% would be earnest students of traditional Chinese medicine, acupuncture and herbal remedies. So how did she get what I am doing here?

She is talking about *bodhisattvas*, and she asks me if I have any questions. I am floored, unable to formulate a question but, in response to one thing she has to say, I ask her why I sometimes have trouble with my 'desires'? (Bravo on Sam, the 'householder', for interpreting my renunciate neurosis.)

'You come in this world, you get everything that comes with it … get whole package, of course!' She scoffs as if that should be obvious. My own words are coming back to haunt me. I often give this example to the premies wanting to move into the ashram. Say you buy a new car, and it comes with a cigarette lighter. Does that mean you have to take up smoking? Just because it is standard equipment, you don't have to use it for the same purposes as others do. Your body is God's gift to you. What you do with it is your gift to yourself. QED.

A young monk has been coming by the ashram to hear about Maharaji. The coordinator tells me that this handsome six-footer was originally a guitar-playing Christian, with long hair, but when he heard the message of the Buddha he shaved his head and became a monk. As a young monk in a Buddhist order he has been assigned a *shīfu*, or master, from among the senior monks, so I am not sure what this spiritual advisor might be thinking when the young monk keeps visiting our ashram. He is apparently eager to hear about our teacher and attends avidly to the talks recorded on video that require Chinese translation each time they are shown.

After watching a video, the monk prostrates to the screen, touching his head to the floor in a lovely submissive gesture, palms facing upward. He speaks gratefully of the warm feeling that listening to my teacher brings to his heart.

We met first in Kaoshiung, a city in the south, but the monk's supervisors moved him to another city and we lost contact. Somehow he has heard that the Western instructor has come back to Taipei and he finds his way to the ashram again. He is very handsome, but what has drawn us together is a mutual interest in something that in Mandarin would be the '*Da zhīshi* (the 'big knowledge' in Chinese, like the 'Raj Vidya' in Sanskrit); what I would call Knowledge of the Self.

On this day the young monk has cajoled his poor *shīfu* to drive us outside of Taipei, to walk up Yang Ming Shan Mountain. We leave the car in a designated car park and start the hike up the path to the summit. On the walk up, I catch a whiff of a beautiful fragrance, off to the side of the path, but I can't spot its source.

As the monk has almost no English and I no Chinese, conversation is limited. But it's enough to sit with the silence. We linger for a short, refreshing meditation at the crest before we start to walk back down the path towards the car. But when I catch a whiff of the lovely fragrance again I pause and turn to locate the source of the perfume: a flower, perhaps, somewhere in the bushes, off to the left.

The young monk notices my distraction. He straightens up to his full height to exclaim briskly, in his rudimentary English:

'A-*ah*! Don't *a-ttach*!'

He is teaching: Let it go. Don't leave the path to follow some passing beauty. Non-attachment frees you to continue on the path. He might have said also—all six feet of him, with his vigorous limbs, shaved head, and perfect features: 'Don't admire my beauty. Listen to what I'm telling you!' Other fragrances will come, sweet *and* sour—let them go, too. Just keep moving on, let it all flow by. This is all temporary, you're just a visitor here, don't fall asleep on the roadside. Everything that has been created will be un-created in time.

Am I so ready to be lured off the path by a fragrance, just as, at another time, I might have been lured away by a beautiful face, or a well-turned limb? Instead, it's: 'Don't attach!' Clear as a bell, my vigorous brother-in-truth delivers the message, in full confidence, and we are both laughing. It's sweet to have these lessons drawn in actual, real-world situations, rather than through reading Buddhist theory. The principle of equanimity: not indifference but not attraction or repulsion, either; I remember that time in Sydney, coming off the roller coaster of LSD, when I saw I had to abandon the pursuit of heaven AND hell and find my way to a middle path. Like Odysseus, perhaps, who needed to avoid both Scylla *and* Charybdis on his long journey home.

I have more to let go of than such simple attachments—to possessions, to things, even to relationships. I need to relinquish the tangled thicket of conceptual formulations that takes the place of direct awareness. I can see the wisdom of having had all the books taken away, for before I moved into the ashram I haunted the spiritual bookstores. Now, it's as though an overriding guiding intelligence simply will not allow theory to overtake experience; will not permit this fresh opportunity to be baffled by my fondness for ideas, nor muffle clarity with doctrine. Making way for the diamond mind of insight to crack the shells of theory—all too often wrapped around direct experience—from the inside.

As if to ensure that I get the point, Maharaji addresses this very process in a subsequent meeting with the instructors in Kissimmee, Florida. Let's take it as given here that the true experience of the core of being is arrived at without the aid of conceptual thought processes. I hear echoes of this in the old commandment: 'Thou shalt not worship graven images. Thou shalt have no other gods before Me.'

I take that more radically than it is usually read, perhaps. Conceptual frames—even fondly held ideas about the holiest of holies—are only a facsimile of the real and can form a barrier between me, the practitioner, and its direct, full-on perception. Maharaji brings it home with an example from one of his favourite pastimes—flying aircraft.

When a plane is approaching the speed of sound, everything starts to shake and rattle. The shaking builds up and up, to the point of breakthrough. When the plane hits that speed, there's a big sonic boom, perhaps you've heard it. But *after* that point it flies into silence, because it is now flying faster than sound itself. A build-up of pressure to a point of intensity, a big boom, then silence. Practising Knowledge consistently can bring you to a point where everything you think you know is challenged and shaken apart. But at that point it's a mistake to stop. If you keep going, right there, when everything is shaking loose, there will be a breakthrough, and you will fly free, beyond all ideas, into the zone of peace.

He calls this process the 'concept bomb', and this apprentice instructor knows, somehow, that while the challenges will continue he can proceed with less baggage, and more freedom.

On the road I connect with John Chan, another instructor sometimes assigned to the Pacific—before taking up the practice of Knowledge, he was a famous, high-concept fashion photographer in New York, which he left behind, happy simply to photograph his teacher. Hearing that instructors receive much *darshan*—the face to face time with the Master—John applied for the instructor service too and, being bi-lingual (born in China, he had grown up in Hong Kong), he spends time in the same region as me. John really travels light; and he seems blessedly free of attachments, his sole suitcase much smaller than mine. His one-pointed commitment to practice has made him intensely concentrated; he eats sparingly and often sits in meditation right through the night. His satsang is brief, almost terse, and spoken only softly, on the breath.

Next to him I feel excessive, grossly undisciplined; but on the occasions when our paths cross John Chan is very good company, with a sly sense of humour revealed mostly in brief, almost monosyllabic, statements. My satsang is florid, overblown, with too many stories about 'me'. I love to hear his testimony because every quiet word he utters derives from a place of intensely focused experience.

People often look to the apparent self-denial, the renunciation, in such a lifestyle. There's no sense of what that *tapasya* is really freeing up: ie, the manifestation of consciousness as the core, the experience of being itself rather than this person: Victor, Australian male, of a certain age, with all the detailed genealogy of an individual of a particular time and place.

Re-focusing my life through these so-called 'disciplines', then, is a way of slipping loose from the personal self, putting the learned identity on hold to make unmediated contact with the 'absolute ground of being' which, as I approach it, is experienced as boundless peace. The intentional disciplines of this lifestyle shifts the focal length of awareness away from the foreground of personal identity and into the whole perception of a source Being from which each little personal self depends for its moment-to-moment existence. Touching base with that deeper stratum brings an intense sense of relief, displacing my former existential angst, and the personal self, with all its fond allegiances, relaxes into the embrace of what could just as easily be characterised as a Mother 'god'.

There I go, creating conceptual word webs again. Mind, spinning.

As I learned with Padarthanand in Brisbane, being harnessed in service assists in moving the focus away from the mere self-satisfaction of meditation towards this state of relative liberation. With deep satisfaction as the centre of being, liberation, if that is what it is, is lived out gratefully in service to others. What did the Buddha do after his Enlightenment? He spent the next fifty years in service, helping others towards the goal.

That shift in focus: it's like those times as a child, when you sit on the grass looking down at the ground, and you fix your attention on a single point. Your eyes go still and as you let your gaze spread you become aware of all the ants moving through the grass. You didn't see them before, because your eyes are themselves dancing. Being still freezes the foreground and what was unnoticed in the background can come to the fore. It's like that in your mind, too. What layer of experience do you wish to focus on? Can you discover, from experience (rather than repression), how universal energy gets refracted and reduced through the prism of your own conditioning and your personal preoccupations; and, further, how to *reverse* that process and recover what is, when *you* are not? 'On the path of love, there is room for you or me, but not you and me', sings Kabir.

In a volume of Taoist verse collected and translated by John Blofeld, I read:

Unlimited chatter and mystical natter
Had best be swept out of the way
Then the radiant orb of wisdom's moon
Will emerge from behind the hill …
—Li Feng.[6]

---

[6] From *Taoism: The Quest for Immortality* Mandala Books/Unwin paperbacks.

reflection

The Buddha nature is in every heart.

Faced with the intense interest of these passionate Buddhist seekers, I sometimes wonder how they can be interested in attending to the teaching of a very modern Master, when Buddhism has its own elaborate and highly evolved philosophies and practices. One day in Tainan, a particularly thoughtful fellow explains that for someone seeking the best place to eat in town, rather than restricting his/her inquiry as to the whereabouts of the 'best' *restaurant,* should instead be asking where the best *chef* might currently be located. (A restaurant's reputation might be based on the work of a chef who has already departed for another establishment!)

So I shared with him this story that really spoke to me when I first came across my Teacher.

An island community of fisherfolk have a very hard existence. Their only diet is fish. So, even on days when it is too stormy to go out in their boats they must gather on the beach to work, patching the boats and mending their nets.

One such day when they are all down at the shore grumbling about the bad weather, complaining through the drizzle about how hard their lot is, a small boat pulls up at the other end of the beach. At first no one notices their visitor, but as he comes towards them, slowly leading a bony creature along the sand, one yells out for him to stop. No one ever has ever come to their sorry island.

They mutter among themselves, suspicious of the visitor's intentions.

'Friends,' he says, 'I've brought you a gift.'

'A gift? What kind of gift? No one's ever brought us any such thing before.'

'It's a cow,' he explains.

'Cow! What's a cow?' cries one. 'Yeah,' says another, 'What use is that? Can it catch fish? Can it mend a net? Can it row a boat?' Some brandish oars, shouting at the visitor to go away; others throw fish-heads at him, voicing their mounting suspicions with resentment.

'It will give you milk,' he tries to explain.

He isn't getting through but, just when all seems lost, he reaches under the cow and tugs at an udder, aiming a squirt of fresh, warm milk to land in the open mouth of the loudest protestor. The rich, creamy taste soon has him licking his lips.

'Mm, that's different,' he says. 'Could I try some more?'

In no time the visitor has produced a bucket brimful of milk, and all but a few take a taste of the new food.

'And you can have cream, and butter and yoghurt ...'

The visitor coaches them in the care of the cow and after a few days of instruction he departs, leaving her with them. Now they can have buttermilk, and yogurt, and grilled cheese on their fish. People vie for the honour of brushing the cow's tail, polishing her horns and hooves. They build her a shelter and gather only the sweetest grasses and clover for her to eat. Their children grow sturdy on the new diet.

As the years pass the community changes. Their vegie patches thrive, with cowpats used for manure. 'Moo' becomes their new word for 'happiness', in time taking on an all-embracing meaning as 'the good life'; 'satisfaction'; 'existence' itself. Each night they gather together to tell stories to the young ones about how miserable life was in the days before the cow. They change their calendar system, with a new era dating from the time when the cow came. Children grow up who have never known any other way of life.

But after many years pass, the cow grows old, and eventually she dies. The fresh milk soon runs out, but for some time they are able to make do with cheese they had stockpiled and they remind each other: 'We should never forget what a difference the cow has made to our lives'. They build a statue and a larger shed to remember the cow and each night they gather around the fire to share the histories of the times before and after the cow. But as the years pass, some of the younger people grumble that they have never seen this damned cow, have never drunk 'milk', and why do they have to sing the silly songs and recite the stories about the cow anyway? All they know is fishing, and all they ever eat is fish.

So the elders erect another statue of the cow, much larger than life, and perhaps a little better looking, too, to impress her qualities on the new disbelievers, who refuse to take their turn on the roster for cleaning the cowshed. Another generation passes and dissent increases. Story-time around the fire is cut back to once a week. Only one person takes care of the shed and the others resent his cushy life. The elders, some of whom never even met the cow, decide to build an even larger statue of the cow so she will not be forgotten. Soon the statue is ten metres tall, has seven horns and nine udders that flow with water to symbolise the milk, and her many eyes serve as a lighthouse for boats at sea.

Life is hard. On days when it is too stormy to fish, they all work on the beach, caulking leaks in the boats and mending nets. One such day, when they are all down on the shore grizzling about the bad weather, complaining through the drizzle how hard their lot is, a small boat pulls up at the other end of the beach. At first no one notices the visitor, but as he comes towards them, slowly leading a bony creature along the sand, one yells out for him to stop. They mutter among themselves, suspicious of the visitor's intentions.

'Friends,' he says, 'I've brought you a gift.'

'A gift? What kind of gift?'

'It's a cow,' he explains.

'Cow?!' says one, catching sight of the rather plain bony brown animal behind the visitor. 'Cow?' he says. 'That's no cow! THAT's the cow,' he shouts, outraged, pointing to the statue.

'Beware of false cowherds, leading false cows,' mutters one. 'Yeah,' say the others, as they pick up their oars to drive the blasphemer away. Smelly fish-heads rain down upon him.

'But she will give you milk,' he tries to explain, to gasps of outrage.

'Sacrilege!' All the frustration of their miserable lives focuses on him. He reaches under the cow and tugs at an udder, aiming a squirt of fresh, warm milk to land in the open mouth of the loudest protestor. The rich creamy taste soon has him licking his lips.

'Mm, that's different,' he says. 'Could I try some more?' In no time the visitor produces a bucket brimful of milk, and all but a few of the most conservative doubters have tasted the new food.

I love this story. It seems to me that everyone is waiting for a superman to come to the rescue. Christians with Jesus coming out of the clouds (what if he came in an airplane?); Muslims awaiting an Imam; orthodox Jews, the Moshiach; Buddhists the Maitreya; Hindus the next incarnation of Vishnu, or Krishna, etc., and the stories (and the expectations) just get bigger and bigger. What if he came simply as a human man (or woman?)—a simple human being, but 'awake', like the Buddha? What characteristics or obvious signs can we go by, if we insist on working from past models?

Meanwhile, there is the milk …

the wobble factor

From the early days of the practice I found that it is easy enough to let go of a thought. Some chains of thinking are more charged than mere daydreaming but even a sticky sequence of erotic fantasies can be released—if I want to release from them, that is, rather than indulge them. To let go of them might mean letting go of desire itself.

Experience also teaches me that *not* to do so will surely put me outside the deep core of peace located within the centre of being. If I prefer this deeper absorption, I let go of the thoughts, and the energy that has been congesting in the base centre—in the region of my genitals—is released, easily, to fold back into an undifferentiated flow of awareness where I can regain the deeply rooted contentment I've been writing about. It's always a choice. And the choice I made ten years ago, to enter the ashram and choose celibacy, gives the moment-by-moment renewal of those choices a compelling context.

I interpret my sexual urges as an unconscious wish to escape the renunciate life, a rebellious set of tricks played out by a truculent mind trying to escape from the focus of discipline. The choice then is either to crush the erotic impulse, or to simply let go of desire and return to a state of harmony, and that is an important distinction. The first option represents mere repression and will almost certainly create some kind of reaction. I have taken on this lifestyle willingly and yet I must choose it again, and again.

'Your mind is like a big rubber ball,' Maharaji tells me. 'Push it down, it will bounce back.' Repression/attraction is the swing of a pendulum: if you push away in one direction it will lead inevitably to a return swing. So, if I treat the renunciate life as a modern form of hair-shirt austerity, refuse to acknowledge desire, even punish myself for bad thoughts, I know that some day the pendulum will swing back and I will start to want what I have denied myself, with a passion.

Detachment, on the other hand, comes from surrender, which I feel works differently from repression. To entirely relinquish the prompting. Instead of the swing from extreme to extreme, letting go releases me and enables me to return to one-pointed awareness. Each meditation can bring me, potentially, to the brink of total absorption within; an integrated focus of all aspects of being in which all of 'me' dissolves into the awareness of the blissful foundation underlying every moment.

If, on the other hand, I allow my mind to operate in its fantasy mode it offers niggling little prompts, habitually collecting around whatever it wants to suggest that I lack. It will propose that something is missing—something out there that I need to pursue in order to feel good. 'Don't you want to go and get it?' But I don't need to move from my seat to go and get it. If I follow the fantasy, I have already left the seat, departing from the contented state of fulfillment itself to pursue something I have been fooled into thinking I lack.

At a birthday party celebration for Maharaji in Miami Beach, we try to entertain him with music and skits. I sing along with a young woman to the Billie Holliday song:

All of me, why not take all of me
Can't you see I'm no good without you
Take my arms, I never use them
Take my charms, I wanna lose them …

I hope that I can intensify my devotion and surrender every aspect of self to my teacher. That is my strategy to overcome the delusion of desire.

You took the part that once was my heart
So, why not take all of me?

But the closer I approach that state of ultimate surrender, the more the ego-mind kicks up distractions to stop me from surrendering, as if the part of me that has learned itself as separate, individual, unique is afraid of drowning, of losing itself, overwhelmed, even obliterated in the flood of bliss. Perhaps this sounds like quietism, but the busy life of service, day in, day out, and the relentless traveling, provides its own *jiu-jitsu* of engagement and surrender.

If I look at my life one way, I *have* virtually nothing—too many clothes in a heavy suitcase and a well-thumbed passport is what it adds up to. Anything else literally becomes a burden, including the suitcase if it incurs excess baggage charges; some poor local coordinator will have to cough up the cash from the community funds. No telephone, no bank account, no fixed address; no furniture to call my own.

I resent the size of my suitcase. Why can't we just wear some simple robes, a heavy one for winter, a lighter one for warmer climes? And in Japan, where I always feel that I take up too much space, the way they sound my name reinforces the feeling: I am 'Big' Marsh.

Yet from the point of view of my heart, I have never been more free, or more abundantly fulfilled by this 'nothing'. I am rich. Ergo, letting go isn't the same kind of manoeuvre as repression. To follow the promptings of desire would be to complicate my life, to cultivate tendrils of attachment in place of this freedom, adding emotional baggage to drag at the psyche, just as the suitcase drags at my physical body.

I rarely feel the urge to masturbate and regret it when I do, not because of any moral compunction but simply because I can't ignore the link between the focused lifestyle and the steady surge of bliss energy I am used to riding. Masturbation dulls my high. I meditate for several hours every day and I am acutely aware of the shifting quality of states of mind and feeling. If I shoot my load, bliss energy falls away noticeably. There is a discernible link between the physical emission and this energetic letdown. In the aftermath, I am left with a dragging feeling, where before I felt buoyant. Then I count the days, watching for the subtle inner cycles of energy to lift me up again. Yes, there is a palpable high that comes from focusing every aspect of being into one-pointed concentration. It is such a silly waste to ditch the constant state of clarity for a momentary splurge of excitement.

I had heard little about Tantra before I came to this practice, and I was intrigued by the mysteries of Taoist yoga hinted at in *The Secret of the Golden Flower*, the esoteric Chinese text that captured Carl Jung's attention. The body is the laboratory for the transmutation of consciousness. I knew that the same energy, if retained instead of carelessly spilled, was somehow recycled as a subtle fuel for the alchemical transformation. The meditation practices draw it deeply inwards and up to nourish higher centres of awareness with a rare form of energy, and I have become attached to the heightened states it opens into.

In Taiwan, I meet an 80-year-old herbalist, a doctor of Chinese medicine who is overjoyed when he receives the meditation techniques we instructors are sent to impart. He recognises their potential, deeply. He looks me straight in the eye and says, frankly (and with some envy): 'You are young, you can *cultivate* ...' using that term in a way I have not heard before. He understands the potential of spiritual practice to develop what is only dormant in the 'uncultivated' mind.

Besides, masturbation is too lonely. Even as a fantasy, there would have to be someone with me. At this point I refuse to acknowledge that the occasional yearning for sex might be masking the desire for love within an intimate relationship, but I have been so demonstrably unsuccessful in that regard. The ashram life seems such a good fit for me, and the benefits far outweigh the apparent sacrifices. I remember the lesson from the monk on the mountain—as you pass them on the path the fragrance of beautiful flowers may come to your attention, but don't get attached! And I press on. Perhaps I should wear blinkers, I think, if beauty is all around.

And then, there's massage.

My body often gets weary with travelling but how can I complain? All I have to do is talk all day. But a strong massage can release a lot of physical tiredness that seems to come with the miles. In Tokyo, one chap drills me with shiatsu, his fingers like steel. No comfort there. Someone with rough hands, too, can make you feel worse, especially if they talk all through the session.

Nevertheless, physical contact *can* open the door to sensuality (surprise, surprise!) and it is all too easy to use that tactile opportunity as a subterfuge to disguise the promptings of desire. I test the waters with a young man in New Zealand but we pull back from the brink. I move on to the next town, grateful for the constant travelling to push me past the opportunity. 'A rolling saint gathers no attachments,' advises Padarthanand, his language skills sophisticated enough to re-write the aphorism. I am a poor candidate for sainthood, but I do recognise his advice as the voice of experience from a fellow traveller in this discipline.

It is not so much that celibacy is an end in itself. The majority of students are householders, after all. My teacher is too, and so was his father. As I see it, I haven't committed myself to a monastic lifestyle, I am serving my Master at an important stage in his work, and I find great fulfillment and excitement in that. Celibacy, here, is simply a means to that end. His work is to teach people the ultimate yoga—that kind of docking procedure whereby people reconnect with the root of being and the ultimate source of peace. As an instructor, I am not teaching a theology but an empirical practice. My job is not to train people to believe in a certain philosophy, nor even to swear adherence to the group, let alone train them in a renunciate lifestyle. I am there, on behalf of the Master, to assist individuals to make a subtle connection within themselves. They are not required to enter into a relationship with me. The meeting between aspirant and instructor is a sacred, trust-based encounter, nonetheless, intimate in unfamiliar ways, and I feel privileged to watch as people begin to locate the exquisite blessing emanating with every breath.

To facilitate that intimate and truly private process I know that I need to be out of the way. My personal story—the clatter of my opinions and the sticky pull of my desires—might provide raw material for satsang but is otherwise irrelevant to their process. I don't want to muddy the waters for people coming into clarity. How gross if I should be there, tugging at their attention: notice *me*, love *me*, feel *me*, touch *me*. I want to become transparent so they can look back calmly within, undisturbed and undistracted by me and, even as I attend to their questions, it is a curiously impersonal task.

The situation is the same with people who are already into the process. They come for inspiration, ask for reviews of the practice, inquire about the ashram. I am there to help them focus, as well. So, even if I want to 'act out' a desire for a sensual or affective relationship for my own personal satisfaction, I can't in all conscience involve any of them in that. I need to re-focus daily, literally shifting the focal length of awareness back towards the deeper satisfactions and relinquish, again and again, the lesser cravings.

But the wheels are about to fall off.

down and out in fragrant harbour

What fortitude the soul contains
——Emily Dickinson

Hong Kong, circa 1979. Perhaps it is the effect of the 'stripping down'. Or perhaps like John Chan, I was drawn to this service because I heard instructors would enjoy many more meetings with the Master. Now I find myself resenting being left out on the road, in the remote reaches of the Pacific, rather than hanging out with Maharaji in Europe, or the US, or South America, as the other instructors seem to do.

But what do I have to complain about? How hard life is for so many inhabitants of the planet. In Hong Kong, it seems the whole damned human rat race is compressed into just a few square miles. Everyone struggles desperately to get ahead, pair off, have a family, work tirelessly to provide for each other, and then … die.

A dark cloud seeps in and slowly takes a grip of my entrails. It is not so much the oppressive crush of human toil all around me that is the source—I believe that Knowledge holds the key to alleviating suffering, after all—it's something inside me that is floundering, collapsing.

I can't work out what is wrong. I continue with my duties but I feel I am sinking. The days drag. Meditation is dull and unrewarding. I prop myself up, going through the motions, with only the dregs of inspiration to motivate me.

Meanwhile, the patient local devotees gather in the evenings, taking rest from their toils to seek spiritual sustenance through me, the visiting instructor, but what is the source of my own inspiration? I hardly ever see my teacher. When I speak, it is as if the weight of five million people is pulling us down. I am deeply impressed by the locals' tireless perseverance and try to take that up as my lesson. 'Perseverance furthers', the I Ching would advise me, yes, but 'it pays to see the great man', too! Stirring myself from the black mud of my own inertia, I am impressed that grace somehow gets the wheels turning and I can deliver as required. Each time I have to speak, for a short while I am lifted out of myself, and what needs to come through, comes through.

As long as I am doing this service, there's clarity, even humour, and a flow of inspiration that carries all of us along for an hour or so. It's a small miracle, every time. But when it comes to my own practice, there's nothing but effort. I do a Knowledge session for three sincere aspirants who have emerged from the masses to inquire about another way of living. They make the subtle connection successfully, grateful to find their way back home. But again, even after the palpable grace of the Knowledge session, when I return to my own practice it's like a damp squib.

My enthusiasm has gone. Hope falters, staggers and falls away. A man could kill himself, feeling like this.

I remember the chrysalis in the garden, when I was a boy. I know I can't leave the process half done, even if the pathway of growth seems to have petered out in darkness.

Am I a hypocrite, I ask myself, to speak about something I'm not even experiencing? Have I been kidding myself all this while? Has denial, finally unable to withstand the onslaught of some lack of belief in this entire process, unmasked me as a self-deluding fraud? Is this a crisis brought about by doubt?

It is more than that. A few niggling doubts would not be enough to undermine everything I have experienced. Is this one great big doubt, then; doubt-as-ontology; doubt as an existential state of being? Whatever it is, it is not like the gnawing anxiety I experienced before, that drained away in the very first weeks of the company of his devotees. No, I don't have any problems with my teacher (apart from not getting to see him enough), nor the practice, nor the service I am engaged with. Perhaps this is not about doubt at all; it is some deeper malaise. If this is depression, how can that be squared with what I am preaching?

Every time I prop myself up, give myself over to talk for others' benefit, there's clarity, understanding, inspiration. For others. Nothing for myself. I go back to meditation and the clarity and inspiration are gone. It's like a slow and thorough death and it drags on me for months. It's as if the whole edifice of identity—all the effective resources I have patched together to cope, through thirty-something years—is simply inadequate to take me any further. Sleep is no escape either; the same blankness and discomfort mocks my hope there, and my days are as dark as my nights.

I have heard of other instructors calling up HQ, asking to be brought in off the road. Should I try to get hold of a phone number of someone close to the centre of operations? If I were on tour in Europe, or the United States, even South America, where the communities are all much closer together, there would be the frequent company of other instructors for inspiration and support, and there are always more events with our teacher in those parts of the world. But characteristically, I go it alone. Perhaps because of the years sitting in ashrams in Australia, going for long periods without darshan, not even seeing an instructor, and just toughing it out with the practice; or because of the history of alienation within my own family, I have not overcome a life-long disinclination to seek advice about what I am going through. For one reason or another, I can think of no alternative but to continue, somehow to work my way through it. Meanwhile, the service moves me through the days, like an automaton.

Instinctively I opt for just going ahead and being 'depressed'—if that is what it is—not trying to push it away. Giving up on optimism and pessimism, both. Relinquish hope itself. No more tap-dancing. Let everything fall down, then feeling what remains. Slowly I become aware that, although all my improvisations have fallen away, something still breathes me, supporting me when all my self-induced 'inspiration' has gone. Beneath all my *doing* lies *being* itself—bedrock. That the 'me' rests on the body of an apparently sleeping giant and this is what underpins me, inspired or not, tap-dancing or not. To persevere is to let all the unwieldy superstructures of the belief in the self and all its needs be destroyed, ruthlessly, and the ramshackle devices of my puny human expectations be blown away. 'I' dies and lives from this place, without any need for embellishment.

Maharaji's father, Shri Hans, commanded his students to 'always have faith in God'. I have always shied away from 'faith' as a religious concept, and taken comfort in the belief that I don't need faith. Or belief. I have a practice, an *empirical* practice—it's about knowing from lived experience, not belief. I don't rely on ideas about 'God'.

Now, from this bedrock place, uncovered over months alone, I find that indeed, I *don't* have 'faith'; instead, deep down, *faith has me*, and reality tips into a new configuration. A faith that is neither a projection of hopes, nor a construct willed into being and kept alive by belief. This new sort of faith is born out of my little death, the fatal intersection of me with the

232 | VICTOR MARSH

apparently indifferent universe; the discovery of what is there when 'I' is not. Something sustains me—has been sustaining me, will continue to sustain me—through the fat times and the lean. Un-asked, un-thanked, it just is, the basis of being and consciousness. 'I' needs to learn to live from here. And perseverance is the only signpost on my path.

Finally, I remember something Maharaji mentioned, almost casually, in a conference more than a year ago. Typically, after a hilarious bout of playfulness, the interaction took a more serious turn.

'What if you had no experience in meditation,' he quizzed us, 'would you still have faith?'

'Oh, we would still have the experience of satsang,' came one intrepid response.

'And if you had no experience of satsang,' he continued, 'would you still have faith?' Gradually, he eliminated each and every element we threw at him.

'Oh, we'd still have you!' we chorused. With the assumption being that, as out teacher and guide, we could always turn to him. But it seems in my case he's even ready to test that assumption.

Not being able to go to see him at will, just pull out of the tour schedule, commandeer the funds and fly to an event somewhere, I have just had to accept it. But in a way, by stepping back and letting me fall, has he been showing me what it is that *he* relies on, perhaps? Has he left me alone, at one level, to discover what supports my life, my being, even in my death. Has he ever left me 'alone', in fact?

A year later, still on the road, I look back and, not for the first time, feel as if a large rock has been shifted from my heart while I wasn't looking. I am fifty pounds lighter, freer just to enjoy, participating in the simplest, pared-down miracle of being and becoming and, at the same time, significantly more detached. All my doing—my comings and goings, my travelling about and talking on this endless round of touring—is nothing more than a puff of cloud drifting through a clear blue sky.

When Maharaji says: 'Even in your darkest hour, I will not abandon you,' I know I have recovered the root of that possibility, but I have had to find it within. And from that place, I appreciate meetings with the Master even more. The next time I see him in Florida, he looks around the small gathering of instructors, asking, 'Where's Vic?' (looking right over my head) and he proceeds to detail every event with him that I have ever attended.

People think that if you 'follow' a teacher, you give away your power, and they readily imbibe the media stereotypes that cannot imagine any other possibility for reading this relationship than through the reflex of mistrust and suspicion. He must want our money. Does he want to take *my* money? What money! Perhaps it's really more serious than that. This is the kind of process you could dedicate your life to, after all. Isn't a life more valuable, by far, than money? That same life you ought to be putting into a career, a family, superannuation and careful provisions for the future.

So what kinds of priorities operate in a life that is devoted in this fashion?

Rather than taking away my power, he keeps putting me in situations where I am thrown back on my own resources, to find my own power; or, even deeper, to find the power on which I depend for my every breath. I remember my university encounter with Blaise Pascal and his insight into *les divertissements*—the thousand things a man will do to avoid being alone in a room. Alone, to face … what? The void? Emptiness? The unreality of self? Certainly, to the ego, it will seem like an annihilation. Perhaps all my little efforts at spiritual practice are just diversions too, fulfilling the need to *do*. But this bedrock experience of being (I could almost call it 'not-being', as it isn't even 'Victor', but something beneath him, before him, during him, after him, now) has only been revealed by continuing with the practice, moving through this recent cloud of *un*-knowing.

Practising knowledge is not just filling 'me' with bliss, then; a deeper process has been unfolding that is re-connecting little me to the greater whole and, in the process, stripping away my dependence on anything but that. Riding out the 'depression' has enabled a deeper centering to take place.

At high school I was a sprinter, but this is the long distance haul.

I have watched how a potter must tame centrifugal force, determined to bring the clay under her hands into centre on the wheel. If she tries to raise the walls of the pot before the clay is centred, it spins off kilter and undoes all her work. That's what the master potter has been doing to me, finessing me into a deep realignment with a centre of being beyond 'me'.

Instead of fleeing, I continued with the disciplines, and when the bottom seemed to drop out of it all for me, that experience has served only to reveal a deeper ground of being which doesn't depend on me or my most sincere and dogged application. I depend on it, utterly. Such a relief—letting go to that—you could almost call it freedom.

Deeper still, I start to understand what he is referring to when he quotes Kabirdas, the mediaeval Indian saint who sang (in this approximate translation):

> That a drop resides in an ocean, everyone knows.
> But an ocean that resides in a drop?
> Only a few know that!

1979. I go to a festival in Miami Beach. At the time Maharaji favours this location because it's a central point for people to gather from across the United States, from South America, and for direct flights in from Europe. It's good for everyone except those in the Pacific, but many make the trek anyway. After the festival, he gathers the instructors for a short conference and, beyond answering the few questions we might have, it's a welcome opportunity for us to bathe in his kindness and soak up some inspiration.

At the conference, even while we are soaking in his presence, he doesn't let the chance go by to teach us a very valuable lesson.

Instructors often ask for advice about particular situations they have faced. We want to check if we have given the right answer, done the right thing in some situation, sometimes even pressing him for a 'ruling' on certain issues, so we might all know what to do if faced with the same situation, or the same inquiry. Sometimes he will respond as requested, but on this occasion he takes us to another place. Typically, this is in the middle of a very playful time when we are all laughing and relaxed. Almost unobtrusively, he introduces a question into the play.

'So, you're on the road, and someone comes to you who is close to death. Do you initiate them or not?' A couple of people essay a response, but he poses the question again.

All of us have heard that on a previous occasion someone asked him about the very same issue, and the word has got around that he said that this would not be a good idea, that the person would not have time to practice, and so on. In the version I heard, he made a joke of it:

'Oh, their ticketing has already been done, their baggage is checked in, and you're just going to mess all that up.'

I don't know if this version is a garbled or accurate account of whatever teaching he gave but the idea has lodged firmly in my memory: if someone is close to death and asks to receive Knowledge, it's not a good idea to give them initiation. They won't have time left to practise.

But on this day he continues to push the question at us: 'What do you do?' A male instructor, from Europe, proposes that this is a hypothetical question but Maharaji insists that we are to take it as happening now, and we have to decide, now. What are you going to do? A courageous few offer answers. Some shrink back, letting others take the lead. Not letting anyone off the hook, he goes around the room and asks each one of us in turn. What do you do?

By the time he gets through all of us, he has heard every possible response or combination of possible responses. But he concludes by saying: 'Well, you're all wrong, because you don't know until you are there, in that situation, what you must do.'

Wouldn't it have been simpler just to give us all a ruling? In fact, he demolished the idea that we already have the answer, from something he is reported to have said previously.

You don't know until you are there. If you have a fixed idea of what is appropriate, you will not be able to respond to the subtle particulars of each time, place and situation. No book of rulings would be supple enough for all contingencies.

So, what I have called the 'stripping away' process is not a gratuitous exercise in demolishing the ego. And even when it seems that he is forcing me to depend on nothing, in fact, I am not alone; the subtle presence is there for me, in ways that I could not have expected. But I won't find that trust, in new situations, moment by moment, unless I can be in the present, not reaching back into memory, trying to recall what he might have said, but clear enough to respond, always, in the moment. In this case, the sacrifice of a kind of certainty is not intended to leave one adrift, but free. Free to be used by a different operation of consciousness—not 'me'. For those souls seeking a little guidance at a crucial point in their own process, my puny little ego will obviously be an unreliable guide. Yet the 'advice', without a rule-book to guide me, is not merely random. He has me spending hours a day engaged with the process of reconnecting with the deeper layers of being, where my wee personal self is refocused, to be more or less re-absorbed within the greater field of which it is already a part. As long as I do my job—which is less about giving advice, or inspiration, than to disappear—the responses to sincere inquiry that come through me, a mere relay station, are more likely to be attuned (albeit mysteriously) to the needs of their deepest selves.

On the last day, just as he is leaving, John Chan calls out for Maharaji to stay longer. Caught by the gentle note in John's entreaty, he pauses in the doorway and turns to look back at us all smiling in the hope of further indulgence.

'I know it's tough being out there, on the road,' he says. (My heart perks up, looking for an extra little puff of inspiration to carry me through the next tour, however long that might be. But the advice is blunt.)

'So, toughen up!' he says, and leaves.

blown out

November 1979. I go to Florida again to join in the preparations for a six-day festival in Kissimmee, near Orlando. A horde of volunteers is setting up a tent city in a hundred acres or so of an orange grove leased for the occasion. Numbers swell daily as the event approaches and everyone is drawn into the buzz of preparations. A small team grades internal roadways; some assemble tent kitchens and others construct a large stage complex, with room for two rock bands—one on either side of the main stage—and above those a platform for our teacher to speak from, providing a good eye line all the way to the back of the field. Participants are drawn in from various parts of the world and the anticipation of being with him over an extended program feeds our enthusiasm. So many different types of people, yet for every one of us, he is the radiant source of inspiration.

Each evening these advance workers gather for satsang in one of the larger tents already erected. Two nights before the official start of the event the numbers have swelled to two thousand or so (of what will eventually become 12,000). Rumours have swirled all day of his imminent arrival. The buzz builds in the tent, speakers alternating with musicians. Soon enough, we hear a thudding beat approaching overhead, signaling his arrival on the scene, and everyone streams out, abandoning the program. A helicopter hovers overhead in the dark. Suddenly a searchlight switches on underneath the chopper, splashing light over the cheering crowd prancing about below. The chopper moves on to land behind the stage area where a team has erected a set of trailers that he and his family will stay in for the duration of the festival. We all crowd back into the tent, jubilant. Everyone has been working to make ready for his arrival; now the final piece is in place.

As we settle down to continue the program, the MC announces that there is a live feed of the audio from the sound system right into his trailer and, should he choose, he will be able to hear everything, virtually attending the event. The excitement rises, but pity the poor person who will be asked to speak next.

There are already a half-dozen instructors from different continents gathered near the rostrum and the MC will pick one to address us happy campers. I'm sure I won't be chosen. I spend most of my time roaming the countries of the Pacific and East Asia and I don't get to as many events as, say, the American or European instructors, who are much better known. Nonetheless, so as not to be noticed I cower behind the person sitting in front of me, trying to occupy as small a space as possible.

Why is it that you can feel the energy fingering you even before your name is announced?

'The next person to speak will be instructor Vic Marsh ...'

Oh shit. I can't believe it. Why should I be the bunny? The mood in the tent is buoyant and everyone is waiting expectantly but what I am feeling is intense reluctance. It's all right when there's no one else available but who wants to hear from me, when the real draw-card is just across the way?

I have to drag myself towards the low platform where the microphone stands and before I get up to speak I pay a long, deep obeisance in the general direction of his trailer.

Really, I should be able to cope, I've been doing this, year in, year out, every day of the year and even if I start slowly, it's always a little miracle when the words start to flow. But on this occasion, is there any need for someone like me to blather on? I for one would rather hear from him, directly, or *anybody* else for that matter ... In my heart I am, once again, pleading:

'Please help me!' I can't believe I'm supposed to say something. 'Just get me out of the way, please, and *you* manifest!' An expectant silence falls as I step up to the microphone. I stand at the microphone, still reluctant, and lift up my head to face the crowd.

But I can't speak. My whole being is being squeezed by the most intense experience of love I have ever felt and it is swallowing me up completely, from within. Every molecule that constitutes me is dissolving; 'I' totally unzipped; all my systems have gone haywire with love. I am literally *unable* to speak—not even a single syllable.

How could I be so instantaneously undone, from top to toe, inside out? I feel the crowd's expectation and I try to force out some words.

'Uhn ...' My very breath is extinguished by love and my effort to say something—anything—comes out as a breathless grunt. All those faces waiting to hear from me but the energy has expanded itself so totally through me that I can barely stand or hold my head up; it requires too much physical effort and I have lost the strength to resist the upswelling energy.

People are looking quizzically in my direction. My mouth works helplessly like some beached fish and my hands cling to the microphone stand for support.

A murmur swells through the crowd. They start to applaud and cheer as they see what he is doing to me and the bliss starts to catch on.

'Uhn ...' Still, I can barely lift my head for more than a second before the sheer effort of holding it up falls back and I dissolve again into the overwhelming experience. After a couple of minutes of conspicuous futility I collapse to the ground and the tent explodes with whoops and whistles and raucous applause. They don't need to hear sentences strung together coherently by me, they see something more direct. I asked him to get me out of the way. My hand flails in a feeble gesture back towards his compound. I see that they see him working directly, through my delirium.

The MC calls for a musician and I crawl back to my place to sit, spent, wondering what hit me yet at the same time in no hurry to come back to 'normal'. Still floating in intense waves of bliss I don't want to emerge. I've been undone by love.

holi holi holi

1980. After all the various highs I have experienced, he plunges me deep into another, beyond anything I have ever known. Rather than in some antique pilgrimage site, these more intense shewings come where you might least expect them. He adapts an ancient celebration from India into a very Western setting: at the Orange Bowl, a college football stadium in Miami, Florida.

Sometimes known as the Festival of Colours, *Holi* is as traditional in India as some of our annual celebrations in the West: Thanksgiving, say, or Easter; but it's quite a wild celebration. As common as it is, many people forget that it was originally intended to celebrate the devotion of a great servant of God, named Prahlad. According to one legend, Prahlad was the son of an evil king, Hiranyakashyap, who wanted everybody in his kingdom to worship only him. Instead, much to his father's displeasure, Prahlad, even when young, was an ardent devotee of Lord Vishnu. So the jealous king enjoined Prahlad's sister, Holika, to sit in a blazing bonfire with Prahlad in her lap. Holika had been granted a boon whereby she could enter fire without destroying herself. (It's complicated, I know, but it *is* an Indian story!) However, Holika was not aware that the boon worked only when she entered the fire alone, so she was burned to a crisp while, due to his extreme devotion, Prahlad was saved by the grace of the god Vishnu. The riotous festival, therefore, celebrates the victory of good over evil and the triumph of sincere devotion. As a spring festival it celebrates the promise of light and summer after the gloom of winter. In India today, Holi tends to be commemorated by a wild free-for-all in which people shower each other with coloured powders, dyes and paint— even motor oil—and in the hands of some, it can get quite rough.

There are marvellous photos of Shri Hans Ji Maharaji—my teacher's father—gathered with his devotees in playful celebrations of the festival, and all are beaming with glee. Everyone becomes a child during Holi. Some of the first generation of Western devotees who experienced the celebration at the ashrams in India ask our teacher to play Holi in the West and it is to be staged this day at the famous gridiron stadium in Florida.

His love of technology has transformed the play, lifting it entirely into another scale—physically, and in other ways too. He has enlisted devotees from Canada, real-life officers in the Fire Department, to rig up a two-jet water cannon, with adjustable nozzles, mounted on a swiveling base. It's gigantic. Water shoots through the nozzles at high pressure, just like the fire hoses they would use on large buildings. Here at the Orange Bowl, the double-barreled cannon is mounted on top of a two-storey stage in the centre of the field. As for the colours, subsidiary lines feed liquid dyes into the jet stream from large barrels off to one side. The stands are empty but several thousand devotees gather on the grass of the playing field, all dressed in white.

Loud music rocks through the stadium's PA system and the mood is as bright as the Florida sunshine. Multi-coloured garlands of flowers are draped over the water cannon and along the rails of the stage and a walkway where, pretty soon, he comes striding with his young family, also dressed in whites. After some preliminary play amongst the family, bucketing each other with coloured water, he mounts the stairs to the topmost level, where the water cannon sits ready for action. A nozzle on each hose enables him either to focus the water into a direct jet, or spray it out in a diffused array. While operating the cannon, he uses levers on a handgrip to select which colours to introduce into the mix from those barrels of dye over to the side.

He turns on the jets, spreading clear water in a diffuse spray across the heads of the crowd across the field. He wets us all thoroughly with a few trial passes, eliciting roars of delight. He starts introducing colour into the mix—a jet of red spreads across one section of the crowd, then a short blast paints another section blue. Changing the nozzle so the water becomes a jet, he takes direct aim at a couple of the security staff and bowls them right off their feet, skidding them across the wet grass on their backsides, cackling with laughter. Soon the air is filled with a numinous mist of changing hues, and the mud underfoot is pocked with small pools reflecting other rainbow colours.

Everyone is leaping up and down, some are calling out for a direct hit. Somehow, he manages to pick out from the crowd those who can handle some extra force and tickles them pink (and green, and red, and every other colour available) with an intense jet of water. Looking around, I see every face turned up towards him, blotched with motley colours and beaming with joy. I look down and see a fine spray of colour has washed my white clothes violet. The rainbowed air all around carries us into a state of wonder and then the drenching wetness of some powerful new blast washes over us, again and again, in the most intense cleansing of body, mind and soul.

Every cell of me is intoxicated. 'More,' I urge, and a solid blast of water knocks me over, spinning my glasses down into the coloured mud. (The sensible ones have switched to contact lenses, but these, too, are undergoing some bizarre colour transformations.)

Pretty soon, all that's left is giddy, dancing ecstasy. Take every drunken party, every disco night danced 'til dawn, every rave, festival and doof and roll them into one celebration. Stretch the exuberance past breaking point, a *reductio ad absurdum* of pure fun played out under the sun, and perhaps you'll start to feel it: the pointless reality of joy. It doesn't make any sense at all.

The local papers glower suspiciously of cultish behaviour and criticise the choice of music. The very concept of such pointless fun is too much for flat-footed journalists in Brisbane, too, after a similar stoush in a farmer's paddock on the outskirts of town adds fuel to their dark, paranoid theories about gurus. What nefarious practices can they have been up to, these orgiastic cultists?

The scene is also played out another time in a stadium in Rome, Italy and, as we traipse back, multi-hued, to our temporary accommodations, Romans catch on to the infectious mood and the local trains bubble with glee. From a similar party, at the main ashram outside of Delhi, where the dyes used are more 'permanent', one gentleman returns to work at the State Department in Washington, D.C., with his white hair and beard tinted shocking purple and a beatific smile imprinted on his face.

But it's not all sweetness and light. In a stark contrast to unalloyed joy, in Tokyo a young firebrand smashes a rather large, framed picture of my teacher—glass included—over my head. He belongs to a New Age group where the followers dress in orange and believe in acting out all your emotions, uninhibited; including rage, it seems.

tail of the dragon

With no fixed base, I continue to live out of a suitcase. It's hard to reconstruct the exact order of some of these events but at the time, the constant movement no longer feels disorienting; rather, it feels liberating. In 1981, four years into my time on the road, I go to Seoul, to prepare the first young Korean aspirant for initiation into the meditation practices.

New regions are opening up all the time and I enjoy the chance to do pioneering work in fresh territories. In such situations there is no support system in the form of an ashram or a pre-existing community of devotees, so one of the dedicated Japanese coordinators, Kimio Ogawa, raises money from the Tokyo ashrams and we fly into Seoul together and hunt down the cheapest hotel we can find on the edge of town.

I'm carrying a heavy cold. For the past two years every time Spring has come to the region I happen to be in, I have been transferred to the other hemisphere. My body pines for summer.

On a previous visit the young aspirant had arranged to screen a movie about my teacher at the university where he was studying, and I managed to talk my way through Customs carrying a canister of film. I was amused when touts stopped me in the street asking if I wanted a 'young college girl' but it became rather tedious when people started knocking on my hotel room door to ask if I wanted a woman for the night. When I showed little interest, even the switchboard operator got in on the act to try to motivate me. At this stage I am so intent on my service, even if they had offered me a 'young college *guy*' I would not have had the inclination (let alone the money).

On that earlier visit, a stranger stopped me on the street and invited himself back to my room. It soon became obvious that this was an undercover policeman of some sort checking out just what this Westerner was doing in town. Perhaps he tailed me after my encounter with Customs. It had been the same in Taiwan. 'Spiritual' groups had been used as a cover for political activities in the past, the coordinator tells me, and sometimes after an event she would report that secret police had been monitoring attendance.

I wasn't military; I wasn't in sales, so I told the plainclothesman honestly what I was doing, enjoying having the opportunity to talk with him about meditation—not a difficult subject to broach, in a Buddhist culture.

Seoul impressed me as a lively place on that first visit. All around, people seemed unusually animated—on the sidewalks, in cafes, they were engaged in intense discussions. But after a while I realised that what I had been taking as excitement was less about enthusiasm than a high that fed on tension and … was it fear? There was some ongoing discontent with the government, mostly expressed as student unrest. The war had left the peninsula divided, splitting families, and the south only existed because it was protected by the US from the communist government in Pyongyang, and the huge nearby presence of China. Seoul, the capital, was in the northern region of South Korea, only thirty-five kilometres from the demilitarised zone and North Korea. Relations were tense. So all the city buildings—even the hotels—had large roller doors at the entrances that could be pulled down in case of emergencies.

For most of the time Kimio and I have been in town, we have heard the boisterous noise of riots rolling around the city like a restless dragon.

After a few days, it is obvious that the sole aspirant is sincere and ready for instruction. He has been a keen student of Buddhism but is intrigued by the method Maharaji is offering and it seems to me that he will practise with diligence. He is still at university. If he had not become interested in this, he would probably be protesting against the government, too, just as his older brother has done before him. After graduation, all young men are required to sign up for two years' military service and many are drafted into the squads of riot police and find themselves spending their training trying to subdue the very riots in which they had been involved in their student days.

Inside the hotel room we put blankets across the windows and try to muffle the distractions from the street. The training session is straightforward and our aspirant has no problem with the techniques. When the time comes to go out for the one meal of the day that our budget allows, he prefers to stay in, forgoing food to continue with the meditation practice. Kimio has located a restaurant about half a mile from the hotel where we can get a more or less vegetarian meal (tofu soup, with the clams removed).

Just half an hour later, after consuming our frugal fare, we start to walk back to the hotel. But half-way we meet a rush of people running towards us, holding their hands over their faces and coughing violently. Within a few steps we too feel a stinging, burning sensation that attacks the membranes of the nose, eyes and throat, inducing involuntary wheezing. I can't work out if it's the bronchitis, or the gas, but it hits me really hard and soon I am heaving for a breath, my chest and throat now throwing off webs of mucous.

Tear gas dissipates fairly quickly into the air, and it isn't always possible to see it, but the body goes into a kind of involuntary flight mode. We have turned to join the rush of people trying to escape the source, following a cluster spilling into the subway to dodge the fumes. I feel, dimly, that the hotel should be our island of safety, but we find we are running in the opposite direction. The dragon has caught us up in its tail.

Air-conditioning sucks gas down into the underground and we emerge again, ducking into a department store for relief.

'Waa …' says Kimio as he wheezes for clean air, 'this is intense!' I am in a pretty bad way, too; my bronchitis exacerbates the problem.

Blindly we find ourselves trying to circle our way through a maze of narrow laneways and small streets, looping back in the general direction of the hotel. We come across groups of students dunking their kerchiefs in public fountains before they plunge back into the confrontation, holding wet bandanas to the nose and mouth.

Even as we get lost among the smaller streets and alleys, I have a pretty good sense where our hotel is located, at the top of one of the main boulevards.

It takes us about an hour to work our way around. We burst out onto the boulevard, relieved to find that we are only 150 yards from the hotel. But our elation is cut short, for the street is utterly deserted—except for a block of riot police about thirty yards away to the right, moving slowly up the street like overgrown black beetles. To our left, in front of the hotel, the rioters have uprooted a tree and set fire to an overturned bus. They have kerchiefs tied over their faces and they're tearing up the pavement with their bare hands to use as missiles against the cops.

Members of the riot squad are dressed uniformly in black—Darth Vader clones with full-length body shields and gas masks—all human expression erased. An armoured vehicle crawls ahead of them, belching out more gas. Despite our desperate attempt to escape the acrid clouds, we have found ourselves back at the source.

The situation provokes a weird shift in perception. It is as though I am out of my body, detached, observing the scene. Everything moves in deliberate, slow motion. Shifted into that state I see there is just enough distance between us and the police to be able to scuttle up the footpath and get ourselves to the front door of the hotel. Fortunately, the police ignore us—all their focus is on the students—and with our bodies pressing up against the buildings Kimio and I make it quickly to the front door.

When we get there we find that the security doors have been rolled down. As the trouble has come so close, the managers have correctly interpreted the situation as dangerous and shut the doors down, barring entry to anyone—rioters and guests alike.

We are on the run again. We scuttle, coughing, down the very street where we had first gone for our meal, completing the circle.

We notice a building where the roller door has been lifted slightly and duck under it, but entering the lobby we find it thickly fogged in gas. We hear footsteps running up the stairwell and follow a couple who seem to know where they are going. Up on the next floor we find a crowded teahouse overrun with people coughing. The poor proprietor is run off her feet, bringing drinks out to her spluttering guests. She seems embarrassed that a Western visitor should be subjected to this disgraceful display of civil disobedience and brings me pot after pot of chrysanthemum tea.

Another hour passes and the rioters disperse to take the battle to a fresh location. We exit the building through the rear, stumbling over a mound of rocks, where some of the riot squad are resting, helmets off. Climbing over rubble I come face to face with one of them, an exhausted young man, wide eyed, more frightened than we are.

Meanwhile, as Kimio and I have been skulking around the city like desperate rodents, up in the room where we have done the training the young Korean sits calmly meditating, bathing in the bliss. The sealed windows have kept out the gas.

The repeated exposure to the gas has me coughing all night. Two days later, when I go to Taipei I limp into the care of one of the young doctors of Chinese medicine among the aspirants. Three times a day he feeds me potent herbal teas prepared on the stove. He needles me with acupuncture, heating the needles with an earthy, burning herb. He cups my back with small glass bowls and drags me out of town to stand naked under a trickle of sulfurous hot water spouting from a hillside.

Even now, when I get a cold, it never goes to my chest.

live feed

On the road, I have to respond to the various needs of different communities I pass through. In Australia, New Zealand, Fiji, Japan, Korea, Hong Kong, Taiwan, Singapore or Malaysia, occasionally Sri Lanka and the Philippines, the routine is the same. I give introductory talks in public, follow up with question-and-answer sessions and one-on-one interviews. I run preparatory seminars, Knowledge sessions and follow-up practice sessions where I review the techniques. I also give reviews of the practice for the older premies and I'm often called on to encourage the residents in the ashrams. No great shakes as a logistics man, I deal only minimally with the organisational concerns of the coordinators, but I help out with fundraising.

Through all this there are some extra-ordinary experiences of synchronisation with my teacher that might be difficult to describe. Such alignment is profoundly revealed, for example, in the silky grace of the knowledge sessions themselves, when the subtlest power of all swells into the room and gathers every stray thought and impulse into the deepest, most exquisite immersion of unity. But it manifests, too, in some of the talks, and the question-and-answer sessions, when my insecurity about the limits of my experience could otherwise totally undermine me. I'm just a boy from Perth, after all, who went looking for some peace of mind. Yet, from the earliest days in Edmonstone Street I have been put on the spot daily, cornered every which way by that very issue: How can I speak about this when my own experience fluctuates so? And: What can I say I *know*, when all normal modes of knowing seem to be undone by the very experience I am talking about?

I have learned, early on, that a sincere prayer for help brings about an enhanced kind of understanding, and that I can be learning even as I am talking. Let me make it clear at this point—I am not 'channeling' a message from some separate, disembodied entity; I am not losing consciousness to be 'possessed', like a medium in a séance. I am present, certainly, but even if the examples I use are from my own experience, it is as though I am being lent the words from a deeper understanding. Coupled with the meditation practice, I begin to see that 'I' exists within a web of consciousness energy, which is the field from which my life and my awareness spring, and to which I will return. 'Return', not at the time of death so much, as in receiving every breath.

So, by asking for my teacher's help to engage in this service, the tight little web of ego identification located as 'Victor'—and what this entity might know, or not know—may relax—like a sphincter, no less—and a greater awareness and understanding can manifest through me, expanded temporarily into grace. In these endlessly re-iterated submissions, 'I'—the personal self—gives way, in trust, to something wiser, more patient, more loving; empty of the petty considerations of me and mine.

A group of aspirants gathers for a weekend seminar in Kyoto, in a spacious ashram near the centre of town that is maintained by a household of dedicated young women for the use of the wider community. Around twenty-five people have shown interest in preparing to receive the techniques. We begin on a Saturday morning, around 9 am, and by the time I drag my body off the *tatami* up onto a chair to start speaking, at around 9.30, there's a rag-tag mixture of people in the room—young musicians, serious students of Buddhism, housewives, and so on. I don't ever discover much about their personal circumstances. At this early stage in the movement there is precious little in the way of tapes or film of my teacher and the main burden of the talks falls on me as the visiting instructor. So I expound on the basics and then take questions until we break for lunch.

Among those present is an intense Israeli woman who came to Kyoto some three years ago to study Fine Arts. In a short time, she has mastered reading and writing Japanese and can discourse fluently with experts on the finer points of aesthetics, which is an extraordinary achievement and a testament to her mental rigour.

Mid-afternoon, during question time, she wants to know:

'What has this all got to do with him?' indicating my teacher's photo. (Her English is excellent, too.) 'I can understand about consciousness, and energy, and I can see that you are having an experience, but I don't understand why *he* is really necessary to the process!'

A common enough question. I respond with an analogy about a powerhouse generating energy, with a number of relay stations carrying the charge along (however that works) but I can see she's not entirely satisfied with the metaphor. All I can say is that without the welcome intervention of the Teacher in my life, I simply would not be here, doing this. Without his guidance, I would still be muddling along, wondering about the purpose of life.

I continue to answer questions for the rest of the afternoon and, after an hour's break for dinner, the rest of the people making up the local community gather for the evening meeting. Having talked for most of the day already, I exhort someone else to get up first, so I can take a swig of inspiration myself, but they are nervous in my presence—I'm supposed to be the expert—and what they have to say is very brief. They're shy and they have all come to hear me, so again I must get up to do my duty. By 7.30 pm, I am talking again.

We are waiting for a phone feed to come through from Copenhagen, where Maharaji will be speaking, live, and we are not sure of the exact time of the hook-up, so by around 9.30, when the meeting would normally be over, most head to other rooms to do their meditation practice. But the aspirants—who have not yet received instruction—can't do that, so I am required to keep going, for their benefit.

By 10.30, the others are creeping back into the room. We are still waiting for the feed to be switched through, via Tokyo. Ten minutes later, the local a/v expert, realising that transmission has already begun, switches the feed through to the speakers. In Copenhagen, Maharaji is already under way and in Kyoto I'm still talking and we are both giving exactly the same example ... live. As we recognise this, everyone is agape—including me, 'the instructor'—especially when he goes on:

'And what good is it to you people in Copenhagen, if there's a bunch of people in Japan!' Double-take number two among us, assembled in Kyoto. Everyone is stunned, including the Israeli woman. Meanwhile, I am left sitting in the chair, with a huge grin all over my face.

'... Or if there's a blissed-out Australian!' he continues, and this visiting Australian slithers to the floor, while the whole roomful of people, students and aspirants alike, roar with laughter.

The next morning the session continues as scheduled and the Israeli woman's husband joins us. He was the first to get interested in what is going on and initially she followed him in, more out of curiosity than anything personal, but yesterday's events have really tickled her interest. The husband is British, he is an architect and their approaches are quite different.

I have been talking about how the notion we carry of 'self' is re-oriented by the practice, and I often give an example about the construction of a new building in the middle of the city, trying to set up an analogy about preparing oneself for 'renovation' but, as this aspirant is an architect, I put the question to him:

'What's the first thing you have to do if you want to erect a building in the middle of the city?' Foolishly, I expected the architect to say: 'Why, pull down the one that's already there ...' but with his first-hand experience in these matters, the architect begins to enumerate the complicated processes involved: obtaining permissions, drawing up plans, and so on, with much information that only an insider would know.

That evening, in the phone feed from Copenhagen, Maharaji gets into a point-by-point explanation of the procedures required for building in the middle of the city, and once again, the room is full of smiles.

For all my dullness, I have to recognise that there is a truly out-of-the-ordinary synchronisation of consciousness when we come to the source, with all the participants: the Master (the powerhouse), the speaker as the 'relay station', and those motivated by a sincere inquiry, all webbed into the unified field of awareness.

Somehow with the service comes the grace to do it. If the master gives his *agya*, or authorisation, to a representative, then it seems the teaching is mysteriously supported by him. Trying to explain just *how* this occurs never reduces the mystery of its daily iterations.

In Kuala Lumpur, after I gave a speech at a local Rotary Club luncheon, a reporter for the local *Straits Times* interviews me. I try to explain what this process is about and I notice that the reporter doesn't take any notes. I become concerned but he waves off any suggestion that he might want to do so in the interests of an accurate report. The next morning an article appears on the front page and his account carries not a single sentence I would ever have uttered; it is a total word salad, a mishmash all of the reporter's own devising, and I am mortified. How do you control what a reporter writes?

Nonetheless, that night, six hundred newcomers turn up for the evening's introductory talk, overflowing the ballroom of a major hotel the locals have rented for the occasion. Something must have come through, in spite of the reporter ... and me. Afterwards, a local Indian devotee approaches to inform me that her nine-year-old boy has told her that he was watching Maharaji walking around the stage, checking out the event, and when the instructor (namely me) walked up to the microphone to begin speaking, Maharaji walked right into him!

The boy seems to have a clearer picture of what is transpiring than the instructor himself.

Most people who begin the practice are not required to take on the life of a wandering, celibate, vegetarian monk to fulfil their life's plan, but as Padarthanand has said to me: 'a rolling saint gathers no attachments.' I'm there to help people re-connect with the simplest part of themselves. While they're not making a connection with me, for a brief while I have to give them my full attention, one at a time. As I move from town to town, country to country, I don't know if I will ever see any of these individuals again, so it is a curiously impersonal, if careful, and even very warm interaction. Almost certainly I will forget their names, perhaps their faces too, but this introduction to the deepest part of themselves is my careful responsibility and it has to be done cleanly. That imperative clears away the necessity for personal friendship, attachment and possible desire.

Detachment comes to feel like freedom to me. Inside, and out.

Shri Hans Ji Maharaj used to say that 'the seed of everything always remains'. I know that any kind of behaviour is still possible, if latent. All of my old trips can be revived and spring back into action in a disturbing irruption of the mind's well-practised tendencies.

As I become more conscious of the nature of the real transaction in which I am involved from day to day, I see that it has always been my choice which seeds I will water and nurture into growth and which will remain dormant. A soothing massage offers some relief from the physical strains of constant travel, but once too often and it gets sticky, so I find I have to avoid them altogether. With more consciousness comes more responsibility and the greater the need for non-attachment. To engage with this service it's best to be stripped naked—if not literally, then in the sense of not looking to anything else for comfort or security—let everything be taken away except that which is needed to remain focused on the task at hand.

Somehow, from out of my own stumbling practice and paltry understanding, night after night I am the window onto another place on behalf of us all—myself included—and each time a small group gathers in a quiet room to learn the techniques that will take each of them back to the simple, subtle essence of being, inside, as the medium helping them to make that connection, I need to be rendered sufficiently transparent to allow that meeting to take place.

On one level it is called 'selfless' service yet, always, I am enriched to be a small part of it. Every session requires a surrender of self that leaves me on the sidelines, in awe, as the miracle of grace occurs. And there are other instructors, serving in this same capacity, travelling all over the world, planting the seed of this teaching.

ego tripping

Shift your allegiance from the activities of your mind to the eternal presence of your Being
—Ganga Ji

The coordinator of the Mission's activities in Taiwan is an intense young woman named Jia Wei and she usually travels as my interpreter whenever I am there. One day we visit a Chinese family who have arranged a meeting for people from their local community. After a luncheon I am to give a short talk. As I am not only the guest speaker but also the honored guest at the table, it causes some consternation when an elderly Buddhist monk, who has heard of my visit, comes to me to beg for help in solving his *mondo*. The hostess is eager to serve the food.

Now, from what little I know of Zen Buddhism (including the frustrations of the book I once found in Sydney: *101 Zen koans, WITH ANSWERS!*) I have some theoretical notion of what role these puzzles are supposed to play in quickening realisation in the minds of practitioners. Yet I don't want to interfere with a process I have not personally engaged with, and one that, in any case, is already under way between this humble monk and his master. He is getting on in age, and there is a kind of desperation in his questioning. Given my background, you might understand that this situation—with the added anxiety from the hostess hovering impatiently in the background—represents a kind of nightmare made manifest for me. I am the boy from Perth, transplanted, temporarily, into a society where the pursuit of truth is an honorable endeavour. I don't speak the language—neither Mandarin nor the local dialect—but I am the 'esteemed guest speaker' at a gathering of seekers and one of them, in utter earnestness, is asking for guidance in a matter of the highest import.

His sincerity triggers my own, and for the hundredth time that week, I die inside.

'You know, I don't really know how to interpret that for you. My experience is very simple,' and slowly, as I piece together a coherent story, with Jia Wei translating, he understands *and I do too*; his head relaxes and, as the rest of the people drop away, we end up smiling deeply, heart to heart.

Whatever I've said, when the words stop flowing he throws himself flat on the ground in an effusive display of gratitude, prostrating to me … nine times! I really think he has missed the point and I become distinctly uncomfortable. For that transmission to occur, I had to be reduced to zero. This kind of thing has happened before. Rather than puffing up my ego, it makes me squirm. I know from the inside what kind of process has had to occur for that 'wisdom light to emerge from behind the hill', as the ancient Chinese poet described it, and I can't pretend to take the credit for any clarity that has manifested for the old fellow. I'm just glad to be learning from the words that sometimes come out of my own mouth. Tonight, when I sit to do my own practice, I will still be 'on my own', in a sense, just me and my lazy, hazy mind, struggling to find my way back to the still centre, deep within.

Jia-Wei nudges me slyly in the ribs. If anyone knows it, she knows that I am not the source.

'Relax, it's not for you,' she says.

There's a deeper reality showing itself to me in these interactions that I still don't 'get' exactly, but some months later, in Fiji, one very focused devotee sets me right.

I am staying with an Indian family in Suva: a businessman, his aged mother and his wife—all fellow students of my teacher and all wanting to help him 'spread the word'. They have given over use of a building next door for the evening meetings and prepared a room in their house for visiting instructors. Householders often provide the wherewithal for us monkish types to take shelter.

I become acutely aware of the wife's workload and the situation becomes uncomfortable for me. As a faithful Indian wife, it is apparently her duty to keep a scrupulously clean house and prepare the meals for her husband. Added to that are the demands of his dependent mother, who has become the wife's responsibility to bathe, dress and feed. The mother-in-law does very little, as far as I can see, to lighten that load, and receives her daughter-in-law's service, night and day, as if it were her due. The wife doesn't complain. But my presence in the house is, as far as I can see, an added burden. In addition to everything else she has to do, she cleans my room, makes my bed and washes my clothes. She also makes three separate meals a day for me, each one a mini-banquet of vegetarian dishes and each requiring many steps to prepare.

I know that to get time to do her own practice of the techniques, before her early morning duties begin—including feeding me—the wife is getting up really early to give herself some space to breathe, in peace, in the quiet retreat of meditation.

I wake up and try to make my own bed, but no matter how quietly I go about it, she appears from out of nowhere, shooing me away, horrified that I would take this opportunity away from her.

As the days pass, I can see that she isn't happy. If I am contributing to that unhappiness I want her to do less, not more, for me, but that just makes matters worse. One day after lunch, as she clears away the *tali*—the metal dishes containing the *sabjis*, the rice, the *dhal*, the *chapatis*—she asks me why I don't like her food. Fiji is very hot and sultry, the humidity saps my energy and my appetite is minimal, but when I merely pick at these carefully made dishes—I could get very fat if I ate all this—she takes it as a kind of rejection. She is irritated and a little impatient with me. The tension mounts, and as I try to help her—'Really, you don't need to do so much for me'—she is increasingly exasperated. Finally, in her limited English, she scolds me:

'It's not for you, don't you see? Is for Him. Please get out of the way!'

The penny drops. As much as ego can block the light, puffing itself up in its ignorance of the real state of play, it is equally ludicrous and distracting for it to always be fussing about, in the performance of humility. Her efforts are aimed not at trying to please me; this work is her worship, her *karma yoga*. Her devotion focuses every moment of her active life in the *bhakti* of devotional awareness, her service opening the doors of gratitude in her heart. Looking beyond me, she has her eye on the target, and all the while here I am, like this fretful little bird, fluttering around:

'Oh please, not for me, I don't deserve that.'

Once again I'm getting my lessons from people with a better understanding than I have.

In the realm of action there *is* food for ego. In Japan they call me *sensei* until I insist: *'Chigaimasu! Sensei wa janai, boku wa gakkusei da yo!'* 'No, I'm not the teacher,' I try to say in my appalling Japanese, 'I'm a student myself.' In some countries they want to call me *Mahatma Ji* and try to touch my feet, but that cultural formality doesn't pull the wool over my eyes. I know who I am, and that often uncomfortable fact is usually sufficient to keep my ego in check.

No single issue causes so much confusion in spiritual practice as the concepts surrounding the inflation and correction of the ego. Given its centrality to our make-up and sense of personhood, there's no wonder that it should be an issue for anyone desiring to grow beyond narcissistic self-absorption. Trying to extricate oneself from its insidious familiarities can be as frustrating and ineffective as the efforts of wily Br'er Rabbit trying to extricate himself from the sticky clutches of the tar baby: the more he struggles, the more entangled he becomes.

I come across some awfully wrong-headed strategies employed in various milieux—a young Buddhist nun, who climbs over a wall and sneaks out to our meetings in Taipei, tells how on occasion she has been forced to lick the spittle of her *shīfu* from the floor, or drink water from a container into which he has expectorated. Apparently this is supposed to help her become humble. It seems to me that it might simply be training the ego to adopt new postures appropriate to the political economy of the nunnery. I hesitate to judge the practices of another tradition, lacking insight into how they might be deployed in re-training the mind, but in Kyoto, one of the brothers in the ashram speaks ruefully of the rigours of his own former Zen practice. He glows when he speaks of the contrast between this and the path of love that he says he is experiencing as a student of our teacher; the path of devotion is more likely to encourage than to punish.

It seems to me that while a true Master doesn't indulge you, he or she won't try to cripple ego-functioning either. As I've tried to suggest in some of these experiences of my own, it seems to be more a matter of *aligning* the smaller self, for all its relatively petty pre-occupations, with a deeper functioning. Working with these aspirants I know that the deeper part of me that I am getting to know, is relating to the deeper part of them and the social self is sidelined in the strict purity of that interaction. That's all. So it's not a matter of crippling ego functioning. If ego is abused or pressured, it will often simply react, and spend a lot of time and energy in rebellion and truculent resentment. Why shouldn't it be cared for and given its due, as long as it's not running you? Years later I am pleased to find Ken Wilber discussing how the notion of 'egolessness' has caused what he calls 'an inordinate amount of confusion': 'Egolessness does not mean the absence of a functional self,' he writes. 'That's a psychotic, not a sage; it means that one is no longer *exclusively* identified with that self.' [7]

In my experience, the various elements of an authentic practice harness all aspects of the self into a better functioning whole. In meditation, as 'me' lets go, I sink into the embrace of a force field that warmly clasps me into itself and I surrender to allow that to happen more completely. Small 's' self dissolves into greater Self—the recovery of one 'I' equally distributed in all. Sometimes it feels like no self at all, in caps *or* lower case. In case any inflation or aggrandisement spills over to feed the ego, service and the company of others on the same path are the perfect correction. In that mode it is obvious that each heart yearns for truth, and each heart is due equal respect. As these Buddhists quote to me from their own tradition:

'The Buddha nature is in every heart.'

Still, I must be careful.

Jia Wei's youngest brother starts to come along to satsang in Taipei, and he asks for initiation. I am a little concerned that perhaps he hasn't been listening long enough and might be easily blown away by the first distraction or small difficulty that comes his way. One thing I have noticed: the insistence on listening for some time before beginning the practice on your own is time well spent as preparation, not simply because necessary basics are expounded. In fact, the receptive state engendered by listening—relaxed but alert—approaches the right state of mind for practice; the deeper the absorption in listening, the more the mind is prepared to let go and attend to what is going on inside, all the time, when they undertake to begin the meditation practices.

For the techniques do not create the experience. The practice is less a doing, than an 'un'doing. For years, I have used the techniques to try to control my attention, as though I could become a perfect yogi, with one-pointed powers of concentration. Gradually, I am learning that when I allow them to shift my focus, the techniques reveal an ineffable something

[7] (*One taste*, p. 276)

that is already perfect and happening of its own accord. That doesn't depend on me, I depend utterly on it.

Besides, it is better if an aspirant remains critical for as long as s/he needs to, and test out what s/he is hearing against her/his own experience. Take your doubts seriously, and then trust your own experience, I would advise them. You can't motivate yourself in this practice if you are just following someone else into it. When a couple comes to this practice together, of course it helps if they are in accord, but in reality each person needs to find her/his own thirst, find her/his own motivation in that, and make her/his own effort. And there is no need to rush forward; every stage of engagement with the process is important, and requires its own time to mature.

Finally I am left alone in making the assessment as to whether someone might benefit from listening more before they undertake the practice. Maharaji has said that he holds us instructors personally responsible for every person we initiate, and sometimes I take it almost too seriously. I ask Jia-Wei her opinion, just as Padarthanand used to ask me, and like him, eventually I have to make up my own mind.

When it comes to this young man—Jia Wei's brother—I joke with him:

'Now you be careful, do you hear me? If you don't practise, I'll come in your dreams and haunt you!'

Some months later, when I return to Taipei, I am pleased to see him in satsang. But to my horror, he tells me he has been sliding away and that, just before I came back to town, he had a dream and *there I was*, wagging my damned finger at him! He has turned up at the ashram for the first time in months and, sure enough, there I am.

Maharaji has an assistant ring around to make contact with each instructor on the road and emphasise that there should be no hint of coercion with the aspirants. Either they come to it willingly, or not at all. As much as he holds us responsible, on the other hand, he explains, it's still just an opportunity. 'It's a crap shoot,' he says. You just don't know whether they will persevere and turn this seed into a life-giving plant. What he offers is a possibility. This is his gift to us. What we do with it is our gift to ourselves.

The lessons continue. On a tour of communities in Australia I visit Adelaide, where the nightly meetings are still held in the Grote Street hall where I was once the local community coordinator. The same striped velour curtains I picked out cover the windows, and here are the chairs I selected, priding myself on them being more comfortable than those in other halls.

I notice a young man whom I haven't seen before and he joins the group of aspirants who are asking for Knowledge. However, as he has only just begun to attend, I ask him to wait for initiation until he has checked it out thoroughly and made a good preparation. Even though he hasn't received instruction, he takes up an invitation to attend one of the overseas festivals; in Kissimmee, Florida. On my next visit to Adelaide, months later, he is still around but he doesn't appear quite ready, so I don't include him in that Knowledge session. However, he follows me to my next stop, in Perth, and this time I do include him in the session.

Throughout this whole period, lasting probably six months, he has been very calm and accepting of the way his process has unfolded. After the Knowledge session he comes up to me and says:

'I didn't want to say anything until now, but I'd like to tell you something of my story. All my life I've had this experience: at night I am woken from a dream, moved by some powerful experience. A few years ago I realised that what was waking me was a voice calling my name. The dream was the same, but what woke me was hearing this voice. Then a couple of weeks before I first went to the hall in Grote Street, I finally saw the face of the person who had been calling me for all those years. And when you walked into the hall in Grote Street, I recognised you. Yours was the face I saw.'

I am shocked silent. Yes, I'm touched by his story and very glad that he has come 'home', as it were. But by now I have been taught that *I* am not doing anything. Perhaps it could be said that something is being done *through* me, often in spite of me. It seems to me my only job is to stay in alignment so this subtle power can manifest. My alignment comes through service, my own meditation practice and listening for my teacher's guidance. And as I found from the experience with the Israeli professor of fine arts in Kyoto, I can safely say that subtle, loving power comes from him. I am certainly not the source.

father knows best

1981. Back in Australia, my itinerary takes me to my hometown: Perth, where I grew up and from which I couldn't wait to flee. Once again, for the 365th night in a row, I will be the guest speaker and the local devotees and aspirants looking for some inspiration have gathered to share the stories of the Master and his message. They have renovated a rented meeting space near the city. It's simply furnished with rows of chairs and with room at the front with cushions for those yogic types more inclined to sit on the floor. On a low dais, a beautifully framed photo of our teacher, and fresh flowers, with a microphone and a chair for the speaker. After some live music, one of the local premies speaks and then it is my turn to get up and address the group.

I am already into my spiel when my parents join the audience. I am staying at the local ashram—a household of devotees in Nedlands—rather than at my former family home. I am the cuckoo who flew away from their nest. My earlier years in the ashram were in the Eastern states and now, as an instructor, I am always on the move—overseas as often as not—so I hardly ever have the chance to see them, and even on this visit the schedule is tight.

Unfamiliar as they are with the format of the meetings—perhaps they think it's like going to church—their humility is natural and I feel a great wave of love for them, even from this distance. I watch as they take their seats and see them surrounded by a nimbus of soft light that suffuses their upper bodies.

I admire their courage in coming: they could have been afraid of throwing themselves into something alien. The movement has been portrayed as being a 'cult' by the news media. At one point my mother has inquired anxiously whether the teacher might ever require us to commit mass suicide, after she hears about the Jim Jones debacle in the South American jungle. While I feel that is a particularly wrong-headed, even insensitive take on what I am up to, given my lack of communication I know I can't blame her. Still, by now I expect them to understand—they did visit me in Brisbane early on and were smothered with attention by Penny and the others; they must realise we are not a bunch of brainwashed zombies. In any case, the simple proceedings here will not require them to engage in awkward obeisances to foreign gods.

Ironically, I have been telling the story of how I came to this path, so I continue—that seems more apt than ever before, and a suitable theme for the occasion. Probably for the first time, they hear the inner thread of my life story: the search through drugs, the frustrated attempts to connect through relationships, and the deep relief on finding my teacher, who showed me the missing connection, within. I use my own story of coming to the practice to illustrate some of the principles of how the process works and the benefits that accrue with perseverance.

As the meeting breaks up, there are a few people who want to discuss various points with me as the visiting instructor, one-on-one, and as I work my way through the line, I notice my dad hanging back, waiting his turn.

'How're you doing then, Vic? Pretty good, I reckon.'

'Well, yeah, just like you heard up there, Frank.'

He shakes my hand and then he says:

'If I had my life again, I'd want to do what you're doing!'

I am shocked and surprised to hear this coming from my father, who is in his 70s. There is so much respect in his look and in his tone of voice, I cannot brush the sentiment aside. Here is the man who had pretty much ignored, even rejected, me in some of the formative years of my existence; whose respect has never before really been in evidence. In my own eyes a failed son, I have been glad to leave behind the family homestead, the town, the state, even the country where I was born, eventually to find my roots *inside*, rather than in any one geographical location. Before that inner re-orientation I had gone as far *out* in the wrong direction—away from centre—as it was possible to go, trying to leave the limitations of my body to find peace, only to meet that figure pointing back at me in the dark room of the stranger's house in Paddington. The 'home' towards which that image directed me was not with my family, in Perth, but located through an internal re-orientation. So now my home is my body and wherever my service happens to take me. The painful anxiety has long gone; so has the dream of drowning and I have a life of perfect freedom, making myself useful by helping others find their way back 'home'.

I remember Frank asking me years before, with his bottom lip jutting out:

'When are you going to repay your debt to society?' It wasn't a question, it was a criticism and a challenge. What kind of repayment would he have expected? To work for his business as a salesman, perhaps, or to go into teaching? Instead I have gone my own perverse way. Now, long after I ceased to seek my father's approval, having found a path which satisfies my inner man, here is this old man seeking me out, unsolicited, and telling me, man-to-man (we have tried to call each other 'brother', awkwardly, since the Lodge initiations), that this very way of living and working has earned his admiration.

At this time, I don't know about Frank's early desire to become a missionary—my sister Valerie will dig that up several years from now when she encourages him to write his story; there's much information in Frank's biography that when I find it will produce a new basis for understanding—so I am not aware what might be the reason for this unexpected respect. I am sure that he was deeply disappointed in me—not without cause—when I left my partner and son to fend for themselves, although he never communicated any of this, but at the time I was accustomed to his tacit disappointment in me. Perhaps there has been something about the teaching the old man has heard tonight that rings true to him. Perhaps he enjoys seeing his son playing the expert, with others listening to what he has to say.

Instructors observe a commitment in some ways equivalent to that of a monk—to be poor, in the sense of having no income; chaste, in having no intimate relationships to tie up their mobility; and obedient, in the sense of going where you are sent and accepting whatever service is given. (Of course, there is plenty of room for initiative and leadership within that.) There might be something about that set of disciplines that attracts the old man's respect but as my schedule doesn't permit much exploration of the new possibilities, I will not get to the bottom of this for several years.

Inwardly I have a mild reaction: 'Well thanks, Dad, I could have used some of that support twenty odd years back'; but more than that, I rather relish the feeling that I have 'hit my straps' utterly without reference to my father and the value system with which I associate him and his peers. If there's an element of paternal pride in this reaction—'That's my son up there; he has something to say, and people are listening to him'—it

doesn't really register with me; it's as if the old channels of conditioning—
the stimulus-response bonds of father-son dynamics—no longer operate.

And it's only a brief interaction. We break off to talk to Tish and then
we go our different ways. Mildly surprised by my father's unsolicited
testimonial of respect, as I turn it over in my mind, it feels irrelevant, our
alienation has been so deep. I know that sounds harsh. Back at the
ashram, as I prepare for the evening practice I see that, in effect, my
father's earlier rejection has been a gift; I was forced to work something
out for myself, and help has come from totally unexpected sources that
have to do neither with my family, nor my country, nor the religion of the
region. If a man is supposed to find his power, then I have found mine.
Secure in my inner bearings, I am less likely to be blown away by the
threat of macho hostility. Enthusiasm is still alive and well, refreshed daily
by the invaluable practices I have learned, and continues to open me up to
new experiences. If I had forced myself to stay in this setting, trying to fit
myself into the model of masculinity my father represented, just as my
brother did, my spirit would have been crushed. I would have been no use
to anybody, including myself. So I am glad to see at least there was no
bitterness in me when I heard my father speak.

his fall from grace

My mother has been calling to me for years. 'When are you coming
home?' She moans, and something in me that needs to be free shudders,
my love mixed with the need to shrug off the ties that bind me, so intent
am I on my need for freedom. 'Home is where the heart is, mother. I
carry it with me, and I love what I'm doing.' I can't dilute the message to
suit her needs and I feel a twin-edged sword twist in me when she wants
me to return to her idea of 'home'. Her clinging hasn't answered my need.
I have found a new strength—a new way to be in my own body, in my
own mind, centred deeply in the matrix of all of being. After years of
confusion, I *have* found out who I am, and what my brother had been, and
I won't let that discovery slip from my grasp.

In fact, I will do something more foolish than merely let it 'slip from
my grasp'.

Sometimes in meditation I catch myself mid-fantasy. My mind has
wandered off and I have been imagining myself selecting pot plants in an
apartment of my own somewhere. Then I recall Padarthanand's advice—
'Wondering is wandering!' he would say—and I bring my attention back
to the technique. Following some fantasies, energy flows down into my
genitals and leads to the familiar stiffening arousal, the body perfectly
responding to the mind.

I decide that if I were to explore that possibility, I would have to do it
in a different sphere, with people who know nothing about me, and
whom I wouldn't be leading off the 'straight and narrow'. But my
schedule doesn't allow much time for deviation and if I want to go out I
have to ask for the money. I am, in effect, poor, chaste and obedient.
Such conditions are a great help if I want to stay focused on my service,
but restrictive if I want to wander. The 'safest' way out might be a visit to
a swimming pool, perhaps, where I can covertly admire the male form or,
as I discover in Japan, I can make a late night visit to one of the local
communal bathhouses.

266 | VICTOR MARSH

I find my way through the back streets near the sisters' house to the *furoya*, the public bathhouse, where I slip off my shoes, place them in one of the empty cubby holes, step up onto the small verandah and slide open the door to the interior. A female attendant perches on a raised seat, a vantage point where she can look down into both the men's and women's dressing areas. Nobody seems concerned about that, so I nervously take their lead. I pay the minimal fee and enter the men's side of the establishment where I quickly undress under the watchful eye of the attendant then go through a second sliding door into the wet section. Around fifteen men of various ages are scattered through the area. Some are seated on low plastic stools in front of shower faucets, soaping and scrubbing their bodies clean before entering the soaking tubs. Others who have been through that cleansing routine move from one tub to another, until they find one at the right temperature in which to luxuriate. Between shower and pool most of the men carry a small hand-towel in front of them for modesty that, once in the pool, is neatly folded and placed atop their heads while they surrender their stresses to the heat.

I wash every part of my body scrupulously, then go through the whole procedure again in a kind of performative display to indicate that I understand the rules: no getting in the soak tub until already clean. After rinsing off, I step gingerly into one of the pools, only to withdraw my foot hastily from its scalding water. I find one tub is just a little cooler than the other two and lower myself slowly into the water, wondering how the other bodies can take so much heat, and I try to relax and enjoy it as they do. Throughout, I avoid glancing at the different body shapes, aware that I am already highly conspicuous as the only *gaijin* in the suburban bathhouse.

I continue to be discomfited by the heat, unable to release and unwind—how can they find this enjoyable? After about ten minutes I get out of the tub and go back to the locker area to dry off and dress. There I notice a young man, perhaps in his late twenties, who has almost completed dressing. He is hovering discreetly near the lockers and he seems to be showing some interest in me. Outside my own culture I can't trust that I am able to read the codes of flirtation correctly. I glance back and he holds my look just long enough to suggest that it might be so, but this bathhouse is in the suburbs and he won't want to be showing his hand. Perhaps I'm reading an expression I have projected into that other, impassive face? Perhaps he is just curious about the presence of this Westerner. At a swimming pool in Kyoto, one man called out: 'You are not white … You are *red*!' hugely enjoying his own joke. (His own skin tone was more like ivory.)

'Arigato gozaimasu. Oyasumi nasai,' I call out to the attendant, ducking my head in the obligatory little bowing gesture as I slide the door to the porch closed. As I find my shoes I notice that the other guy, who has left before me, is lingering a few yards down the narrow suburban street. That heads away from where the ashram is situated. The guy takes off, pausing to look back to see if I am in tow and after just a moment's hesitation I follow, something gentle in his manner telling me that I'm not walking into danger. Nonetheless I *am* wandering off the straight and narrow of my chosen lifestyle and I'm conscious of that fact as I head, literally, away from the ashram. At the same time I am caught in a buzz of excitement.

I try to make a mental map of the turns we take so I can retrace my steps, but we are scooting through narrow streets and lanes for six or seven minutes before the other man slows. He is waiting at a corner for me to catch up. He can't speak English, so there is still no chance for clarification of his intentions.

'Chotto matte, kudasai,' is all I catch of his whispered Japanese. I am supposed to wait. When he sees that I understand this, he smiles and crosses the road. He looks around to make sure no-one is about and disappears into a doorway among a row of small, single-storey houses crammed tightly side by side.

'What am I doing here?' I wonder. I don't find the fellow particularly attractive—he's a little nondescript to appeal to me, erotically—but I'm sufficiently surprised at this turn of events to go along with what is happening. Both of us have been on a fishing expedition and caught more than we bargained for.

He re-emerges and comes over to draw me back to the doorway.

'Irrashaimase (Welcome)', he says, as he hurries me inside, where another man in his mid-thirties is waiting. So, he must have gone inside to consult with his roommate. His lover? I don't know enough Japanese to ask and, even in this irregular context, it seems impolite to inquire.

In their single room apartment, a futon is already spread out on the floor for sleep. The other man is wearing a cotton *yukata* and is obviously ready for bed, but smiles broadly, apparently eager to welcome me too. The three of us look at each other awkwardly for a moment, but a current of erotic energy flashes among us, drawing us into a huddle, scrambling to undo each other's clothing, all vestiges of politesse cast aside with our remaining garments. Thank God the Japanese are not prudish about sex.

After years of abstinence, it's an electrifying encounter. Nonetheless, I am glad that my schedule sweeps me past considering other potential outlets for my newly aroused sensuality, at least for the time being.

My touring schedule moves me on from Tokyo and I am busy speaking at public events, meeting with aspirants, interviewing candidates for the ashram, and so on. Soon I am called to a three-day event in the US that attracts several thousand people to the Miami Beach Convention Centre. After the main event, my teacher pulls together a short conference where he meets with the instructors for two more days. During one playful interchange, he draws attention to the new moustache I have grown.

'So what's this?' he asks. I try to make my own joke of it. 'Oh, that's to keep me warm,' I say, conscious of the increasing size of my bald patch. 'It's winter where I've been.'

'Oh, come on,' he says, undeflected. 'You? With your hot breath!'

If I thought there was anything he didn't know about me, surely that cover has been blown away.

At another meeting with instructors, one of the men from South America tells Maharaji he has been having trouble with the occasional massage that has got out of hand. I am amazed at his honesty. Even if I know at some level that your teacher is the one person you don't try to hide from, I am still trying to be the best little devotee in the world and I'm too used to hiding anything to do with my sexuality, even from myself. I feel that I should somehow cover up my lapses, but at the same time as he shows this acute awareness of the slightest events, as long as I am making a sincere effort he offers compassion and the tacit opportunity to try again. I'm impressed that as Maharaji addresses the topic he treats us all as adults. 'Don't make an issue of it,' seems to be the message, 'if you fight it, it will only get worse'.

These remain tacit understandings rather than explicit rules, for he has always eschewed giving us rules to live by, challenging us to base our standards of behaviour, and our ethics, on the insights derived from our daily practices and the development of conscious awareness they engender. In some ways it would be easier if he *did* give us a list of dos and don'ts but that's not the way he operates. I know a little about obsession and where you put your attention. With the one-pointedness this line of work brings, you have to be careful what you focus on. If you're walking a tightrope, a wobble can become a disaster.

The issue remains unresolved. I feel that if I just ignore it and sublimate *eros* through service, as I have been doing more or less successfully now for ten years (with some lapses), that I can somehow transcend its demands. I'm not sure I subscribe to the Freudian theory of 'drives', and feel that I am operating in a sphere where such things can be over-ridden by what I might call my 'higher calling', if only I could use the term without the religious overtones …

As long as I let myself stay wrapped up in the routine, my focus remains clear, and I can do the service effectively. Massages are to be avoided. On occasional nights off my mind starts to wander. 'An idle mind is the devil's playground,' I have heard and the cliché threatens to manifest in action. Even if I haven't received much formal indoctrination into Christian beliefs, such tropes persist in the wider culture, but I reject the adage out of hand because I don't believe in 'devils'.

In Kuala Lumpur I stay in a household of young men who form the nucleus of the ashram in a large and enthusiastic community. A handsome fellow among them looks like he could be a Bollywood film star. He has huge eyes, long black lashes and a lustrous moustache over a splendid set of brilliant teeth, and I detect a certain weak-at-the-knees response from some of the young women when they talk with this Tamil Nadu Adonis. But for me, the attraction is more in the nature of an aesthetic appreciation.

Some space opens up in the seven-days-a-week routine of evening satsangs. After the Tokyo bathhouse I find I am open for action. I am not inclined to rock the boat with anyone in the ashram. I feel that I can't create waves in the very centre where people are trying to maintain focus, for I value that and its benefits for them and myself. If I am to dally with sensuality it will have to be away from people who know me and respect me for the role I am playing. In my idle hours I plot to get access to one of the cars, in a surreptitious bid to step out from the shelter.

There is a small, pale blue Datsun which has had an intermittent problem with the ignition, or the battery—I can't ascertain which—so it isn't being used much. One night I excuse myself, begging the keys for an outing into town, with a lame excuse about visiting a shopping mall. I don't know if there are any eyebrows raised behind my back, but I hope I can get away with the occasional oddball requests.

I've heard of a small dance club downtown, called the Blue Boy, which is rumoured to be gay. I find my way there and park the car on a street with a slope, in case it needs help starting. I go into the club and buy a soft drink from the small stash of *ringgit* I have begged for petrol money and take a seat in a booth to survey the scene. There are twenty or so young men, mostly Chinese, some gathered in small groups at the bar, others bobbing about to bad 70s disco on the dance floor (it is 1982). A nice-looking young Chinese man with an open face and black hair flopping over his forehead smiles shyly at me. I buy him a drink, further depleting my dwindling cash resources.

'Would you like to dance?' I ask, after a few sips of the drink, and the young man, whose name is Kim, acquiesces readily. Communication is not a problem, as it might have been in Japan. A hangover from colonial times, English is widely spoken and understood, and provides our makeshift *lingua franca* for basic communication.

Ten minutes later we are outside the club, trying to negotiate a location for the staging of our passion. Kim is from Port Kelang, miles away, so even if we were able to pass the scrutiny of his family we can't go to his place. The ashram is out of the question. We are both out-of-towners and equally ignorant of further options. Each of us has landed a juicy catch but neither of us has a clue what to do next. Perhaps he hoped that by snagging a Westerner there would be a chance of sneaking into a hotel room together, little knowing that he has caught an *orang puteh* still wrestling with the tacit vow of poverty, even while considering renouncing his other commitments to celibacy … and obedience.

I have heard sniggering references to a kind of lovers' lane on the other side of town where young couples in parked cars take the risk of a cuddle, or something more. I try out that idea with my young Chinese friend, hoping for a better read of the appropriateness of the location, but the guy is too passive in the company of a Westerner to have an opinion either way and he seems to know as little about KL as I do.

We drive out of town to find the area, on the edge of a large, hilly park. Within the prevailing climate of strait-laced Muslim morals, it's a risky location, even for 'hetero' liaisons, and it doesn't feel like a place to give full expression to our desire, even at night. So, after a few minutes' nervous necking and clutching at each other's bodies through our clothing, I decide to get away from potential prying eyes and move the car further up the hill into the parkland. Luckily, the car starts without any fuss. I take one of the internal roads that turns and winds up away and pull off to the side of the road under some over-hanging trees.

The area is quiet and completely deserted. We climb out of the car and cross the road to walk down onto a spread of lawn among some shadowy trees, where we soon start to kiss and fondle. Our hands reach hurriedly under each other's shirts, hungry for the frisson of contact, skin electric to touch in the warm night air. We undo each other's trousers, letting them fall loosely around our ankles and press our bodies together as the waves of passion mount.

Suddenly a figure appears, striding towards us. A man in uniform; military or police—it's not clear. His face is wide open in alarm. He is moving quickly, and he has a gun!

In our unfamiliarity with the surroundings, what we have taken for a public park is in fact the grounds of the Sultan's palace. The dinky Datsun parked by the side of the road has drawn the attention of a security guard who is as astonished to see us as we are surprised to see him. His brain is racing to size up the situation, hastily prioritising his choices amidst our mutual confusion. I pull up my trousers and split off one way, looping back up the hill, wondering what the hell he might do with that gun, while the Chinese boy scuttles off into the parkland down the hill. The guard decides to pursue me. With a Westerner in his sights, who knows what he is hoping for.

He sees that the looping path I am taking is actually a deceptive attempt to get back to the car and he easily heads me off. I give up trying to escape and he puts the gun back into its holster. How do I get out of this mess? I become still, compliant, waiting for some cue how to proceed. A van full of guards drives slowly by, pauses to ask if they can assist their colleague, but he waves them off. He wants this catch all to himself.

He asks for a driver's licence and takes it to the rear of the car to check it out. I curse myself for being slow to pick up the cue—I have heard that this is the common ploy whereby a policeman can pocket a bribe, and I realise too late that I should have put some money in the fold of the licence. He brings it back, open, and he's plainly disappointed. I scramble through my pockets to retrieve the last eight ringgit—all that I have left from my night on the town. He is incredulous that it's such a miserable sum. His repeated requests fail to produce any larger amount. I turn out my pockets to convince him that there is no more to come and open the door to show him the glove box. His expectations are dashed, he has no precedent to go by, and the associates who might have helped him he already sent away. In addition, by coming back to the car together we have left the young Chinese among the trees, so the guard's attention is divided. He still has to work out what to do with him, as I have turned out to be such a dud.

The flush of stress hormones has thrown me on hyper alert. Paradoxically, given the intense risk I have been facing, my mind has gone into quiet, still clarity. I see my best moves as if they are being laid out in slow motion along a line of least resistance, to get myself out of there before the situation gets any worse.

In his confusion, the guard decides to help me. The car's ignition fails and he assists me with a push start. He might have just arrested me, with God knows what consequences. I reckon that his own self-interest in trying to take a bribe has confused the situation for him and I escape through the loophole of his own ethical dilemma.

An hour later, back at the ashram, as the adrenal steroids gradually leave my bloodstream I try to take stock. I know it's possible that he has taken down the licence plate number but the poor fellow was so flummoxed, at first by his surprise discovery and then at the disappointing lack of cash, that he helped me leave, in spite of himself. To say I have escaped scot-free—by 'luck'—would be an understatement. Could it have been my teacher—apparently sensitive to the very changes in the temperature of my breath when I am aroused—exercising some supernatural invention? I tremble to even think about it. Somehow that consideration seems like an appalling abuse of the concept of grace, given the context. What I have risked de-stabilises everything about my situation and my status. 'Shelter' is a concept I have felt as a practical experience, but according to the rules, as I understand them, protection is afforded by following the teacher's direct 'agya', or instruction—not by abusing it. I can't twist the notion by reading it as a force to be called down when you get yourself into a huge mess. Besides, I have been trained not to operate under the assumption of supernatural intervention.

I have really stirred up a mess of confusion for myself. My recent experimental strategy of keeping the two parts of my life on separate tracks now seems dodgy, at best, and dangerous at worst.

I'm also extremely uncomfortable with the recognition that, in trying not to involve anyone from among the aspirants, I have led an innocent outsider—young Kim—into an encounter with the law, and I can't even guess how that affects him in the context of his own culture. However I parse the events, the scene is a tangle of ethical impasses and I have blown it, big time.

After a couple of days, I sense that the cop won't be tracing the car back to its owners. A part of me feels that for whatever reason—call it good luck—I will be safe from any embarrassing repercussions. But my visceral feelings of guilt are compounded as I consider the broader implications of what could have transpired—not only the personal humiliation of court appearances, but the scandalous fall-out for the movement in Malaysia and the subsequent problems it could have caused for my teacher's work there. These factors are almost unbearable to contemplate. When I was fully surrendered to the rules of the renunciate life I was not plagued by this kind of guilt; I felt liberated.

At this point I feel like a real hypocrite. Instead of having to keep two sides of my being partitioned off one from the other, some part of me is insisting on integration. Obviously, my recent experiments in extra-mural flirtation have been a failure. While I know from experience that traveling as a celibate monk has been necessarily part and parcel of helping to spread the word, to continue to drive a wedge between spiritual practice and the sensuality of the body now seems inherently unhealthy and I reject with all of my being the familiar dichotomies of a religion I detest. Even if my shame is to some face-saving degree 'private', as far as I am concerned my tour of duty in East Asia has ended in ignominy. I know I have done some useful work in my years as an instructor, but I am shocked to see how easily it might all have been cancelled out.

In the early years I decided that if I was to be of any use to my teacher I couldn't remain a whiny, clinging dependent. (Do you want to be a 'vic'tim? he challenged me in one talk.) From the time of the event at the Sydney Opera House he forced me to look for the connection within. And the repeated shewings of intimate presence on the road have been clear indicators how close he really is at all times. By taking on the responsibility of representing him and his teaching I feel I have 'stood up' to be counted for him. When I have moved forward in confidence I have felt the grace move with me but now I have come close to throwing the whole thing aside.

I have read about developments in the 'gay liberation movement' in magazines on airplanes and felt a little curious, even envious, as *Newsweek* or *Time* reported on 'alternative' lifestyles, uninhibited guilt-free sexual liaisons and the frequent use of pot. In the decade I have been dedicated to the monkish way of life the sexual revolution has almost passed me by. It isn't as if I have had no experience with other men. Since late puberty that had gone on intermittently, and even flourished, uninhibited, with Helm. Somehow I felt that the time with the mother of my child had been an interregnum, a deviation from my own 'norm'. I recall the visit of Dennis Altman to the Pram Factory Theatre, when I was trying to pass for 'straight', and turn over in my mind the mixed emotions his visit had stirred for me.

Remaining in the ashram, I can still see sex only through an imposed system of values which distorts its meaning. Worse, it is opposing the two possibilities against each other: either you practise Knowledge, *or* you have sex. It is a contradiction that I don't believe in. I don't want to fall into worshipping a lifestyle—celibacy—but I want to continue to grow in experience (and understanding). I could never imagine abandoning the practice. While I have come to understand that my body is a laboratory for the transformation of consciousness, no less, I hope that process can continue in a more integrated fashion in a healthy lifestyle that enables a balance between the complex elements of being human. I fear I am probably taking a retrograde step, but I can no longer pretend that I don't want to pick up the threads of my sexuality again. Sex has been a guilty secret in my life too often, something I have had to do in the shadows, something to be ashamed of, and here, the very practice which has helped me come back to face my real self and integrate every part of being is in danger of reinforcing my shame.

If I want to come to terms with my sexuality, before I can sort it out I have to *own* it, rather than pushing it away in denial. The so-called renunciate lifestyle, which has given me the time, the space, the focus, to put a tap root down deep inside the experience of contentment could begin to work against me, undermining my growth. That's how I rationalise it. The possibility of quitting my service goes against every argument I have called up to help me keep a foothold in the practice. Now I consider abandoning the disciplines that have transformed me from the hippie seeker—looking for the sublime through psychedelics— into a patient practitioner, and instructor. I have to sort out which disciplines are essential to the practice from those that are required only to do the instructor service.

Following his *agya* has given me an enhanced quality of life in tangible ways. The ashram has been a shelter and an opportunity for service that has taken me on an exciting journey through a dozen or so countries, opening my mind and heart to realms of experience in ways that I could have never imagined. I know, clearly, why celibacy is required to do this particular service, yet I don't know to what extent it's a requirement to do the practice, *per se*. Every day I see people all around me who live as householders, presumably having sex even while they continue with the practice. They have worked out their own way to remain involved in service, even with all the complications their family duties require. Couldn't I have some of that too?

The choice is complicated by the fact that I am undeniably queer. The practice of re-union with the divine essence inside has neither enabled me to transcend desire, in the long run, nor has it 'converted' me into becoming a respectable heterosexual. Playing at that possibility has already complicated two other peoples' lives. I wonder if in some way it would be a betrayal of my former partner, and my son, if I were to quit my renunciations. I know they have moved on, and the preoccupation is all within my own head, but some part of me has felt that my failure in abandoning them has been ameliorated to some extent by my service to what I see as the greater good. But to remain ambivalent, now, is simply no longer an option. Whether or not my queer relationship with social living is a fault within myself, or a distortion built in to the bogus two-dimensionality of conventional existence, doesn't matter. These years of intensely focused practice have given me a rare opportunity to learn from the ground up what it is to be alive, and to realise that I do 'belong', for that deep ease of being, fully accepted already by the original Source overrides the old, insidious feeling that I was not one of the real people. Now, given the shocking encounter with the law, I am afraid of what mess I might get into if I continue to deny the newly revived urge. I start to review my choices, using some of the flabby pop psychology that floats freely through everyday discourse. Repressed desire will find expression, willy-bloody-nilly, and if it doesn't find a healthy outlet, who knows what other nasty events might ensue?

But how to justify these needs? What waves would it create if the love that has previously dared not speak its name were to shout it out loud? Would the ashram fall down? Why go 'gay' now, after having a taste of real 'liberation'? Isn't the personal self a carefully sustained delusion? Why go back into delusion? For it does feel like a regression. If I were to find a guy to hang out with, would I keep secret from him what I have learned over the past eleven years? Hardly. But if I were to get him interested in that path, wouldn't he graduate beyond needing me? How could I keep the two things apart? Years of practice have taught me how (and why) to bring my separate self back into the integrative embrace of an undifferentiated ocean of awareness, and I know that as a deeply felt experience of simplicity and peace. To choose to come out of that contentment just to embrace a particularly difficult form of queer individuality seems doubly perverse.

For a year I try to deny the possibility, wrapping myself in the disciplines all over again, even while I consider the possibility of leaving. I hope I can do it without losing the thread back to what I have worked so hard, over a decade, to recover. It is that possibility, that I might lose my own 'Ariadne's thread', which keeps me hovering at the edge of a decision: either to stay, or to move on.

A storm blows through Tokyo. In the small back garden of the brothers' ashram in Kichijoji, strong winds uproot a small tree. I can tell, looking at its exposed root system, that this plant has been used to getting all its moisture close to the surface. Perhaps because it rains a lot in the area it has never needed to put down deeper roots. So when a strong wind comes along, it has been toppled too easily. I am glad to have had the opportunity to cultivate a deep rootedness in the experience of being beyond all forms and I wonder if I am sufficiently strongly connected to risk re-engaging with the tempest.

I write a letter of resignation to Maharaji from the Brisbane ashram.

I feel I can no longer continue in this service. You know I love you and want to serve you but I would hate to become a thorn on your path. Thank you for the gift of Knowledge, without it I would be dead. I owe you my life. You saved me from destroying myself. I do want to continue in the practice and I hope that you will always allow me to come to your feet. Please understand what I have to do.

Your premie, Vic.

I am too embarrassed by my own actions to spell out exactly what I have done. 'Becoming a thorn on your path' is my code for creating a scandal, and I bank on his understanding. I have struggled with the decision for a year, yet I haven't ever felt I could discuss it with others without confusing them in turn. I don't notice the pattern: when I decided to leave Helm, to go to graduate school in Sydney, I thought about it alone and I presented it as a *fait accompli*. Similarly, with the mother of my son; I came to the decision without consulting her. The only time I can remember ever trying to discuss my problems with anyone else was with the high school teacher, Mr. Styles, back in the late sixties, and he had totally missed the point.

Some things have become very clear. The focusing power of the practices are invaluable aids I will carry with me, even as I leave the ashram lifestyle. I feel full of hope and high expectations, assuming that I can re-enter the marketplace with ease, as long as I continue with the basics I have learned. I feel incredibly lucky that, in place of the conventional nostrums and moral chastisements of religion I encountered in my upbringing, I have received practical, long-term training in an alternative, completely empirical way to approach the existential dilemma of being in the world. I feel utterly disinterested in the old dichotomies: belief or non-belief; atheism *vs* theism. This is pragmatic. Just as a musician would not attempt to perform unless his/her instrument were in tune, I know how to tune myself to the deeper frequency of reality, in which I live and move and have my being, quite independently of the ridiculous dramas whipped up around these bogus issues.

hometown blues

'home'

1983. I ring my sister and ask her to pick me up at the airport, then fly back to my hometown to start a new life. I am thirty-seven going on thirty-eight years old and I have been in 'the monastery' since I was twenty-seven. As I think about the possibilities of starting a new career, I am optimistic and I feel that there is nothing I can't do if I simply apply myself.

Returning to my former bedroom seems grossly inappropriate and facing my parents is jarring. My mother responds instinctively with non-judgmental, loving concern but my father glowers mutely in the background. I feel like a giraffe in a goldfish bowl.

Before a week has passed, one of Maharaji's key assistants, whom I know from the instructors' conferences, tracks down my parents' home number and rings to tell me that my teacher has received my letter and wants me to know he is sending me his blessings. I am thrilled that he has understood, that he has accepted my resignation so graciously and that he has taken the care to let me know. My meditation practice has continued without interruption but if I had any doubt that I could go forward with confidence, he has dispelled it.

During the call my father hovers by the phone. 'Well, are they going to give you any money?' he needles. I want to tell the old man to back off. Doesn't he understand this isn't about money? Time given in service is given. To me that is axiomatic. It is crass to think that something would be 'owed' in return. Either you give yourself freely or you don't. It was always voluntary, and when I wanted to leave, I was free to do so.

The Knowledge practice is a gift from the teacher. Through the practice I recognise that every moment of my life, breath by breath, is truly a gift, and that very particular awareness has been transforming me, from the inside out. To offer my time, some money if I have some, my paltry set of skills—any part of my life back in service—could only ever be a token of gratitude and appreciation for what I have received.

Here is my old man, the former business manager, anxious about money. What is he expecting, 'severance pay'? The misunderstanding is a real clash of cultures, a mutually uncomprehending encounter between two different orders of reality but I am too touched by the phone call to give his concerns more than a dismissive grunt. We withdraw in silence to our respective corners.

Much later I hear from John Chan that during a conference with instructors, our teacher has gone so far as to praise my resignation, saying that in fact I have done the right thing. I don't get any details but I presume that it has been better, after all, to get out of a situation where I could have caused him huge problems than to stay and live a duplicitous 'double life'. Within a year, most of the ashrams are closed down in the West and most of the instructors are let go. An experiment has run its course. The message seems to be: 'If that doesn't work, let's try it another way.' These are the benefits of following a living master. Nothing is set in stone, and he is remarkably able to drop a system that isn't working, ready to try a different approach, even while the focus on the empirical practice will always be upheld.

While I don't claim there is a direct link between the choice I made for myself and the subsequent wide-scale closure of ashrams in other countries outside of India, I do marvel at my teacher's resourcefulness. I have traveled through many different cultures, each with its own historical traditions and witnessed, first hand, how effective these practices are for people across all cultural, linguistic and religious boundaries. But his focus is always further ahead; he is considering how to streamline a process that may have come from one culture yet make the essentials available in any context. His long-standing interest in communications technology produces unconventional solutions at a time of unprecedented growth of interest in practical spiritual techniques. Beyond audio- and videotape, he will start to make use of MP3 players; recording equipment is always updated and with the rise of the Internet, websites, live-streaming events and so on.

Notwithstanding this, in the short term I do feel that I have failed on one level; failed to rise to the challenge of the rare opportunity I was offered, but realistically, one that I went so close to blowing. Perhaps this master needs devotees who are more dedicated than I have been able to be. I should have been a better example and risen above the craven call of the flesh, but instead I have compromised. If I can't meet the requirements of what I continue to see as a 'higher' path, I am determined at least to put the practice of Knowledge at the centre of my life, no matter what kind of work I find to do.

When I sit to practise the techniques, I find the thread has not been lost, and the exquisite inner experience is always present for me to receive. Whenever I go to satsang, or watch a video, my mind is stilled and my heart opens to drink of the inspiration I have always found there. In my alleged 'fall from grace' I have, in fact, been caught by a safety net: the practice of Knowledge; and I realise that my teacher is indeed compassionate. If it weren't for that ongoing practice, what I have done would have been the equivalent of stepping from one moving train onto another that was passing in the opposite direction. After all, for eleven years I have done virtually nothing else.

I have no car, no phone, no credit card, no knife, no fork, no spoon; no career history that any employer can relate to. In one act I have relinquished the entire basis of my way of life. But I do have the practice, and I am to learn the hard way how to juggle the demands of working in a new career with the needs of my heart.

For now I need the time to unwind, to remember what it could be like to simply relax and do nothing until I can figure out what direction to take. But I am also restless to get on with it, whatever 'it' might be. Life seems wide open with possibilities and I feel ready to meet the challenge of any kind of work. Within a few months I send out two dozen job applications but offers are not forthcoming. I don't get a single interview. The case-worker at the government employment service cannot relate to how I have spent the last decade, and my time as an actor in a political theatre company before that is not much recommendation either. I cook up a resume that threads together a plausible narrative, finding ways to re-phrase the description of my duties and responsibilities. The 'initiator', or 'instructor in ancient meditation techniques', becomes a 'personal development counsellor' and 'seminar leader and lecturer' while the 'ashram coordinator' transforms himself into a 'community organiser'. But these word games don't reflect the deep shift in priorities that I have lived through and, somehow, even though confronted with the major challenge in how to interface with a world that seems to have no room for me, I can't take the rejection too deeply to heart.

Back at the family homestead, my father is not making life any easier. How can I blame him? I shouldn't be here but I do need some time to fluff up some new options.

'This will always be your home, darling, no matter what,' my mother assures me. She has welcomed me back, even though I am in my late thirties, and she acts as a buffer between my father and me. But the old man resents this invasion of their routine and he is clearly wary of me becoming a drain on their finances (they are now pensioners, dependent on government hand-outs for the aged) so he sulks and grumbles until he can get rid of this parasite, this grown-up son who doesn't know what to do with his life.

I don't grasp the real source of his dissatisfaction.

One morning I am sitting on the back steps of the house, catching the warmth of the sun. The old man comes barging through the back door en route to the toilet, his face glowering, with the morning newspaper clutched in one hand and the other holding up his pajamas. I stiffen as I feel his resentment boring into me.

'Mmm, isn't the sun good!' I say, as I try to remain relaxed.

A pause, as the old man rustles together a retort.

'Bah! … WHOSE sun?' He tosses off, and withdraws to his morning's reading in the 'library'.

It is an accusation, a blunt attack and an insulting pun, all at once. My body is still sprawled on the step, but my mind curls up as I pick apart the layers of meaning, spoken and implied. 'Why should you sit there enjoying yourself?' He doesn't want to see the younger man idle. He doesn't want me eating their food.

But it's not that the sun isn't free. 'Whose sun?' I realise, has nothing to do with whether or not it is free, nor whether I have 'paid my way' to enjoy it. It is also an implied attack on my love for men, never addressed in open conversation: 'Whose *son* is it that you want to enjoy?' (And worse: how can a man who abandoned his own son be interested in all that!)

We've simply never communicated on this issue and, given our alienation, the old man is unable to confront me directly, but his disgust is clear and it comes out obliquely. As long as I made the choice for celibacy, I had his respect; quitting that, what do I have to show? The accusation reaches out and pokes at my vulnerability; in his eyes, my queer choice has been a kind of relapse, a falling back.

I suppose he has a point. I couldn't stay and look after my child; now I have thrown aside my nobler alternative for … what? But still, why so much hostility? I should remember the occasion when he came to the public satsang and said: 'If I had my life again, I'd want to do what you are doing.' It was at the talk my parents had attended, here in my hometown, while I was still an instructor. But for the time being I am unaware that obliquely, in his typically gruff way, my father might be expressing his own disappointment that I have fallen from the 'high standards' he once set for himself. Could there have been a sense of respect, even admiration for those very aspects of the renunciate's life I have been living but now quit? He needed to find a basis of respect, a reason to admire me, his remaining male offspring, but I have disrupted the projection, disappointed the heroic model of renunciation to which he could relate. By falling away from such 'high standards' I have failed not only myself but some unfulfilled aspiration of his own. As we have never talked about anything, and I haven't yet read his life story, I can't test these theories.

At this point, as our paths intersect again, our relationship continues to be distant, guarded, hostile. Do I really need to internalise his disappointment, mixing his hostility with my own sense of failing?

I don't want to let sex interfere with my spiritual practice any more than it need but, having given myself permission, I am now more than curious to let my sexuality breathe. I hook up with a guy from Malaysia, but he storms back home to the Peninsula when he realises this former monk has no money. The sex is exciting, if short-lived, but the one-to-one relation is an emotional roller coaster that I am reluctant to ride, and too volatile for someone used to flying solo.

Which door will open for me? My sister and mother give me some money, and the financial coordinator back in Brisbane sends me $500. I buy a queen-sized bed and mattress, thinking I will stay in Perth, but I can't even get a job in the Public Service, so I flee to Melbourne, leaving the furniture in storage. A professional marketing manager, Elaine, whom I had met when I was still an instructor, takes pity and offers me a rent-free room in an apartment situated on a corner opposite a park in South Yarra. Every morning at 5.30 the first tram of the day grinds by noisily under the window.

I get onto the dole, Elaine asks for rent, and money is extremely tight. One weekend when she is away I go to an ATM machine to withdraw money for food but there is less than twenty dollars in my account. If the bank were open, I could ask a teller to give me five or ten dollars, but it is a Saturday and this machine only doles out multiples of twenty, so I have to go without. One week the dole office decides I don't actually live at that address and peremptorily stops payment, convinced that I am ripping them off in some way they are not obliged to explain.

After a previous marriage, Elaine is in another stormy relationship and I don't feel inspired on that front. My grand plan for a love affair and a brilliant new career has ground to a pitiful halt; but I can't go back. At least Elaine's invitation has lured me out of Perth and back into the swim. Ideally I would like to work at the ABC, with the vague hope to work in documentaries, but they are not offering cadetships to someone my age. I am ready for anything, so when Elaine recommends a job working with a wholesaler of giftwares to department stores, as strange as it feels, I have to accept. He is gay and lives in Toorak; perhaps she thinks we will get along; that this could be a suitably 'gay' career path for me to pursue. Or perhaps she just wants me to get off my arse.

Stanley, the boss, is a tight-lipped fellow who is slowly smoking himself to death. His only food intake seems to consist of white-bread sandwiches with sliced banana and sugar, washed down with instant coffee, black. Out of the ashram I am now a lapsed vegetarian, but I still feel an allegiance to wholesome food. As I pick up his custom lunch order from the deli next door to the showroom I think: 'No wonder the guy is always terse and angry. Doesn't he know anything about the body/mind connection?'

I am a conscientious employee, but I am not good at the things that count, such as dusting the showroom shelves. He scorns my attempt to use a feather duster: 'That just moves the dust around! You have to *wipe* it away. Don't you know anything? What do they teach you in those ashrams, anyway?' Stanley's tetchiness is short-fused, and he is prone to black moods. After two tense weeks on the job, I finally give myself a lunch hour (how many times can you dust the same little alabaster boxes?) but Stanley blows his top, so I walk out, unwilling to accommodate his toxic moods any longer. I can't tell if he is glad or sorry to see my back.

Whatever I am to do with my life, it appears that it won't be in wholesale giftwares.

living in the material world

1984. Even if my monastic days had their own rigours, there are so many elements of practical living—simplified for me while on the road—that I now need to take up as my own responsibility. I have to get some traction in a career; almost any kind of job will do. But after the brief interregnum with Stanley I hope to be able to exercise some choice about working conditions. My applications to the ABC for jobs in television or radio, and for cadetships in newsrooms, are all rebuffed. Once again I do the entrance tests for the Public Service but they, too, pass on me. I wonder if I should lie about my age; I am 38 and counting, and people look at me as if I have come out of an asylum, which in the strictest sense is not far off the mark, but that is certainly not the usage they have in mind. Clearly, I have entered a world where a different set of values applies and I have to fight the feeling that I should apologise for 'wasting' the previous decade, which in terms of a career path now seems to have been an out-and-out disaster.

This indemnifies the nagging sense that I have failed where it really counts: to go beyond the demands of the body and the emotions; that anything I might do will only be a compromise and can only ever be second best. The ashramic life was the high bar and I failed to rise to its standards.

Yet the practice continues to bring me back to the same blissful core. If I focus on the success or possible failure of my external pursuits I can collapse into worry, but my essence is always joyful, whether my fortunes go up or down. I have a strong instinct to honour the truth of what I have gained through my ashram training. Whatever opening has occurred inside of me over the past eleven years I want to never let it close down again. I believe that if what I have understood there was true, then it continues to be true even though the lifestyle may have changed (albeit radically). It's a salutary period.

I know two or three of the premies from the local community in Melbourne who work on a popular TV show and on previous visits to the city, when I was an instructor, I initiated the wife and son of the host, John Young, who started the meditation practice himself under the instruction of one of the American women who spent time here too. I remember John from his time as the lead singer of rock and roll band, 'Johnny and the Strangers', who used to play gigs at surf clubs around Perth, but I have never seen his show, *Young Talent Time*. The director of the show, Ray Belcher, has also started the practice of Knowledge and when the woman who has been working as an associate producer on the show quits for some reason, Ray recommends me for the job and John agrees to try me out. Perhaps Ray has too much respect for me as a former instructor; the only television I did before was a couple of years in front of the camera as an undergraduate back in Perth, through ABC TV for schools, playing Victor, the hayseed Australian visiting his French *cousines*, à Paris.

Young Talent Time is a high-rating weekly show suitable for family viewing, airing on Saturday nights on Network Ten, and it has already been running for fifteen years without the benefit of my interest. Based on its national profile it has launched entire careers for some of the talented child performers coming out of the 'team'. In its heyday it has out-rated every other show the networks have programmed against it, including the anarchic *Hey, Hey, It's Saturday*, on the rival Nine Network.

I start work on my birthday, with the title of Associate Producer. I rent a small apartment and Ray Belcher, the kind director, who pays for the phone to be connected, refuses to accept repayment from my first paycheck. My nine-month period of unemployment ends, then, not with an entrée into the elite corridors of the ABC but willy-nilly in the deep end of mainstream commercial entertainment.

One of my responsibilities as an associate producer is to get together the talent quest segment which runs through the year. The contestants booked previously will soon run out and I begin holding auditions in several cities. I also have to engage all the guest acts—jugglers and magicians, snake charmers, animal wranglers and whatnot—suitable for a variety show.

There are few openings for team members, who usually only leave the show when they turn sixteen. Boys are harder to find than girls, especially boys who can dance as well as sing. But John, who is executive producer as well as the host of the show, would rather find boys who don't look like they come from a dance school. If they look like they prefer football but have a voice, all the better, there is a red carpet just waiting to lead them to fame.

I hold auditions for the talent quest in different parts of Australia. I tend to pass over little girls who look like clones of Shirley Temple, trained to belt out tunes like tiny Sophie Tuckers. But if I find someone who can really sing, the executive producers can become annoyed—really good singers threaten to make the regular team members look somehow less brilliant and the regular team members are the stars of the show, after all. So I look for kids with talents in different areas. Classical musicians get a generous hearing, especially if they remember to smile to camera while showing off their technical expertise. A competent young magician or a puppeteer is a welcome alternative and is probably surprised at the enthusiastic reception from me, if not always from the judges.

Occasionally auditions do turn up the kind of talent that recommends someone to be a potential member of the regular team. Natalie Jane Miller, who can also sing as well as dance, is moved to Melbourne with her family to join the team, and we bring a fourteen-year-old boy named Mark from Tasmania to Melbourne, with his family, after the promise of a cassette tape recording of his voice is backed up by an equally promising photograph. We try them both out first as contestants in the talent quest before they make the move. Maggie Burns, the tireless choreographer of each weekly episode, has to sort out how to get Mark's feet moving to the rhythm. We don't have long to groom them in the pragmatics of performance as, according to the show's format, they are required to leave the team when they turn sixteen, or if their bodies show signs of blooming into maturity, earlier.

In auditions, the same songs keep appearing. The theme from 'Ice Castles' haunts my meditations, unwelcomed. I hear a hundred renditions of a duet by Joe Cocker and Jennifer Warnes about love lifting them up where they belong. Meanwhile, the team sings and dances to the Pointer Sisters and some viewers worry that the kids are growing up too fast. The boys get into Michael Jackson's 'Bad' phase, and Vinny del Tito masters the modern movement arts of moon-walking and break-dancing, while the girls either just want to have fun with Cindy Lauper or vamp about as Madonna clones with big hair, layered, trampy clothing and too much jewelry. Karen Dunkerton covers Madonna's 'Material Girl' and the costumes, accessories and choreography are a direct imitation of the video clip (itself an homage to a sequence in a film starring Marilyn Monroe) in an endless chain of image sampling and recycling.

After being axed by a rival network, the family soap opera *Neighbours* is snapped up by Network Ten and, as a cross-promotion for a sister show, our host invites Jason Donovan (a gentle, vanilla blond dream boy) and Guy Pierce (darker, more intense) onto the show to meet the team, thereby expanding their fan base and boosting their profiles within the same demographic that watches the already well-established 'YTT'. One of the permanent team members is Dannii Minogue, who is extremely popular and, like most of the others, already has her own fan club. Dannii's sister Kylie is part of the cast of the new *Neighbours* so it is a natural match to bring her onto the show as a guest too. John sets them up as a duo to perform the Annie Lennox and Aretha Franklin hit, 'Sisters are Doin' it for Themselves'. There is pandemonium among the studio audience and at home it comes across brilliantly, too (even if the musical director allegedly has had to work hard to get them singing in tune).

I have barely found my feet but after a year they promote me to producer of the whole show. I never get over the feeling of being out of my depth, struggling just to stay afloat. In my experience, creativity has very little place in production work, for it seems to be mostly about logistics, and every question from the staff and technical crew is a problem for which I don't have the answer.

'There's no money left in the budget to build a staircase in time for the opening number; is that alright?' (This, after the cast has rehearsed their dance numbers.)

'What happened to the last one we paid for?'

'There was no room to store it, so it was trashed.' Apparently the production budget can't accommodate more than one staircase per season. Or:

'Unless she gets a solo, and soon, we are going to pull our daughter from the team!' Or:

'Don't you think the girls' dresses are too short?' etc.

I become almost phobic about phone calls. Each time the phone rings, it is another catastrophe looming but I soon learn that problems multiply out of control if you don't face them immediately, so I steel myself and always pick up. They must know that I don't know what I am doing but they keep me on anyway, and I stumble through the second year exhausted.

Each week of production is like a giant hand squeezing all the breath out of me. I meditate every morning before I go in to face the music, and again at night, if I don't fall asleep first, and that helps me keep my sanity. Luckily the hall where satsangs are held is within walking distance of my tiny apartment and I cling to that as my lifeline. As I am no longer an instructor, I am relieved from having to speak at length in public, but I can't 'hold my breath', as it were, and keep my spiritual life on hold. In fact, the practice is a perfect way to find my balance through these intense times and it would be folly to let it go. Rather than practising 'spirituality' as a separate discipline, a kind of parallel track to mundane living, I am being led through a new initiation into what I might call the spirituality of everyday life. Thus, the daily practice of attunement is crucial and even more helpful than before. The image of tempered steel comes to mind. Whatever moulding or shaping was going on in the previous years is now being rigorously tested in the so-called 'real' world.

Yet sometimes I have to speak the truth, unalloyed.

It's Saturday morning. I'm in a taxi heading out to the Channel Ten studios in Nunawading. Tonight we will tape an episode of the show before a live studio audience. The show is so popular we have to allow an extra 100 seats to cope with the endless, growing list of requests to garner a precious place in the studio audience.)

I'm trying to review the schedule for the day ahead of arriving at the studio. We plan six shows in advance and last week's show is already ancient history. I need to get my head around the schedule for this particular episode so I can spot the potential bottlenecks before the problems start to hit me in the face, fully fledged, as the day unfolds. When I get to the studio I know the pressure will kick in immediately from 8 am and accelerate relentlessly through the day, without relief, until the crew walks off the set 12 hours later and the show is, hopefully, in the can.

So, which contestants will be up first to record their spots at 8.30? Good there's that juggler, a bit of variety. Hmm … and there's an earnest 15-year-old classical pianist who looks like she has forgotten how to smile, and a ballroom dancing duo from Perth. Hmm … will the set allow that pair enough room to work their routine? The Team will arrive before 9 am for costume fittings and to start the camera rehearsals for the numbers they have been rehearsing with Maggie after school only since Thursday night.

When the taxi driver has something to say, I am more annoyed than attentive to his remarks.

'There's another one,' he says.

(Another what? I just want to concentrate, thanks.)

'Yep, I reckon I see one every week now. Churches closing down all over the place.'

(Why is that a problem? I read on, hoping that Malcolm will remember to meet the elephant handler at 3 pm or will I have to find a place to hold the animal when I should be doing something else?)

'I think it's a real shame, you know.'

(For a moment I reluctantly give up trying to penetrate the potential problems in the schedule.)

'Don't you think so?' he continues unprompted. 'When you see a church close down and they buy it and use it for something else?'

(Now I hear him. I guess he wants a response.)

'Well, I guess I don't see it as a problem; no, I don't … I mean, what did Jesus say? "This body is the temple of the spirit", or something like that? And the Buddha said: "Within this body, even though it is only this tall and will die one day, is the whole universe, and the path that leads to all goals"? If the body is the temple, then the heart is the altar and that's where we make our devotions, isn't it? This precious body is the house that God built; whereas, THAT'S the house that Jack built. How can God be contained by a building? Anything we create will be undone in time.'

My concentrated outburst renders him speechless; he has the answer for which he was looking but he is surprised … He leaves me alone to ponder the ponderable while he chews over what I've said.

If I wasn't so into ironing out the kinks in the schedule, perhaps I could have told him that when you realise that you have to find it within you there's always a teacher somewhere on the planet who exists just to help you find it. I hope that cabbie finds the connection he has lost.

Out at Nunawading, the day's unrelenting work comes to a climax in a studio packed with fans. The live performance is a paroxysm of energy that brings everyone—performers, audience and the production crew (if not the technical crew, who somehow always maintain a certain macho

292 | VICTOR MARSH

sangfroid)—to the edge of frenzy. I prefer my carefully cultivated state of calm detachment but if I try to disengage from the madness, something always goes wrong. What has happened to equanimity? If I leave the studio floor, instead of joining in the effort to whip up the audience, I'm failing in my job. I have to wade into the maelstrom and cope— detachment be damned. The production budget, and a delivery schedule that leaves no time for post-production, mean that what is recorded on tape is what goes out to broadcast. If there's anything wrong, we can't do fixes, the crew has gone. Next week's show is already in process.

Forty-four hours of this content every year.

My young friend returns from Malaysia and we decide to try living together. Leon is slim and fond of fashionable haircuts, which his abundant black hair holds very well. It's a decided contrast to my thinning, male-pattern baldness. With a brilliant smile and an agile brain, Leon is an animated conversationalist and a wonderful companion, and his outrageous humour often has me laughing out loud. He is immediately popular with my small group of friends, too. Flirting and flattering with the women, he's just as ready for a game of poker with the men. In Malaysia he trained as a croupier at the casino in the Genting Highlands and had a stint on the floor of the Stock Exchange. He's used to taking risks. I take risks, too, major ones but where I tend to seize up with fear that I don't know what I am doing, Leon breezes confidently into new situations without missing a step.

Taught to cook from a young age, he concocts great meals from the rich store of dishes he learned from his grandmother, using cheap, fresh ingredients. Things have certainly improved since the first time he came to Perth. I have my own apartment and John has given me the use of a company car. I have rented a television, as I can't afford to buy one yet, and am constantly on the look-out for bits and pieces of furniture. As my salary is modest, the shortage of money continues to be a source of tension between us. Leon gets some work cleaning friends' houses and saves every cent. As a baby in Penang, an aunt and uncle adopted him. His adoptive mother was very thrifty and encouraged him to save. If he saved three *sen* from the money he earned from doing little chores for neighbours, she would give him a matching amount for his bank account, training him very early to make money grow. Unfortunately, his adoptive father was prone to gambling and drink and he would sometimes raid the stash his wife had saved to fund his binges. In trouble with the police after a bar-room brawl, the father was jailed and when Leon was fifteen he had to leave school and go to work to raise the money to bribe the police to get his father out of jail.

This information on his background comes out only slowly. He has a lot of emotional issues around money and I can understand that he would want to seek security, financially. But he never seems to understand that my priorities are different, or make allowances for the fact that I am paying the rent, providing the furniture and so on. When I came out of the ashram I owned nothing, had no credit history and I am coping with all the expenses at a time in life when normal people are established, in the material sense. On another plane, I don't think he appreciates the value of what my ashram years have 'established' to provide a different basis for my own kind of security. He cooks wonderful meals, we have great fun in bed, he utterly charms our small group of friends, and so as long as we steer clear of money issues, we get along. After starting from scratch I'm living from paycheck to paycheck—I don't know how else to play it—but I do have an expectation that my home life should be peaceful and supportive, as the job is very demanding.

No matter how hard I try to keep on top of the myriad demands from week to week, something always escapes, and there's often a crisis. On the other hand, sometimes I am praised for things over which I have no control at all. I come to see that praise and blame are equally meaningless. I know how steep my learning curve is; how hard I work; how much I'm putting my arse on the line; if I have come up with an idea that proves effective; if I help a performer pull out a good one; if I'm slacking off; and when I'm in completely over my head. In the middle of all the frenzied effort, that disconnect produces its own kind of detachment. Effort must be its own reward?

We plan the show from production offices in Richmond and mount it with the facilities and crew of the local Network Ten affiliate station in Nunawading. After two years of relentless stress, meditation or not, my back gives out. (The standard, New Age metaphysical interpretation indicates: 'lack of support'; and the lower back in particular indicates lack of financial security!)

At the same time, a member of the technical crew in the direct employ of the network, rather than the production company, has become suspicious of having a gay producer running a show which involves children and, unknown to me, has been campaigning to have me fired. When my back gives out, I am quietly and diplomatically retired from the show, ostensibly to give me time to recuperate, but I suspect to rid the show of any association between children and homosexuals and like Caesar's wife, the show needs to not only be above board but also be *seen* to be above board. When I see my boss's lips moving and hear the words that mean I don't have to do this anymore, my true feeling is one of overwhelming relief, and I have to resist the urge to smile. I remind myself to look disappointed instead of overjoyed.

Some of the team parents hear that I am leaving but I am unable to give them any reason for my departure other than 'health'. They have seen producers burn out before I came along and expect the juggernaut will roll on regardless.

At home, Leon is freaking out that I will have no income. I do a course in *reiki* healing and start to give treatments out of our apartment and I go to work part-time for some girlfriends who have a florist shop in Brighton. We're making the rent. Despite this, Leon's insecurity about money comes up strongly again. One day in the supermarket he screams at me, unprovoked. He must have been worrying even more than I realise. Perhaps he is afraid that I will try to go back into the ashram. Whatever the reason, he erupts like a potent volcano that has been bottling up magma for centuries, berating me in front of the other shoppers about my irresponsible finances.

'How unseemly', I think, and go to satsang. I have my solution to feeling insecure in the world. Leon relies on a different set of resources.

So, from the sublime if simple life in the ashram I have entered into the complex and ridiculous world of television. It is not a career that I had ever planned but the only one that has opened up for me at the time I needed a job. It is difficult to reconcile all the time and energy and passionate belief which so many talented and well-intentioned people pour into for what to me are often tawdry results. As busy and demanding as the work is, just as draining of energy and optimism as the most noble of endeavours, in my heart I can't believe in it. Three years after quitting the ashram I am still finding it hard to shake off the feeling that I have failed the real test I set for myself; that coming out of the ashram to come into one's sexuality figures as a kind of failure; a *relapse*. Worse, that so-called 'sexual orientation' might indeed be a kind of failed heterosexuality, rather than an authentic path in itself.

When did I internalise this psychological revisionism? What body of theory can explain me to myself? I read somewhere an interpretation of homosexuality as a psychological regression, a case of arrested development, a failure along the pathway of 'normal' development, 'side-stepping the onerous demands of authentic maturity'. If I look at myself through a Jungian lens, perhaps I am overwhelmed by the *puer aeternus* archetype, the footloose Peter Pan, the little boy who refuses to grow up. Yet I seem to be capable of taking on responsibility, so how does that fit? Maybe I have an emotionally withdrawn and unsupportive father and I am 'overwhelmed' by my mother. That seems to fit. Perhaps the conventional, neo-Freudian psychiatric model is correct, then. As though the meaning of life is to reproduce and the goal of all striving to come to terms with being is to achieve a satisfactory adjustment to heterosexuality. That seems like a limited template to me and, after all, the human breeding program seems to be doing just fine without my help.

Of course, it is not an ideal time to leap into exploring my sexuality: it is now the mid-80s and the HIV/AIDS virus has only just been identified. Outside of its place of origin, later revealed to be Africa, I am entering one of the host populations in the West where the virus has taken root, a sexually active sub-community dedicated to exploring its own form of liberation. For the duration of the virus' incubation period, I was in the ashram, so my sometimes-reluctant celibacy has proved to be a protection. By some good fortune (and with my teacher's help) I have been spared that risk. But now that I have taken my life back into my own hands, I am forced to take responsibility for my choices and see those choices have potentially drastic consequences, like playing a form of sexual Russian roulette. So when I split from Leon to take up a job offer in Sydney, my little experiment with relationships has to go on a hiatus, taking a back seat to an urgent exercise in getting my professional life together, as a forty-year-old producer with too few production credits.

Ray Belcher recommends me for a job as a segment producer on a late-night talk show, hosted by Don Lane, which will go live to air, on

Network Ten, with audience feedback via the phones. The host, who is also one of the executive producers, has a reputation for a volatile temper, but he soon takes a shine to me and likes enough of my segment ideas for me to find a place among the motley production crew. I am still doing my daily practice and going along to satsang events whenever I have a night off.

One day Don comes storming out of his office and he's shouting, furious that I have apparently been chasing up the wrong guest for that night's show. A producer had come out of a production meeting earlier to tell me to set up a singing taxi driver who was featured in a story in the morning paper and I have gone ahead and made arrangements, tracking the guy down and booking him for the show. Apparently this isn't the person Don had in mind and he is very annoyed. He towers over me, shouting at the top of his voice. The arteries in his neck are pumping, his face is red and his eyes are bulging but I have the peculiar sensation that his anger is all his own business and his ire runs over me like the water off a proverbial duck's back. When he sees that his anger has no effect on me, he storms off, looking for someone else to shout at and the producer who assigned me the story gets to work with me organising the replacement. Whilst getting that in place, I am wondering what I will say to the taxi driver I have already booked; that's the next problem I'll have to deal with. Television is always a very urgent environment; more so when the show goes live to air.

The phone rings. It's for me. The singing taxi driver is calling to say that he has spoken with his agent—who knew that a cabdriver would have an agent? but this *is* Sydney—and the agent doesn't feel that it's the right career move for him to appear on the show. He's apologising that he needs to decline our request to appear and I'm thanking ... my lucky stars? Does a guru, even a very modern guru, really have a handle on the world of entertainment too? My gratitude, albeit sincerely felt, remains non-specific. 'Do your best, and grace will take care of the rest,' he once advised me. Perhaps it works in all settings.

He once gave an example about two types of birds: There are those whose feathers become wet when they plunge into water; the wet wings mean they can't fly away. But others, such as sea birds, carry a naturally oily coating to their feathers so that, even when they dive into the ocean to catch a fish, they can still fly away (and be safe). The oil forms an impermeable barrier that repels the water. So the image of water off a duck's back is more than just a cliché in my case. If I were not meditating every day, this stuff would get on top of me, soak into my feathers, bring me down, and the ire of the Executive Producer host would really trouble me. But I'm not slacking off; working hard is my part of the bargain.

I am having an intense experience of being 'in the world, but not of it'. I can't stand back and adopt detachment as my modus operandi, it's relentlessly busy work; but how much do I let it all get to me? If I fail to head off a problem that I haven't seen coming does that mean that *I* am a failure?

I remember a story about someone getting angry with the Buddha; who is reported to have said something along the lines of:

'I have searched within and find there is nowhere in here for your anger to reside, so you must take it back, it's yours.'

The story is probably apocryphal, and I am never permitted to work from theory or secondhand experience. As long as I continue to do the practice, and give my best effort at work, I seem to have a keel fitted that stabilises my journey through distinctly stormy seas.

After that, and another similar incident, Don's respect for me grows. He gives me my own segment, on-camera, doing movie reviews. We call it 'Vic's Pick of the Flicks' or just 'Vic's Picks' for short. I have to get out and see movies all weekend to gather material for my segment, which I prepare on top of my other duties. If it airs, I get paid an extra appearance fee. If it's cancelled, all the extra work was for nothing. Meanwhile I hustle to find stories to pitch, pre-interview my guests, arrange for their transport, brief the host and concoct a series of leading questions for the on-camera interview.

I have studied numerology and Tarot and it seems to me that TEN is not an auspicious number for a network; Ten is the number of the Wheel of Fortune in the Tarot pack and indicates upheaval. I go to see a psychic, who tells me that the show I am working on will soon be closed down, but that I am not to be concerned, because I will have a job just two weeks later. The network itself will go into upheaval, and 'those who are high will be brought low'.

One Friday we leave work, with our guests lined up for the first two nights of the next week of broadcasts, but on Saturday each of us is called at home to say that the show has been cancelled. We are told to come back in to cancel our guests and clear out our desks … and collect two weeks' pay.

I start applying for other jobs. I have an interview at Channel Nine for an afternoon news magazine and another at SBS, neither of which eventuates. But the producers of *Beyond 2000*, a science and technology show which has been winning great ratings since it moved from the ABC to the Seven Network, are hustling together a production team to make a similar show for the FOX Network in the United States and they need people to start work immediately finding stories for the pilot of the new show and setting up shoots in various countries.

I am interviewed by two production managers, one from the flagship show and one from the new version. I am filled with my customary self-doubt (I left science behind at the earliest opportunity when I finished high school and know nothing of the show's field of interest) but they like the fact that I have lived overseas and have production experience and they call me back the next day to meet with the Executive Producer, who is due to return from Los Angeles, where he has been in meetings with the US network executives. Peter Abbott interviews me standing in the doorway, still wearing his shades (very LA of him) and decides to take a punt on me.

'Can you start today?' he asks. It's a Friday, two weeks to the day since the late-night chat show closed down. The psychic was right.

Two weeks after that I have a crew on the road shooting stories in five countries. Trying to set up stories in different time zones, in advance of the crews' arrival, means being awake at times of the day and night that are convenient at the other end so, like the rest of the hastily assembled production unit, I work seventy-to-eighty-hour weeks. The situation is drastically accelerated by FOX's decision to switch from making a pilot to delivering a full series, for there is a writers' strike under way in Hollywood and production there has been grinding to a standstill. So our show is fast-tracked. Reporters write their own stories and they are not members of the Writers' Guild; as a so-called 'reality show', it is unaffected by the strike.

FOX is planning to launch us as part of a new 'reality programming' block on Saturday nights. The American reporters' contracts are re-negotiated while they are on the road shooting what they thought were to be stories for a pilot, while back at home base we are gearing up for full production. The salary is considerably less than what I was paid on *Late Night Oz*. But I feel lucky to have a job. I still don't know anything about science and technology, but I gradually learn to recognise a good story for the show's format.

The concept of 'reality television' is new at the time. Now re-named *Beyond Tomorrow* in the United States, we are launched on Saturday nights, in a programming block with a show called *Cops*, in which TV crews accompany the police on location making arrests. TV shows in the United States are not produced in full year blocks as they are in Australia and their seasons are shorter. When the first twelve weeks of shows have aired, the production goes on hiatus while the 'suits' at FOX ponder the ratings. Typically for television, everyone on the production staff is let go, presumably to be available six months down the track, if and when the network decides to mount a second season. But for some reason they keep me on, moving me over to work on the flagship *Beyond 2000*, which coincidentally is popular on cable in the US, and given much publicity by The Discovery Channel. I am assigned the States as my beat, so my life is turned topsy-turvy, trying to be awake to speak live to the East and West Coasts, coaxing people to make themselves and their research available for our nosy crews.

'We would need to have the whole TV crew in the operating theatre during the operation.'

'Will it be possible to fly the experimental aircraft in the second week of May? That's the only way we can fit it into our schedule.'

'What are the strongest aspects of the technology, visually? Television is a *visual* medium and we can't just shoot talking heads.'

Even though I am working in television again, the format of the show is completely different from the two I have worked on previously, and Sydney is the third city I have lived in since I left the ashram. This is becoming a bit of a pattern: at different points in my life, I go through major shifts of locale and lifestyle, mostly to do with kick-starting a career and, strangely enough, it's the practice of Knowledge and my connection with my teacher that are proving to be the constants. I could write another book about the experience of working in television, but all I have tried to do here is to respond to the question: what happens to someone who has spent a decade in an ashram, then moves into commercial TV? (The path usually heads in the opposite direction.) And: what is carried forward from one lifeway to the next? What proves useful in *both* situations?

Living and working in the ashram was certainly not a soft option; in some ways it was quite intense; comfortable for the soul, say, but not for mind/ego/emotions, or even the physical body. The image that comes to mind again is that of tempered steel: much stronger because it has been treated by heating, then plunged into cold water (again and again). In fact, looking back I feel that this is just what *should* have happened: everything should be tested under more difficult circumstances. Even though in one sense I 'left the path', I have *not* done so. Rather than being a 'fall from grace' I find, very slowly and incessantly questioned by doubt, that the safety net of grace is there for me as long as I continue with the practice. Everything that was true as an instructor is true as a 'civilian', even if the lifestyles are drastically different. I suppose I should have more faith but every situation is so different, with its own built-in challenges, that I have to face my fear each time.

Early the next year I grab a chance to sit in on a conference with Maharaji, in Sydney, and he announces that he wants to hold a large international festival in July in Miami Beach, Florida, a location that we had helped become chic when we developed a couple of rundown hotels in the Art Deco district of South Beach as large ashrams. We usually get a good rate at the Miami Beach Convention Centre because we hire it in July, a time of the year when sensible people stay away from the intense summer heat. Miami is a good site for North Americans, South Americans and Europeans to collect, but a long haul for those of us in the South Pacific. I have sometimes gone to see him there from Perth and been so disorientated by the jet lag and time-zone differences that I promptly nodded off as soon as he started to speak, a deeply embarrassing situation for a devotee.

He broadcasts an invitation, opening the event in early July for anyone who wants to come. We haven't had a big international gathering for some time and they are usually great affairs, but as my career is just getting established and my finances are in a state of perpetual crisis, I ignore the invitation. My newly-acquired credit card is already charged up to the maximum level, and the production schedule proceeds full-steam ahead. Of course, I would throw in any job if I thought it would stop me from 'following my heart', as they say, but it seems to be going against all good sense to dump the job and borrow more money to get to Miami, with no prospect in sight of being able to pay it back. So even when he re-iterates the invitation a month later, I brush it off as an impossibility for me.

By the time he issues the invitation for a third time, a week before the event is to occur, I finally hear the call. I see that every time I hear the invitation I have been focusing on money, on 'the how', in fact, and I have allowed that to dominate my thinking, closing off the full range of possibilities. I recall him saying in that recent conference that while it is easy to know what you *don't* want, it's much harder to get clear on what you *do* want. Somehow the principle seems to apply in this case. I see that I have been ruling out the possibility on the grounds of a lack of funds, without really considering the basic issue, namely whether in fact I want to be there with him. Recalling some of the occasions I have seen him in the past, I drift into a reverie, within minutes finding myself in a state of bliss. Of course I want to come! I realise.

That night, it is a Thursday, my boss calls me.

'Hello Victor, this is Peter. I'm calling from LA. How are you?'

'Oh, I'm fine Peter, what's up?'

'Well, what I really need to know is how you are situated. Fox has decided that they want to produce the second season of *Beyond Tomorrow* out of here. How soon could you be here?'

'Well, I guess I don't have anything stopping me ...'

'I would like you to head up the Research Department of a production office here. Call John, the production manager. I've told him that you will need a ticket. Try to get here by Tuesday.

'There's just one thing ...'

'What's that?' asks Peter.

'Well, would it be possible to go via Miami? Something I've got to do there first, if that's okay with you ...'

'Okay. Get John to let me know when you're arriving. I want you to meet the new staff producer they've assigned to the show.'

By Tuesday I am on a flight to Los Angeles. I have packed up the US story files and anything else I thought I might need from the office for shipping, sold my furniture to my flat-mate, and packed up some clothes and CDs. I land on the West Coast without much sleep. Selling my stuff clears my credit card. I have nothing, again, but neither do I owe anything.

A clean slate. I feel lighter and freer than I have for the entire five years since I left the ashram. I arrive on July 4th, the biggest national summer holiday in the United States, the home of my maternal grandparents.

Independence Day. It always has a personal resonance for me after that. I take a hire car at the airport, drive up to Hollywood to dump my bag, have a shower at a company apartment and head out to Malibu to meet the show's new producer. He has been looking over a potential story list I faxed ahead and wants to talk over what we might use.

July 4th in Southern California is prime beach time, of course, and I am soon swallowed up into a traffic jam that is bumper to bumper all the way from Hollywood to Trancas Canyon. Two hours later I am sitting on the beach with my new producer, Ron Vandor, for our meeting. I am acutely aware that my teacher's California base is just a mile or so away. Then, as night is falling, I have to head back to Hollywood to pick up my bag and get to the airport for the red-eye to Miami.

The next morning when I get to my hotel, there is a message waiting for me: Do I want to help out, backstage at the event? Ray Belcher, the director I first worked with on *Young Talent Time,* is the event director in Miami, and he asks me to get over to the Convention Center as soon as I can make it. Part of me just wants to just crash and sleep, my body is dragging for attention, but I don't think twice about it. After a shower I head over to meet up with Ray.

The event is quite a complex affair to coordinate technically, and Ray is overseeing the operation. A stage has been constructed at one end of the giant arena; lighting and sound rigs are already in place, and they are setting up a large projection screen above the stage. Ray tells me that he needs me to act as a kind of floor manager, lining people up to speak as they are called to the microphone, between videos, films, live bands and whatever else is included in the program. I am to wear headphones ('cans') to stay in communication with him as the program unfolds. Next day is to be a full rehearsal of all the links before the event begins in the evening and I should be there at 9 am. I go back to the hotel, looking out for a cheap place to eat on the way and try to get some sleep. Jet lagged, when 9 am rolls around, whatever sleep I have managed to get hardly seems enough. The rehearsal slowly gets into gear and I hope I won't fall asleep on the job.

Ray is determined to get in a full technical run-through before the main event, rehearsing every sound, video and lighting cue. The musicians have to get on and off their stage, the MC has to learn the sequence of events, and videos and films have to be cued in before and after the main speaker, Maharaji himself.

During the rehearsal I hear the MC announce that the next speaker will be Mahatma Charananand, but Ray tells me through the headphones:

'Mahatma Ji's not here. You need to go out there and talk for a few minutes, we're still checking audio. Get out on stage and talk, okay?'

So instead of tapping the kindly Mahatma on the shoulder and opening the curtain for him, I stumble out onto the MC stage myself, wondering what I can talk about to an empty auditorium. What I don't know is that Maharaji himself has come to watch the rehearsal. He is sitting with a couple of people in seats on the auditorium floor, and when I appear on stage instead of Charananand he cracks up, slapping his thigh and laughing.

'You gotta talk,' Ray says through the cans.

'Um ... Pranam Maharaji,' I say, recoiling to hear my own voice reverberate through the cavernous space. But I have the use of an entire public address system to tell him the story of how I have managed to take up his invitation, finally, and get to Miami, even when it seemed utterly impossible. Remembering something he had said, I had got clarity. When I realised that I really did want to be there, I had my own little parting of the Red Sea.

That night we are backstage as the event is about to get under way, and Maharaji is waiting to go on after the video being screened.

'That was a pretty good story,' he says, mischievously. 'Was it true, or did you make it up?'

I know he knows exactly how true it was but I guffaw at his question because one thing I have failed to mention was that at some point in the preceding twelve months I had said to Peter that if any opportunity ever came up for anyone to work overseas, I would be available. He must have stored that bit of information away and when they needed to set up a complete production office (on a Fox television lot in Hollywood), he called for me. Maharaji, I know, is sensitive to the slightest nuance of shading the truth. If you want to omit a fact to make the story sound even better, somehow he is always hearing you on *both* channels. It is a lovely, subtle dig. He appreciates how the grace has worked, even on a so-called 'worldly' plane, to make it possible for me to get from Sydney to Miami, but he also lets me know that it will not be necessary to gussy up the tale!

greybeard

December 1991. Graying skin hangs in folds on my old man's face. It's still a handsome head but gouged now by age and signs of neglect. White hairs sprout awkwardly from places where his electric razor's cursory passes seldom go. He leaves his false teeth out, finds them uncomfortable. The remaining teeth are like lonely tombstones scattered through an old churchyard. His eyes are dimmer than I recall, unless a spark of interest summons his mind back more fully to the present.

His shoulders have curved and stiffened into place, shrinking his chest and crowding his lungs' valiant functioning. He has emphysema, yet he still smokes, and hacking coughs wrack his bony form. Drowning tissue gurgles in mucous and regular expectorations rumble up to be collected in the throat with a grating cough, then spat into the nearest Tupperware spittoon.

The room is configured around an aging television's mesmeric eye. He's positioned in a line of sight with the TV and within range of the Tupperware. The fabric of his favored chair has lost its original colour, like the rest of the grubby furniture, its arms covered carefully with graying handkerchiefs. Wrapped in a thinning, ancient robe his octogenarian body huddles into the grimy chair and a grubby knitted cap covers his thinning hair.

Tishie's hand once worked these spaces clean but as her own health deteriorated the circle of cleanliness shrank and then she was gone. A woman visits now, once a week, to check up on his progress. She's from a home nursing service, the Silver Chain. He injured his heel, a few months back. Initially she came to change the dressing of his wound. Now she comes to check he's ok and does a little tidying up.

I wrestle with mixed feelings. His once strong body seems to be deteriorating fast. I'm forty-six, he's eight-one, and in the past nine years I've only rarely been to see him. Los Angeles is a long way from Perth, and my salary is pretty basic. I am pained by his solitude, ashamed of his decline, yet even as I ponder my neglect of my father, I wonder if it could have turned out any differently. I look for things to do, try to clean up where I can, repelled by the dirt, I make a note to throw out the toxic dishwashing rag at the kitchen sink when I can get to the supermarket for some supplies. Otherwise I don't want to give offence to my old man's well-worn routine.

In the corner the television grinds out daytime dramas.

I observe him from across the room, watching as his well-shaped fingers count off an invisible abacus among themselves, the thumb beating out an invisible order, but I can't de-code their ritual.

'What are you …um, doing?' I try, at last, disturbing the count.

'Eh …? Ooh, how many …' The old man responds, starting over again, forgetting to explain.

The fingers are at it again. I turn back to watch the tube, trying to find something interesting there, but my eyes slip back to observing Graybeard, trying to read the finger *mudra*.

Everything has its place, I see, and all actions their appointed time. He rises early, collects the morning paper from the front yard, browses the news, completes the crossword (the straightforward one, no patience for the cryptic kind.) Food is carefully apportioned: two Weetbix with sugar and milk in the mornings (a small can of apricots measured out over days); lunch is delivered from Meals on Wheels service ('Two dollars fifty and you get three courses!' is his testimonial.) The lunchtime dessert is saved until evening, held back until he has served himself up his main course: a slice of white bread, thinly spread with Vegemite, cut exactly in four, each piece bite-sized to slide down an obedient throat.

He has already explained his afternoon routine to me, time meted out in tidy allotments, each half-hour marked off by his choice of shows. He falls asleep in his chair in the early evenings, with the tube still blaring. A coughing fit, or a particularly loud snore will wake him up and he will shuffle off, first to the toilet off the back verandah and then to his lonely double bed, the same one he slept in with Tishie for forty years, after they bought it to go with the new house. At night he uses a bucket beside the bed to empty his bladder and the permanent sour smell in the bedroom is a broad hint that his aim is not always good. I've added a note to my shopping list: something to clean the carpet.

His fingers are at it again and stooped shoulders pull down his chin, his gaze woven into the countdown.

'How many what?' I'm probing, again. No response. 'What are you trying to work out?'

'Whether it's time for the next one,' Graybeard mutters, half present. He grumbles around in his throat, hawks into the Tupperware.

I consider this key. It was there in the cashbook I browsed through earlier, so exactly kept, like his former office accounts. All expenditures entered in lists, under dates: bus 50c, groceries $16.32, cigarettes $3.62. Weekly totals at the foot of each column, his fortnightly aged pension cheque recorded in 'incoming'. He trained himself in accountancy and bookkeeping at night school and through correspondence courses. Even in the army he had been a quartermaster, with the rank of staff sergeant. He still writes in a fine, upright Copperplate script and prides himself on keeping meticulous records.

'Time for the next one.' How many are left. It's the *cigarettes*!

We both know he's systematically poisoning his lungs. The emphysema has rendered large areas wet and spongy, better now at weeping mucous than exchanging gases. So this countdown, then, to the next cigarette, his personal variation on some internal biochemical clock, is this about vestigial respect for the needs of veteran lung tissue, an agreement with himself to have only so many a day? Unable to give it up for the third time in his life, but cutting down his intake, in token regard for failing health? Or is it, rather, that weekly countdown on another abacus clicking away, that $3.62 so carefully noted in the weekly record? Of this brand, how many packs to last the week, allocating so many each day; it now being 3 pm, ten having been sucked on already (since the acrid fumes silenced the nocturnal coughing, at 4.30 am); check that ten are left (fingers weaving) and, as bed does not call for another few hours (thumb beats out its part of the pattern) … Hmm, have to hold off a while longer yet. Damn! Lost the thread; let's go through that again. How many are left? Suck on one now, means nine are left, and for another seven hours, one every 46 minutes … Fingers count down to the next scheduled drug delivery. This body is being run by nicotine.

I remember how as kids we had to sneak into his room and raid the pockets of the trousers he'd worn the day before, to get our bus fares to school. Now, for all his scrupulous accounting, it has come down to this. A few shabby clothes, a couple of rooms in use in the old family house; a trail of repetitive activity worn into the carpet; and this countdown, each hour, to the next cigarette. Life ticks away, the hours and days marked off by racking coughs and the inane chatter of the television. And always, behind the action, the scraping sound of forced breathing.

TV does offer one reward, though. In LA I'm working for an Aussie show (*Beyond 2000*) and my name comes up in the end credits, although there's barely time to catch it, it whizzes by so quickly: 'Los Angeles Coordinator'. He says he watches the show just to see my name there. He's proud of that at least, finally something he can point to, to boast to his cronies about his son.

Each year, in December, the production office in Sydney arranges a ticket for me back to home base. It doesn't cost them anything, they use the frequent flyer points that the travelling crews have accrued and signed over to the company. But after a week or so of catching up, meeting new members of staff, discussing prospective stories to be shot in the US, I take my annual vacation Down Under, maintaining more than a nominal connection with my country of birth. I try to get to the West Coast, on my own time, to catch up with my remaining family. My sister lives down south, in Bridgetown, with her lover, Kaite.

I try to contact my son to let him know I will be in town. His mother and I meet for lunch, but he usually makes himself unavailable. It's summer in Oz, and he is an avid surfer. I wonder if he is avoiding me and what issues my visits might bring up for him, but he doesn't reply to my letters. She has adopted the conscientious position that she should not influence his attitude towards me, either way, and wants to leave it up to him to decide if he wants to re-connect. It has been a long time and I don't feel that I have any 'rights' but I want to leave the door open for him to do just that, whenever he feels the need. From my aunty Lucy I hear that he is good at lacrosse (she has a grandson who plays, too). Otherwise, news is scrappy. His mother answers direct questions, offering little other information, but she does pass me some recent photos.

I've also been writing to Frank, occasionally phoning him, making a late attempt to acknowledge the support he provided when I was growing up. I've been doing a lot of soul-searching, trying to look into my chequered history with a sterner degree of self-scrutiny. In the past I tended to focus exclusively on my father's emotional distance and what I felt he failed to provide but as I go through my own changes, ruing my neglect of my own son, I simply must acknowledge what my father did for us and how hard that might have been for him, given the facts of his early life: his illegitimacy, a series of foster parents, and the tough life during the Depression; the loneliness. Unlike his father, he stayed and took responsibility, which I failed to do, whatever my reasons. I am trying to find a way to balance this recognition against what I still remember as his rejection of me. What had been brutal, at first impact, feels more like a rebuff. There's a wound there, no doubt, but I can't hang on to resentment, given my own sorry record.

I don't know how to open a conversation with him about his own lonely journey and there's an awkwardness between us that our minimalist chat avoids addressing. I can't sit out the evenings as well as the days watching television with him, so a couple of nights I escape to pay social calls.

One night I come home from visiting an old friend, and as the bus pulls up across the road, my heart is unwillingly wrenched with pity as I see the living room from across the street, blinds wide open, lit coldly by a single fluorescent tube, revealing my father's form asleep, in the dirty armchair, the knitted cap pulled over his head. Too vulnerable to the impersonal gaze of the world outside, he sleeps unaware, and it hurts to see this life so starkly lit, exposed for all to see. I cross the road and go in, close the blinds, and gently shake the old form awake enough to get him off to bed.

The next day I survey the sterile back yard, the ragged Hills Hoist still in place. I have never been able to bring any life into this place. Every tree and fragrant creeper I've planted on my sporadic visits has met the same fate. My mother would write to me of the plants' progress and then report reluctantly how they had to be chopped down for one reason or other. A lovely flowering gum needed to be dug out because of some parasitic growth or other. Father detests the leaves the liquid amber drops. He would rake up the leaves, indignant, and burn them in a makeshift incinerator.

These days, weeds compete unchallenged with the patchy lawn, and the dry earth, scratched and raked and burned clean of its natural cover, refuses to flower.

I try to get some conversation going between us, side-stepping the familiar uneasiness that blocks our every move. I feel I should address some of the pain around his early rejection of me, perhaps get him to talk about his own missing father. I've picked up some pop psychology—I live in California after all—and instead of allowing the quotidian TV viewing routine to glide over my need, smoothly excusing us from having to interact, I want to make a rapprochement, even at this late stage. I hope that dredging up old material might clear the channels and something less uncomfortable might flow between us. We have little common base to work from.

I try it out one morning in the kitchen. He's seated at the table, doing the daily crossword. I remind him of the time he laid the floor tiles here, with the help of his friend. I'm hoping to let him know that that's where it had started to go so wrong, where rejection became the rule.

'It's "deny". Eighteen down ... it's "deny"'.

We're sitting at the kitchen table together. I try to speed up filling in the puzzle. 'The clue is: "Say it isn't so" ... Do you remember when we laid this room with those rubber tiles, when we first moved here?' I slip it in.

'Uh, does that fit?' Long pause. 'That'd mean twenty-nine across has to finish with a y'.

'Yeah, it's *bluesy*.'

'Bluesy? No. What's that?'

'Like blues music. Blues-y ... Those rubber floor tiles, grey in the centre, red around the cupboards.' Some later layering of linoleum covers them now.

'What tiles?'

'Don't you remember? That first floor you laid ... Don't you remember the rubber tiles? Gray tiles in the center and those plum-colored ones around the cupboards.'

'Can't say I do.'

'Tishie used to polish them up to a really high gloss. The tile company wanted to take a photo for their catalogue.'

'It's lino now.'

'Yeah, but before that, remember the tiles? That bloke came in to help you lay 'em down, glue 'em to the floor. Remember? You had to cut the red ones in a curve, to go around the cupboards.'

'Did we? Think so ...'

'Yeah, and you shoved me away when I tried to help you. Don't you remember?'

'Can't remember. But the Taj Mahal. That's in India, isn't it?'

'Taj Mahal. They're a band, or a musician, anyway. Folksy blues, bluesy jazz, I guess, or rhythm and blues. So it's "Blues-ey".'

I give up.

'When are you gonna get your hair cut?' He pokes. My thinning hair is pulled back in a ponytail. I like the sleek look around my head.

'Aah, why would I? Think how much money I save!' And I win for once. He glares at me. We both back off.

'Is there anything you need?' I ask him later.

I've been fantasising about taking the old bloke half way around the world to live with me in LA, dreaming how I might re-organise his entire life, tend to his every need. As if. He would have no friends there, no bowling club, no football, no Lodge, no history, no … context. So for today, I'll trim my ambition and try instead to fit into his spartan frame of reference. What does *he* think he needs?

'Not really. Got everything I need … Oh yeah, I could use a pair of shoes. Black ones. For Lodge. Ernie Hillman picks me up to take me to Lodge. First Tuesday of every month. Black shoes.'

His car sits, unused, in the garage. (The garage doors succumbed finally after he collided with them once too often.) My sister Val tells me he was arrested 'driving under the influence' after one of these outings with his cronies, wearing those aprons, drinking too much beer. A Tuesday night, it must have been. His car left the road on the way home and drove into a lamp pole. Another time he drove clear through the back wall of the garage ('The accelerator got stuck!' He explains defensively) and the car pushed on all the way to the back fence before coming to a stop. After each event, insurance patches up the damage, but when he started to come to the notice of the police and the local magistrate, his driving privileges were cancelled. So the ruin of the Triumph now sits ensconced in the door-less garage and he is housebound, unless one of his mates, who still has a licence and some control of his vehicle, comes to his rescue. Meals are delivered on weekdays and he takes the bus up the hill to the nearest supermarket when his pension cheque arrives. Even there his reputation precedes him. He cleaned up the front door of one of the stores with the aforesaid vehicle.

'They certainly see me coming now! It's that bloody accelerator pedal,' he explains.

So we agree. We'll use the bus to go into Fremantle to look for a pair of black shoes for Lodge nights. As a pensioner, he can ride for 50c, and the ticket is good for two hours. Waiting at the bus stop across the road from the house, we're glad to be out and about. He carries a cane now. I'm enjoying the early summer sun on my face, welcoming the chance to do something else than sit in the house counting off the hours, and the chat shows, and the cigarettes.

There's a poster in the shelter publicising special services for the aged and I'm grateful that even though my old man is virtually abandoned in his life of solitude, he is still mobile, and a safety net is there in government services to make up for the failings of negligent offspring. Although he is a longtime Liberal voter, my father is very pleased with the new Labor State Premier, Dr. Carmen Lawrence. When he was hospitalised for the heel, all Val had had to do was find the money to rent him a TV; the rest was covered through subsidies. Lawrence's state government policies are kindly disposed towards services for the aged. She explains that's one reason why she likes to work at state level because while the Feds disburse the funds, the states decide the priorities. While my knowledge of government is virtually nil, I am grateful.

Going over the way things are, I can't see that it could have turned out any differently; that we should live so far apart. I've had to go where the work is, yet the old man's lonely routine still twists a blade of guilt in my gut.

A pair of shoes. That at least, is within my power.

The clean, new bus surges up the hill, right on schedule and after paying we move carefully down the aisle as the bus pulls off and sit together, half-way to the back. I take in the passing scene through the window, surprised how the size of everything seems to have shrunk, compared to my memory of it. Smaller, kind of pinched. Parched dry, just like LA. Everything so neat, the houses, the gardens, the cars. No peeling paint here, certainly no graffiti. I'm impressed by the industry of everyone I see. People sure of their lives, content with what they have earned, apparently not too interested in a world beyond their routines, peaceful and well-adjusted in that very milieu that triggers an old restlessness in me. How far did I have to go, to find my own way?

A young guy boards the bus. After paying the driver, he turns to walk down the aisle, eyes searching out a seat. His skin is dusted with an early summer tan and his limbs move easily as he saunters past. My gaze takes him in, quickly noting the details, measuring the age, assessing the attitude. In his early twenties, there's a calm intelligence to his face. I look to the eyes, perhaps to catch a flicker of interest returned, the old game playing out for the *n*th time. When they look my way, I catch my breath. A stunning mix of greens and grays colours the irises, tourmaline beauty in a well-proportioned face. Such loveliness blooming in this remote place; unappreciated, I presume, then cringe at my own condescension. Hadn't I grown up here, developed my bent aesthetic in this very place? Nearby is the swimming hole at Point Walter, where I first admired Terry Johnson's limbs gliding through the water and the beauty of the male form that shaped my earliest devotions. But the constraints of a harsh culture that always denied beauty in men, preferring to rough it up, expunge any pretty boy weakness, harden gentleness with a tough carapace of masculine denial, had trained me to deny my yearning, and I learned to avert my gaze.

The young man's eyes stonily reject my inquiry.

Next to me Frank stiffens noticeably, recognising the energy that flashed between us. I don't need to turn and look at him to register the doughty disapproval revived in his face. I always had to hide my love, learn to play the game …

We're in his car, driving to work, during one of those school vacation jobs. I'm sixteen and I know, from the same trip yesterday, that there is a building site coming up on the left. Yesterday, when we passed, young men were working there, with their shirts off in the sun. There was one among them whose muscles lightly graced his frame. I'd like to see him again, sip secretly from the cup of physical beauty, re-capture the grace. But to do so openly would be an insult to my father's stern values. So I pointedly look around at other things, to cover my tracks, intent on throwing him off the scent as I steal one glance among the many.

That became a lifelong habit. Even now, whenever I am out and about, if something catches my eye—a flashing smile, a well-turned limb, a sculpted set of buttocks flexing beneath blue jeans—I also look at something else, at random, in another direction, with equal attention, to disguise my interest and deflect suspicion from anyone who might be watching. Furtive devotions, acted out in shame.

Back on the bus I pull back my gaze, no interest returned in kind from the new arrival. I shrug off my father's disapproval as the young man passes on to another row of seats, behind me and out of sight. Now I remember some of the feelings that had driven me away.

'Fuck you!' I think. 'What did you ever do for me that you didn't resent, you mean old bastard. Go to hell.' Underneath the conscientious sense of gratitude that I have only recently retrieved, old resentments seethe at hints of old provocations. Will I never be rid of reaction?

As the bus rounds a bend near the traffic bridge at North Fremantle, the afternoon sun glimmers off the blue waters of the river. I catch a whiff of the sea and let the memories drift loose as I relax into the washed-out azure sky. Picking over bitter memories is a thread of thought I have followed too far before, to no fruitful end, so I release the ties to the past, to let my mind fall back into the other familiar embrace, the one folded intimately within my breath, to soothe me.

We reach the terminus and Frank steps gingerly down onto the pavement. His heel's obviously still causing him some soreness.

'This is where Mercantile Press used to be, on this street, eh?' I say, fluffing up the dialogue. 'When you first came to work in Fremantle.'

'Queen Street, yeah.'

'Before you moved down closer to the Roundhouse. Near that jail. Was it Cantonment Street?'

'Yeah.'

We find our way around the streets of the crisp little port town. Spruced up for international attention on the occasion of an international yacht race that had caught the nation's pride, it has benefited from an influx of money, sprouting some expensive restaurants and a bevy of bars and bistros. Some of the investment seems to have gone into restorations, too, and the scale of the buildings has not been spoiled with tacky high-rises. Traffic is diverted into a system of one-way streets and pedestrians make easy progress. It's a pretty place, small and user friendly, with a quaint maritime charm. At fourteen, when I went to work here in school holidays, I thought it was a bustling city.

Several onlookers smile with approval as we pass, father and son together, and I feel the invitation to an unfamiliar sense of pride walking with my old man. An awkward rehearsal for a play on irony perhaps, but not a life I've ever lived. I push the feeling away.

We find the shoe store and quickly discover a reasonable pair to fit his requirements. They are quite cheap, only forty-five dollars, on special. I want to spend more, lavish at least some kind of fiscal attention on the old codger, but his modest needs are easily satisfied with these, and we're soon sitting down on a banquette to try on a pair his size. A young shop assistant comes to our aid and squats at his feet to help with the fitting.

'How do they feel?' She asks solicitously, with respect for the white hair. 'Your big toe comes to here. Are they comfortable?'

'Yeah, they feel alright,' he replies.

'How are they here?' She feels the sides at the broadest point of his foot.

'Good,' the old man replies, distracted. 'Have to be careful of that heel, you know. Had an operation on that. They had to take out a piece of bone.'

He's so chipper.

'Slipped and fell on the steps outside the bloody doctor's office, would you believe it?' He snorts.

'Well, if the heel feels too tight, you know you can always use the end of a broom handle to soften it up. Just slip it in there and rub it around to soften the edge,' she offers.

'Oh, I'd like to put a broom into *you*, young lady …!'

'Whoa …what? DAD!' I protest. 'For God's sake!' Hardly able to believe my ears, I puff my disapproval, all the while grimacing, embarrassed, to the shop assistant. She brushes it aside with a gracious shake of the head.

I'm thinking: You're eighty-one years old, for God's sake! Doesn't it ever stop? I'm just as uncomfortable at this outburst of (geriatric) sexuality as he was with mine, on the bus, just minutes before.

Apologising to the young woman for my old man's outburst, I pay for the shoes and we beat a hasty retreat out of the store. What else is going to come popping out?

'Um. Would you like to go for coffee, or something … a cup of tea? Shall we sit in a café, watch the world go by?' I suggest, thinking of ways to prolong the outing and put off the return to the stultifying routine back at the house.

'Well, we can't stay too long,' the old man complains, 'this ticket is only good for two hours.'

'Never mind, I'll buy you another one.' I steer us up the street away from the scene of the crime, to an outdoor cafe on South Terrace where I hope we can just sit. Unable to get any traction for extended conversation, the chat comes only in short spurts. We compare shreds of memory, remark on how much the street has changed over the years.

'The footy club's near here, isn't it,' I try.

'Yep. South Fremantle. I'm an honorary life member,' he chuffs. After decades of membership and his years of helping out with the accounts they've found a way to stop charging him dues.

Football is always worth a few sentences. I can check out the progress of his two teams: South Fremantle in the local league, and the West Coast Eagles in the national competition. I have become an enthusiastic AFL spectator. I tape broadcasts from cable TV sometimes to boast to my Yankee friends that it's a vastly superior code. I admire the very qualities I was not able to find within myself to succeed in the game and I really enjoy the pace and excitement. I can bullshit on about it, like men are supposed to, and I like to explicate the more skillful points of the game to look out for, while putting down their own ridiculous version, gridiron.

'Look, no padding, and they play 100 minutes. They don't go off the field unless they're actually injured. It's much more athletic. See how lean they are? Half of your guys look like they're ready for a cardiac arrest. There's no action in your game, it's constipated. As soon as anything happens, the bloody game shuts down and the whole team goes off the field. Now Aussie Rules …This is a real MAN's game!' My friends yawn at my lingering parochialism and change the subject. (And the Aussies wear more revealing uniforms, too. So much more to enjoy.)

The warmth of the afternoon slips away with the breeze coming off the water, so we make our way back to the bus stop and then home without further event, and all within the two-hour limit.

There is no way I can take it for more than a few days; it is clear that the old burrs still rankle. I wish I could do more, but I see already that I have to respect my old man's ways. It's cost me nearly a thousand dollars from my own tight budget to come to visit but it still seems tokenistic.

I pay a visit to my sister and her lover in Bridgetown.

'Tell him what it did to you,' Val advises. 'Make him remember something.' But I explain that when I try to talk us back to one or two of those times when the wounds first began to fester, his memory just won't respond.

'It's the bloody anaesthetic,' she says. 'They knocked him out when they did his heel. It affects the memory when they get older.' Val works in a Federal Government program for funding aged care. She has kept up her daughterly duties, uprooting from Melbourne and moving back to be close to them when our mother fell ill. She is the one who prodded him into doing the shopping and helping out more around the house when Tishie was still around, but now she has retreated to the South West with her new partner.

I'm becoming increasingly uncomfortable with this tendency to see my parents through my own childhood narrative, refusing to liberate them from my own neuroses. They made their effort, and lived their lives with dignity. What have I done that can hold a candle to that? Clearly, it's hubris on my part to think that I have much to offer. We spend our last days together shuffling cards, swapping versions of Patience, racing each other through the crossword, shopping for the simple necessities, retrieving shreds of conversation from the silence that engulfs us. Actions speak louder than words, but the life these actions speak of now is a set of habits, re-played in a jerky silent movie, with the laugh track supplied by the telly.

Still there's something in me that won't settle. All the while, internally, I'm asking for a proof of love. My meditation practice has done much to heal my brokenness but I don't know how to square away the painful memories when I'm actually face to face with him. I won his admiration when he heard me lecture as an instructor here in my hometown, but our connection has been fitful for years.

I fossick around the old house to check the state of his supplies. I go through the linen closets to dispose of threadbare bedding I know he will never use and I'm surprised to find a packet of letters, tied together with a ribbon. All those times I picked over every corner of this place, I never found this cache.

As I break open the secret stash, I recognise my father's fine Copperplate hand moving at a stately pace across the pages, written on both sides of the paper in wartime frugality. They're dated '44 and '45. He was in the Army during the Second World War and he is pouring out his heart to her from a barracks in Northam, some sixty miles away, and

York. He is an ardent correspondent, expressing his feelings unguardedly, and the power of their connection with each other sings through the lines. I find photos of them together, first as newlyweds, with him in uniform and then another, taken a few years later, staring lovingly into each other's eyes.

Wherever it is they have been hidden all this while, these letters have turned up in a spectacularly synchronous way. These dates; this would have been around the time when I was born, and it occurs to me, suddenly, that I was really conceived in love. Rather than prodding at my father's patchy memory, I have pulled down this synchronous hint from the linen closet and shreds of resentment sigh free in me. What have I been holding so close to my heart that I couldn't recognise this before?

On my last night, I have my things packed ready to go and I come back to the house to find him asleep in his chair, with the TV blaring inanely from the corner. We've already gone over the timetables and we know what time I have to make my exit to get to the airport by bus.

I gently shake my old man's shoulder to rouse him and say good-bye. I can hardly bear to see him so old. The strong male form which had once threatened me so, is now shrunken and bony, wracked with coughs.

'Whaaat?' he says feebly, his eyes coming into focus, waking from his sleep as innocently as a child. I'm looking down into his face and see the little boy there.

'I've got to go now, it's time. The bus'll be here any minute.'

As he recognises me, the old man beams and says: 'Thank you for coming, son. Thank you for being here, I really appreciate it,' with more emotion than I've ever seen.

I stifle the sob this wrenches from my throat. There's nothing but love left hiding in the old man's heart. Here's the boy, with the same need for love and attention. He, who must have had such a hard life when he was young. I'm crushed to say good-bye, praying to be forgiven myself for holding on to my pain for so long, content to keep so much distance between us.

funeral suite—my old man

Six months later, I get a call at my apartment in Hollywood. My sister couldn't find my number and rang the production office in Sydney, who pass on the message. Dad has died, two days short of his eighty-second birthday. He'd gone to see his old team play in South Fremantle, the team he'd supported for fifty years. He was proud of his long membership at that club and that's where he made his exit. It was half time, and they were ahead. A member of a junior team, the Colts, tried to give him mouth to mouth, the 'kiss of life', but even loaned a breath he couldn't be revived.

After the funeral and the painting of the house and sorting of items, before heading back to LA I spend a few days with Val and Kaite, trying to smoke my way through a baggie of weed. Futile. Feeling alone is the most familiar state for me but it's how I feel comfortable; it's my 'home' state, not this family thing, but Kaite skillfully walks us through some grieving processes. She knows how to instigate a healing and in her ramshackle house, with its tangled jungle of a garden, they have spun a warm and loving space. If the family you come from is a broken thing, you find your kin where you can, especially if you're a cuckoo.

As Val and I haggle over photos from the family albums, I find a photo of myself taken in the sitting room of the house in Victoria Park. Seated on the sofa, dressed in Sunday best. This was the room where as a boy I used to wear the yellow dress. Look at him, he can only be three, or at most four, years old. The man came and put his head under a black cloth bag and Whoosh! He exploded a bright flash of light. That is why the boy is smiling, the flash prompted him to recall his safe place. Being with the light was being with himself. That's why he looks so hopeful.

I can't put the picture down. Look at those hands grabbing for what's already gone. The eyes are a too-naked testimony of a guileless heart. To me the photograph insists: the child is here, he was never gone. A deep sigh shudders through me. I close my eyes, to follow the thread of breath back home. In the quiet shade of the formal sitting room the touch of golden fabric is cool against my skin, the long dress spills past my feet onto the floor …

The past steps back softly into the present as I accept the risk of owning self—back then, and now, again.

I wanted to comfort the child, instead I find that he brings strength to me.

They never looked beyond the dress. If they saw me slip into the sitting room, in an altered state, eager to catch my ride back home, they didn't think to ask where I was going as I acted out my little home-made ritual. Perhaps they were horrified that their little boy was showing signs of effeminacy. Whatever I was exploring with the help of the yellow dress was transpiring at a level of awareness beyond the crude social divisions of gender and a long time before sex reared its head.

As the boy, I recall wholeness, not division, as my primary state of being.

Twenty years of meditation practice and, finally, I recognise the connection. No wonder I took to Knowledge like a duck to water. At some level I recognised a homecoming, a return from exile. The little boy was naturally at home in his Eden state: undifferentiated light. His very core. Before male and female are, this is. So when he was shamed and sent into exile from his soul nature, he yearned for what was missing, like a lost twin self. Separated from an innate, natural spirituality that collected all the binaries in one embrace, his 'perversity' in yearning for the state of unity was socially transgressive.

And what was he offered in its place? Gender, a bifurcation sanctioned by repeated, coercive indoctrinations and enshrined in countless social rituals. If his instinct was to reject the half-truth of two-dimensionality, why was the only option to be cast as 'pathological', an example of failed development, as a biological error? An outlaw, too, according to the criminal code. But most of all, a sinner, an abomination before God Himself.

All my training, in the ashram, and tested in my recent, 'worldly' phase, has been preparing me for this restoration. This little boy was alright. It was the simplistic, two-dimensional society and its repressive gender modeling that were warped. The two strands of my being are being woven back together, my return from the years in exile guaranteed.

Shamans cross-dress. They take on the clothes of the opposite gender, shift into altered states so they might access the mysteries and perform their sacred functions on behalf of the tribe. I grew up in a place that would, perversely, recognise only two dimensions: male or female, either/or. If this, not that. Certainly not both. And all the time, at some level, I knew it was a lie, or at least only a partial version of reality. The strange alchemy of soft and hard, masculine and feminine, blending in one integrated spirit.

In this reconciliation I know that my original nature is *not* sin. And it should have been safe for the boy to be who he is. My healing has come about neither through psychology, nor the Church, nor even in a misnamed 'gay' community. My teacher and guide showed me how to learn to be myself again, from the ground up, from the inside out. I remember the powerful experience of peace that flooded me when I made contact again in the early days of satsang, and those first experiences of meditation, and the gratitude almost overwhelms me.

Val slips a present into my hand. It's a modest signet ring in old gold, with a thin worn band and my father's initials, FDM, engraved on the top surface. Inside the band, there's a dedication: 'Love from Letitia. 13.5.42'. She gave it to him a year after their wedding and he wore it right up until his death. Worn smooth by the years, and bent to fit the shape of his ring finger, it fits perfectly on my own.

Back in La La Land

It was as if a magic flame dwelt within one, burning, burning,
which one could not put out, and yet whose existence
one might in no way reveal.
—Edward Carpenter, *Days and Dreams*

I'm standing on the sidewalk in West Hollywood. The annual Gay
Pride parade ambles along Santa Monica Boulevard, passing the bottom
of my street. It's a rather tame affair compared to the energetic display of
Mardi Gras in Sydney, or even Halloween here in 'boys' town'; more like
your average Independence Day parade through any middle-American
town on the 4th of July. It's a bright June morning, the weather is balmy
and nobody gets too excited. The disco music and glitter seem a trifle
tawdry on a quiet Sunday morning.

It's the early 1990s. The battles with the police and authorities which
gave birth to the movement, post-Stonewall, have been won long since—
at least as far as obtaining permits for parades goes, and this *is* West
Hollywood—but I'm glad to be here, to show solidarity at least, because
there are still many issues that make us feel like second-class citizens.

Among the floats a gay-friendly radio station blares out disco music to
pump up a group of semi-clad, buffed-up gym bunnies; a welcome relief
from the more earnest displays. There are marching bands, always a
feature of any American parade, and a bizarre group of cheerleaders, too,
complete with authentic pom-pom girl outfits, gaudy make-up, hairy legs
and prominent moustaches. Their energetic routine is well-rehearsed and
raises by far the biggest cheer, after the 'dykes on bikes', a squad of stern-
looking lesbians driving motorbikes.

One or two local politicians have come out to show their support and
secure the rainbow vote. A very small group of 'out' gay police officers
attracts a round of applause but groups of gay Christians from different
denominations evoke more ambivalent feelings among the onlookers,
drawing only tepid applause. There's a rare sighting of a pair of minor
celebrities, actors from an ancient sitcom showing their solidarity, too, but

no 'openly gay' male stars are seen peeking out of any closets right around now.

My ho-hum attitude is soon disrupted when a group calling itself P-FLAG (Parents and Friends of Lesbians and Gays) passes by. A gaggle of gay men and lesbians stroll arm-in-arm with their parents. When I notice a man carrying a placard stating: 'I'm proud of my gay son', I find myself crying.

It must be delayed grieving, I think. I didn't feel particularly devastated by my father's passing; I knew it was inevitable and that he had reached a certain satisfaction with his life. I have found my way in life with little help from him and to a degree I have made my peace with that. He was rather pleased that I work in a job that he could point to with some pride. I know, rationally, that there will never be that 'home', or family, to go back to; I am now, presumably, fully grown up.

But the tears keep coming. Something has been flushed out and it won't go back into hiding. That father's acceptance of his gay son in the parade undoes me. I am grieving for something that has *never* been, rather than something that I have lost. I write to the local Hollywood chapter of PFLAG, thanking them for their visibility, and enclose a cheque. They run my letter in their monthly newsletter and I start going to their meetings to offer my support. These are my new culture heroes.

It seems to me that much of the damage caused to people in my situation occurs at very close quarters; as children, often we have to hide who we are from those nearest to us, and we are cut off from the kinds of support that heterosexually-inclined children usually can take for granted. I see the activism of these parents as working at the coalface of change and their courage in defending their children from ignorance (including their own) is truly revolutionary.

I get more traction for my own little healing journey when I recall that I had decided around age eleven to shut my father out of my life, and I wonder if I have ever completely reversed that decision. By shutting down on him, perhaps I shut down on aspects of my own nature; skills I associated with an authentic masculinity, which would therefore be unavailable to me because I wasn't properly qualified to be one of the 'real men'. Areas of experience and expertise that I associated with *his* world, framed within his version of the masculine, have been out of bounds to me for too long. After all, he contributed half of my chromosomes. Is it possible that my own wrong-headed choices are blocking out much of what I could achieve? I remember in woodworking class that I performed incompetently. While I was worried about being 'outed', confused about the colour of my work apron, the teacher called me a butcher. Yet without anyone looking over my shoulder I built the large aviary for my budgerigars: designed it, budgeted for it and did the construction. Perhaps there are parts of my self that don't fit into the picture of the girlie man. If I hadn't had to spend so much psychic energy hiding, maybe my competency would have improved. Could I be sabotaging myself, not allowing myself to succeed? How do these scripts work, subconsciously?

I start to look out for opportunities to accept challenges that will take me into unfamiliar areas of experience. My father has died, and his funeral was on my *birthday*. Can I dare to assume that there is nothing holding me back now?

Every time I dive deep in meditation, I am absorbed into an experience greater than little me. That absorption quenches my anxieties, nourishing me from within. I feel that I am re-connecting with an indefinable whole, like the 'ground of being' pointed to in Aldous Huxley's précis of Vedanta that I read about all those years ago in psychologist Jim Coventry's room. Without knowing that, as palpable, lived experience, I wouldn't know wholeness. But when 'I' emerges again, albeit refreshed by its encounter, it picks up its usual chain of associations, the predicate of particulars that pertain to my 'personal' history, identifying me as a separate individual. And that includes what I might call my 'desire nature'. Even the most profound meditation doesn't transform me into a well-adjusted heterosexual. Perhaps this 'homo' thing isn't pathological; perhaps it's a normal variation in human sexual behaviour. Rather than being an 'abomination', perhaps it even has 'spiritual' roots. So where is the sin? And why is the church still so intent on driving a wedge between people and their sexuality?

In the final analysis, making peace with my father (which will take a few more decades) is not the issue. In fact, I regret having focused as much as I have on what went wrong between us. It will be a long time before I will understand his early rejection as a gift, in the same way that I have been learning that my differently ordered queer sensibility is a gift, too, and learn to recognise the true goodness of this man who played my father. Only God knows what privations young Frank underwent as a ward of the State, yet I never heard him complain. He conducted himself with dignity and stoicism and he strove to keep a roof over our heads, unlike his father, who had abandoned him (just as I did with my son). I could never indulge in the New Age nostrum of 'forgiveness', then. How could this child condescend to grant forgiveness to a parent? It would be churlish of me to hold anything but love in my heart towards my father, who did so well through a difficult life. As for the lingering effects of his rejection, I have had much very effective help, even if it has come from an unconventional quarter. Otherwise, these are my issues, and I'm the one who has to deal with them.

In perfect timing, my sister sends me an autobiographical sketch Frank had written for her when she was studying family relations as part of her studies in sociology. In his late seventies he wrote his story across eight foolscap pages, back and front, in the proper Copperplate script he had taught himself when he was a quartermaster.

'*It appears that grandfather [Myrtle Ivy's father] was a very hard man,*' he writes. Grandfather Marsh was so upset about the stigma of an illegitimate child, he insisted that baby 'Franklin' be handed over to the Child Welfare Department soon after birth. From what he writes even decades later, the shaming had real consequences:

Illegitimacy, when I became aware of it in my early years, was a handicap, a stigma, a sword of Damocles hanging over my head, & when I thought it was forgotten, would occasionally spring up and bug me. It prevented me, at one stage, applying for a job in the State Government. (That was over 50 years ago.)

All through my youth, living under his roof, I failed to recognise any hint of his shame, so well masked by his manly stoicism, or hear anything of this poignant testimony of loneliness. He makes no reference to his missing father, Harry Christensen (spelling unconfirmed), whose absence must have left a wound.

He lived in various foster care situations as a child of the State until the age of two, when a Mr. Thomas William and Mrs Ruth Holmes successfully applied to have him boarded out in their home in Duke Street, East Fremantle. They were not permitted to adopt him, he explains, as they were then over fifty years of age. Not able to have any of their own, in the previous twenty years they had brought up two other 'State children' and, even after taking him on, they boarded out two more

326 | VICTOR MARSH

boys, one of whom (Harold) was a wild one, 'becoming uncontrollable', as my father puts it, and 're-committed to the State' at about 14 or 15 years of age.

If Harold was wild, Franklin now Francis wasn't about to throw away his chance at respectability. He conformed to their strict expectations and at around the age of sixteen Mrs Holmes influenced him to join the Plymouth Brethren, 'an evangelical group'. While studying accountancy he enrolled in courses with the Perth Bible Institute and also attempted to learn Spanish and ancient Greek but found he had taken on too much and dropped accountancy with a view to becoming a minister or, preferably, a missionary.

Growing up with him I saw no signs of this religious calling, perhaps because he 'fell short of that goal', in his words 'unable to attain to the high standards' required. Now I can recognise the seeds of his interest in my ashramic existence. But he says he encountered 'short-comings, failings, incapabilities' in himself, giving only a few clues as to what they might be:

> For many years I regarded homosexuality as a crime, pre-marital intercourse as a sin, as was masturbation, forbidden in the Old Testament. That & The [Great] Depression, I consider was the cause for not getting married until nearly 31.

I see why he was disappointed when I had apparently fallen away from the 'higher calling'. What I couldn't share with him, because I didn't understand it fully myself, is that in 'falling' I found that, rather than depending on 'good' and 'moral' behaviour, grace is a constant, like a background radiation underlying all our doing and that, if I can tune into that reality, I am aligned with the primordial fact of existence: unconditional love itself.

Frank's birth mother Myrtle Ivy grasped her opportunity for respectability when, at the age of twenty-seven, ten years after surrendering her baby, she accepted a proposal of marriage from a man named Vic Tresize. When she told him about the child she had had out of wedlock, he said it made no difference to him, that it was all in the past. But he also said that what his own sons didn't know wouldn't hurt them either, and they agreed never to disclose the nature of the relationship with 'Francis', especially when he sought her out.

In 1933 (in his early twenties) Francis went to Kalgoorlie in search of work. The thought of his mother had haunted him and while he laboured as a mechanic, a window-cleaner and wood-chopper, he searched the Registrar of Births, Deaths and Marriages for a copy of his birth record and his mother's marriage certificate. (Again, he never reveals the same curiosity about his missing father.)

His inquiries led him eventually to Grandmother Marsh, who was still living in the area. Through her, he traced his birth mother to the town of Jardee in the SouthWest and he summoned up the courage to write to her. The response must have been positive because the following year he went to Jardee to live. He found work at the local timber mill and agreed to be known as a distant nephew. (He must have got on well with Vic Tresize, because he named me, his second son, after him.)

Frank's hopes of settling into some approximate version of a family life were soon disrupted by the miseries of the Great Depression. His work at the timber mill ran out and he had to move towns to eke out a living making fruit-packing cases for orchards. With the picking season over, he sought seasonal work on farms: ploughing, seeding, cultivating, harvesting, and driving teams of horses at Perenjori, a wheatbelt town some 300 miles north of Perth. He mentions driving 'Bulldog Lang' tractors at Morowa, another sheep and wheat farming town in the area, 'International' trucks at nearby Belleranga Station and 'John Deere' tractors at tiny Minnivale, also close by. Between jobs he would live on his meagre savings.

In all this hard labour there was little comfort for a young bachelor:

Most of the time I was alone, except when more than one was employed. Working from daylight to dark left little time for much else but a little light reading & then sleep. One farm provided only a bough shed & bush bunk (2 poles & 2 wheat bags).

There's no hint of complaint in his stoic account, and I admire the humour in his account:

Got a centipede in my pants—it stung me in a very private part of my anatomy—I was very proud of the swelling for a short while.

He went on to make something of himself, putting himself through accountancy at night school, working towards a career in business management, but the spartan survival training continued:

The Depression taught me nothing much more than the necessity to keep body & soul together, to maintain a faint hope of better things to come, to work at anything for any sum, however small, going for as long as 3 days without a meal. I would not beg, but did accept small charities. Ninepence could buy a 3-course meal, sixpence a big savoury dish. I worked in Kalgoorlie doing things like sinking a shaft, in Perth in a billiard room as a marker, and then I stole a feed in a restaurant & shot through without paying & I felt as guilty as hell. I did not attempt to relate religion or belief in God with the Depression. I felt I could not blame God for a man-made Depression.

In 1939 he returned to Fremantle and got a job as a storeman at Spicers, paper merchants. He began to eat at the Roma café, which became an oasis of companionship for him. He met his future mother-in-law there: Edna Evans, a warm and vivacious American woman who drew a large and lively circle of card-players around her. She introduced him to her daughter Letitia. Soon 'Tishie' was shampooing his hair in the kitchen of a friend's house. *'The Evans family were wonderful,'* he writes. *'I felt what a lot I had been missing in my life, and every opportunity I went to visit them.'*

When Frank came to the Evans family he found a warm and welcome contrast to the wintry guilt of his mother's world, the stern, religious values of his foster parents and the lonely life of a bachelor eking out a living during the Depression.

Having my heart cracked open to him on my last visit to Perth, then again, from another direction, by the PFLAG parents, this basic biographical information floods in to fill the gap that has existed between us for too long. I wish I had known more about his life before I had to manage his funeral. More than that, I wish I had sufficient compassion to break me out of my self-preoccupation and recognise a life well-lived. Although he has departed and I have missed the chance to deal with him directly, that has not stopped the relationship evolving. If the psychologists' diagnosis of 'father hunger' scarcely covered the anguish over my father's rejection of me that I have masked for decades, now I can begin to feel my way towards what my own father might have gone through. And what my own son, in his turn, might be feeling through my own absence. These are bitter issues to contemplate. But the healing begins now.

coda

sitting with the practice

I am reminded of a story (some say it's a Sufi tale, others that it's Welsh!) about someone who has lost his house keys. A neighbour notices him searching in the street and asks what he is doing. When he explains that he has lost his keys, she offers to help. Before long, other people are involved in the search, too, but even with their help he has no luck in locating the keys. Eventually one of them asks:

'Are you sure you lost them here?'

'Why no,' he replies, 'I lost them inside.'

'Then why are you looking for them out here?' they demand to know.

'Because the light is better out here!'

I am told these stories work on more than one level, but just to take up one aspect, it would be futile looking for what has been lost in any place where it simply isn't. The search for a solution to so many problems can easily be misdiagnosed, and if the problem is to find meaning, it's important to know *where* the missing piece of that particular puzzle can be located.

Perhaps it's less a matter of locating a missing element than bringing about a certain re-alignment. The original disconnect happens within. I can spend all the time I like trying to re-orient the world to fit my needs; fix what I perceive as the breaks; challenge gender politics; resolve conflicting ideologies; build bridges; make connections; bring world peace: all from the outside. But if the fundamental disconnect was within, those efforts will be futile. It's like pulling beyond the reach of the vacuum cleaner cord. If the plug has come out of the socket, I can mimic the movements with the cleaner, even vocalise the sounds, but it won't function to suck up the dust. If peace resides at the root of being, and I am casting about outside? First things first. Peace nurtures me, from within. That's the starting point; originally, and right now.

The material universe is irradiated with energy, and this includes my existence. Sitting with the meditation practices is the ultimate docking procedure, re-aligning my little self within the greater reality. This way, I may withdraw my attention from the trivial, if dense, preoccupations of everyday life into deep communion with that original source of being, in the same way that the focal length of a lens can be adjusted to reveal deeper layers to the field of perception. Here, the re-focusing is inward, and deeply refreshing, for this homecoming is saturated with peace. The boy in the yellow dress was at ease with this state but was shamed and sent into exile. This book has been about the original dis-location and the odyssey of return.

Perhaps if you picked up my book, with its title suggesting a boy inclined to cross-dressing in a frock, you might expect that at some stage I would have tried to change my gender to recover the missing dimensions of being. When I found the photo, I rediscovered the boy who was so deeply content to be seated in the circle of wholeness. The missing piece of my puzzle was not the feminine then, so much as it was the origin state of unity. Now, in maturity, I can recall the bleak feeling of his exile *and* reach back to recognise the reality before that. *Undifferentiated unity.* Before Victor was, this is. This is the *primary* state, and my original home. When I came into the world of dualities and ate the fruit of the tree of the Knowledge of Good and Evil, I was cast out East of my Eden, separated from my original (and ultimate) homeland. Gender was a *secondary* development, and sexuality, which only came in fully later, a *tertiary* development. To try and inhabit an identity without full awareness of its proper foundation would be like trying to build a building with only a second and third story. How could that stand? Is it supposed to float? Those later developments are an inadequate basis for integrated selfhood.

So for me to recover the experience of unity, deep at the centre of awareness, has been to come home, not through 'regression' or by clinging fondly to childish delusions. That subtle source is where integration and the deepest healing occurs, and the little personal self, Victor, with all the anxieties and obsessions of his personal history, is re-aligned, shifted into a meaningful relationship with the greater reality.

Grounded in that awareness, I might do more good than harm in the world.

This contact manifests in my daily existence as an unreasonable energy of joy. Thus, while some people assume that I simply have a cheerful disposition, my optimism stems entirely from this source. Even if my meditation doesn't really seem to *improve*, in a sense, when I *don't* do the practices I sink into relative torpor; but as long as I persevere, my outlook remains robust.

In replaying these tapes for myself I have been engaged in a project of reclamation then, recovering the lost parts of self that the conventions of social living have been configured to make me forget. In several ways this has been a risky project, to shed the protective layering of irony and focus on the journey of the heart. For hasn't the noisome testimony of cynicism and despair been more than adequately documented?

When I affirm the heart story, it is not at the expense of intelligence, as some may fear, for those other capacities of mind are *not* diminished by authentic spiritual practice, which actually enhances sincere inquiry. I know that I owe a certain loyalty to that child's heart and any intelligent inquiry into the nature of being would be incomplete were it to ignore that testimony.

To recover direct awareness of the nature of unity is more than just a mystical dream; it is a life-saving enterprise. With the tireless assistance of my life guide, the challenges and insights inherent in the process have saved me from throwing this little life away. For I grew up in a society spiked with deeply embedded, toxic and coercive teachings centred around sexuality and explicitly underpinned by Church teachings. Bigotry often dresses itself up as righteousness and that may be reinforced by psychological medicine, too (my 'syndrome' results, allegedly, from a failure along the normative developmental pathway). That I have survived (and thrived) is entirely due to my teacher's compassionate intervention in my life, which has not focused on correcting my 'deviant' sexuality but on recuperating the deepest connection with the ultimate ground of being. That's where healing occurs. Righteousness ought to stem from a deeply realised compassion. First things first, and credit ought to be given where it is due.

For those who still regard my devotion to my teacher as a mystery, then what can I say? I remember the example from Taiwan, of the difference between the restaurant and the chef. The chef whose brilliant work gave rise to the restaurant's reputation may have moved on, and anyone in search of the best food would be better advised to seek the current location of the chef rather than linger in buildings where she or he once worked. I was restless with the traditions emanating from the teachers of the past until I came across a teacher for my own time and, despite him initially confounding my expectations, or perhaps partly because of that, he has really delivered.

Sitting with the practice each day is not always spent gambolling in the bliss-fields. It can be confronting, showing up the real condition of my mind from one day to the next. Yesterday's experiences are not here now; I always have to begin at the beginning and I'm still a 'work in progress'.

Once he told me, in the days when we were all so concerned about the 'God' question, that if you want to meet God, you need to know his address. And, if you need directions, the first question you will be asked is: where are you now? Begin here: this is where the finite self intersects with what is greater.

I find a 10th Century poem from South India, called 'This Miracle':

I'm the one who has the body,
you're the one who holds the breath.
You know the secret of my body,
I know the secret of your breath.
That's why your body is in mine.
You know
and I know, Ramanatha,
the miracle
of your breath
in my body.
—Devara Dasimayya[8]

He continues to function as a tuning fork, sounding a note of rigorous honesty to purify and re-focus my intention. Rather than strengthening the carapace of the personal self, then, formed of its interactions with the social world—reinforced with cynicism, strengthened with competition,

---

[8] from *Speaking of Shiva*, translated by A.K. Ramanujan. New York: Penguin, 1973.

334 | VICTOR MARSH

seduced by a tantalising array of sensualities and deluded with all the little ego gratifications—the work carried out within this relationship develops the very core of being, rather than the husk. This is the zone where the Master's ability to guide is made manifest.

Your smile blooms, a silent sun
releasing my heart's bud free
to intermingle with infinity ...

The work continues, inside and out. Ahead, there will be challenges to confront, and some surprising gifts as well. An unexpected rapprochement with my son. But that's another book. Meanwhile, the practice continues to influence every aspect of being and doing in the world; a kind of spirituality of everyday life, if you will, albeit one rooted in the core practices.

Today, when people ask me: are you a believer, or an atheist? Do you adhere to the theory of evolution, or to creationism? Are you a rationalist, or superstitious? And so on; those bogus oppositions have no traction for me. Similarly, the question of whether I am Christian / Buddhist / Sufi / Taoist / Jewish / New Age hippie / whatever, simply don't apply. I don't really identify with any of the above; nor, I should add, am I 'anti' any of those positions, either. If you find your way to the heart of love, there'll be no brand names there.

The true teacher doesn't tie you to him/herself but gives you the tools to free your mind from rigid thinking. The meditation practices do not operate from a belief or set of beliefs. (If you make up your own set, it will be tested in the crucible of everyday living.) Rather than being concerned with God/not God then, it is the empirical, root practice of a self-directed inquiry into the nature of being and that is why, as a primary tool of insight, it can be equally useful to a scientist or a theologian.

If I want to get soaked in the bath, or in the shower, I don't wear a plastic mackintosh and gumboots and open up an umbrella. I shed my clothing so I can get wet. In a similar fashion, when I dive into meditation, I'm not a 'gay man' meditating any more than I am an atheist or a believer; that's all part of the clothing that gets dropped so that I may be properly soaked (and cleaned).

The understanding that informs my living flows directly from the empirical, daily reiteration of the core practices, and close attention to the advice from my guide. While I do catch glints of insight from the sayings of others who have traveled a similar path, when I try to describe how that process works for me, my inspiration must come from first-hand, lived experience.

I recall how I wrestled in my university days to understand my life in existential terms and I know I have been blessed with a more thorough resolution of that struggle than I could ever have guessed would be possible. I grew up feeling cramped by social expectations of the authorised compulsory forms of sexual expression and the moral strictures of Christian churchmen, which combined to produce the sense that I was not one of the 'real' people; that my life experience didn't really count in the search for meaning. As kind as some its adherents are, Christianity and institutionalised religion are not the exclusive pathway for spiritual inquiry, any more than normative sexuality is the universal expression of *eros*. I have been given the chance to sort through the patchwork of values received from my culture and test them both against my lived experience and my repeated exposure to different cultures. Rather than living and dying as a tragic old queen, I couldn't be a more fortunate human being.

Finally, I must say that I am not completely comfortable with 'gay', or 'homosexual' as an adequate identification. Who is a 'homosexual' when he is not having sex? I have been so-called 'gay' *and* so-called 'straight', as well as formally celibate. Which one is the real *'me'*? Please don't mistake my meaning: I am not trying to abjure my sexuality, nor am I demeaning the work for gay civil rights, to which I have contributed; but I am learning something about the rich, complex and, in some regards, fluid experience of being human.

In my experience the relationship that really counts is my relationship to the source and to the companion guide who leads me there. Getting *that* relationship right seems to me to be the most important of all the relationships that make up a life. 'Straight' or 'bent' doesn't matter, ultimately. We all draw breath from the same source; what causes that brings life, regardless of our tottering hierarchies.

My mother taught me how to tie my shoelaces, my father how to drive a car. More than that, I am deeply in their debt for the support and the shelter and the love that enabled me to survive. Beyond that, it is my beloved teacher who gave me the tools to discover who I really am and my pitifully simple offering to this true friend who has been encouraging me through the process, so patiently and with immeasurable compassion, and who has literally saved my life, is my deepest gratitude.

Acknowledgements

I want to thank my publisher Gordon Thompson, Helen Bell and Ashley Sievwright at Clouds of Magellan as well as the indomitable Kaite Hansen and my unflappable sister Valerie, who urged me to write this down in the first place. Edna Carew and Shelley Kenigsberg gave me invaluable editing advice and the Australian Society of Authors made Shelley's services available under their mentorship program. Others who were kind enough to read the manuscript at various stages were Stephen Muecke, Alan Close, Rob Cullinan, Baden Offord, David Lovejoy, Glen Whittaker and Wendy Lovejoy. The School of English, Media Studies and Art History at the University of Queensland provided a protective aegis while I worked on an earlier version and I particularly want to thank Venero Armanno, Ruth Blair, Angela Tuohy, Stuart Glover, Jan McKemmish and Gillian Whitlock for their respect and generous support.

Excerpts have appeared previously in various journals and collections, including *Griffith Review*, *Life Writing*, *TEXT*, *Polari*, *Heaven Bent*, *Gay and Lesbian Issues and Psychology Review*, and *Queer Religion: LGBT Movements and Queering Religion*.